SHADOWTIME

To Jän
I second that emotion
and to Adrian Poole
with thanks

SHADOWTIME

History and representation in Hardy, Conrad and George Eliot

Jim Reilly

London and New York

First published 1993
by Routledge
11 New Fetter Lane, London EC4P 4EE

Simultaneously published in the USA and Canada
by Routledge Inc.
29 West 35th Street, New York, NY 10001

© 1993 Jim Reilly

Typeset in 10 on 12 point Garamond by
Computerset, Harmondsworth, Middlesex
Printed in Great Britain by
TJ Press (Padstow) Ltd, Padstow, Cornwall

British Library Cataloguing in Publication Data
A catalogue record for this book is available from the British Library

Library of Congress Cataloging in Publication Data
Reilly, Jim,
Shadowtime : history and representation in Hardy, Conrad, and George
Eliot/Jim Reilly.
p. cm.
Includes bibliographical references and index.
1. English fiction – 19th century – History and criticism.
2. Historical fiction, English – History and criticism. 3. Hardy, Thomas,
1840–1928 – Knowledge – History. 4. Conrad, Joseph, 1857–1924 –
Knowledge – History. 5. Eliot, George, 1819–1880 – Knowledge – History.
6. Literature and history. 7. Mimesis in literature. I Title.
II Title: Shadow time.
PR878.H5R4   1993
823.009′008–dc20

ISBN 0-415-08597-7

CONTENTS

v

There is no act of creation that is not transhistorical and does not come up from behind or proceed by way of a liberated line. Nietzsche opposes history not to the eternal but to the subhistorical or superhistorical: the Untimely, which is another name for haeccity, becoming, the innocence of becoming (in other words forgetting as opposed to memory, geography as opposed to history, the map as opposed to the tracing, the rhizome as opposed to arborescence) . . . Creations are like mutant abstract lines that have detached themselves from the task of representing a world, precisely because they assemble a new type of reality that history can only recontain or relocate in punctual systems.

Deleuze and Guattari, *A Thousand Plateaus*

When philosophy paints gray in gray, a form of life has become old, and this gray in gray cannot rejuvenate it, only understand it. The owl of Minerva begins its flight when dusk is falling.

Hegel, *The Philosophy of History*

The sun rises under the pillar of your tongue.
My hours are married to shadow.

Plath, 'The Colossus'

1

'WRITING THE EVENT' OR 'THE TEXT WHICH DISAPPEARED'

History and representation in the nineteenth and twentieth centuries

What happened most recently in the broad daylight of modern times in the case of the French Revolution – that gruesome farce which, considered closely, was quite superfluous, though noble and enthusiastic spectators from all over Europe contemplated it from a distance and interpreted it according to their own indignations and enthusiasms for so long, and so passionately, that *the text finally disappeared under the interpretation* – could happen once more as a noble posterity might misunderstand the whole past and in that way alone make it tolerable to look at.

Or rather: isn't this what has happened even now? Haven't we ourselves been this 'noble posterity'? And isn't now precisely the moment when, insofar as we comprehend this, it is all over?

Nietzsche, *Beyond Good and Evil* (original emphasis)

The human nature unto which I felt
That I belonged, and reverenced with love,
Was not a punctual presence, but a spirit
Diffused through time and space, with aid derived
Of evidence from monuments, erect,
Prostrate, or leaning towards their common rest
In earth, the widely scattered wreck sublime
Of vanished nations . . .

Wordsworth, *The Prelude*

who may tell the tale
of the old man?
weigh absence in a scale?
mete want with a span?

1

> the sum assess
> of the world's woes?
> nothingness
> in words enclose?
>
> Beckett, 'Addenda' to *Watt*

> The coming extinction of art is prefigured in the increasing
> impossibility of representing historical events.
>
> Adorno, *Minima Moralia*

HE RAMBLED FEEBLY ABOUT HISTORICAL EVENTS

Although this is a study of how history is inscribed in fiction – and vice versa – focused on Victorian and Edwardian writing, it is not a study of that eminent form of the period 'the historical novel'. It is indebted to Lukács's classic study of that title and is, in part, a sustained dialogue with this and other of his works but does not follow the precedent of that text in addressing avowedly historical genres. Adorno, as important a figure to this study as Lukács, suggests a rationale to this omission. He argues that in the nineteenth and twentieth centuries it is in avowedly historical works that history – and more particularly the issues surrounding how historical meaning and representation are now felt to be simultaneously crucial and in crisis – is most conspicuously absent. Indeed historical literary works are actually to the fore in facilitating an evacuation of history congenial to capitalism. 'History is extracted from tales which have become cultural commodities, even and especially there where historical themes are exploited. History as such becomes a costume identified with the individual concealing the frozen modernity of state capitalism' (Adorno, 1991, pp.66–7).

I readily concur that it is not in the historical novel that fiction in this period gives its richest account of that most nineteenth-century of concerns, historical meaning. To take my three authors as instances, the works recognisably conforming to historical genres – Eliot's recreation of fifteenth-century Florence in *Romola* (1863), Hardy's Napoleonic projects *The Trumpet-Major* (1880) and *The Dynasts* (1903–8) and Conrad's last, uncompleted novel, also with a Napoleonic setting, *Suspense* (1925) – are not now the works on which these authors' reputations rest, which is just as well for them. Conforming to historical genres seems to require ugly distortions of their art, producing their most feeble and uncharacteristic work. Few would want to contradict the view that these works are variously strained, turgid, slight or overblown and rarely redolent of their authors' characteristic brilliancies.

In these historical forms these authors' command of tone goes awry. *Romola* is too stolid and stately to afford much reading pleasure, indeed the novel seems curiously concerned to make a show of denying such pleasures. *Suspense* is too vapidly boisterous. It is hollow and heartless as adventure modes tend to be, but without the self-assurance essential to the form. *The Trumpet-Major* is overly rosy and decorative and somehow falls short of the bucolic charm it intends. Anne Garland falls for the dragoon John Loveday, or rather his waxed moustaches, blue coat and glittering 'arms and accoutrements' (T. Hardy, 1974, p.42) which are much stressed as if the narrative itself is half in love with a lost glamour of military/historical appearances. There is something faintly repulsive about the novel's monotone pleasantness and one sees dimly within it the origin of 'the historical novel' as we now know it in its most enfeebled and quietist form as the costumed sub-genre of romantic light fiction.

The only one of these works I shall study at length is the most apparently achieved, *Romola*, which I find a paradigm of the problematic structuring of the historical literary text in this latter half of the nineteenth century. 'Achieved' is perhaps precisely the wrong word as my interest here is in what can be seen, in the light of Eliot's subsequent development, as a profoundly instructive and liberating failure of the novel's historicist ambition. The oppressions of historicism are an issue at two levels. At one level there is the narrative crux of a daughter's fraught relation to her patriarchal historical inheritance figured in the reluctant responsibility Romola takes for her father's antiquarian collection. At the other there is Eliot's own titanic struggle to complete a project calling for Casaubonian labours of research and reconstruction. The failure is that of the historicising ambition 'To reconstruct a past world' (G. Eliot, 1981, p.40) which, subjected to profound intellectual reassessment and brilliant permutations of presentation, remains perhaps the mainstay of Eliot's entire artistic project.

Eliot forced herself to complete *Romola*; Conrad evidently did not feel that *Suspense* was worth comparable effort. It seems peculiarly telling that Conrad, for whom composition was characteristically an agony yet who regarded the completion of a novel as an urgent moral imperative and who in the figure of Captain Mitchell in *Nostromo* (1904) – 'He rambled feebly about "historical events" till I felt I could have a cry' (Conrad, 1986, p.421) – had parodied the tedious spinner of epic historical narratives, did not find the will to complete this most aptly titled work. This abortive yarn sadly illustrates Virginia Woolf's observation that Conrad's last few works revisit his early romance forms, but lifelessly. Lacking the buoyancy and conviction essential to romance they render history not as adventure but as 'stiff melodrama' (Woolf, 1980, 'Joseph Conrad', p.305). The abortion of this boisterous historical project is entirely predictable. In 'Heart of Darkness' and *Nostromo* Conrad had already given exhaustive analysis to the debilitating paradox at the root of his fiction's representation of history whereby novels simultaneously deconstruct prevailing historical rhetorics and dramatise their sense of implication within them. *Romola, The Trumpet-Major* and *Suspense* would be instances of how in these three authors we sense the strain of artists labouring within the conditions of historical genre forms – the historical novel/epic/romance – against whose innermost presuppositions about historical meaning they inwardly rebel. Perhaps, in a revealing perversity, we have to go back to Scott, originator of the historical novel and seminal figure in the nineteenth century's profound historicity, to find a major writer in English whose best and most characteristic work can be done within this form.

My focus is for the most part elsewhere, with the justification that it is precisely when freed from the presuppositions of the historical genres that these writers can address the fraught and unexpected forms historical meaning begins to adopt in the nineteenth century. Writing of the Second World War Adorno has said that characteristic of it as a modern historical manifestation is precisely its lack of conventionally historical qualities – of 'continuity, history, an "epic" element', of the ability to leave a 'permanent, unconsciously preserved image in the memory' (Adorno, 1974, p.54). All these now absent qualities would seem equally prerequisites of a viable historical fiction. Adorno's oeuvre can be read as a sustained protest against 'the dawning ahistorical character of a condition in which men experience themselves solely as objects of opaque processes and, torn between sudden shock and sudden forgetfulness, are no longer capable of a sense of temporal continuity' (Adorno, 1983, p.55). He argues that, with Beckett as an honourable exception, art has merely exhibited its inability to represent such a history. 'There is no adequate drama about Fascism' (Adorno, 1974, p.143). We might extend his argument – and backdate it into the nineteenth century – to suggest that it is this very absence of tangible historical qualities in modern experience that prompts the insistent historicity of nineteenth-century discourse. As with Captain Mitchell's tedious historical yarning, the nineteenth century's proliferation of historical genres compensates for the inexplicable absence of 'epic' history with an interminably voluble historical discourse.

Such also is the argument of Foucault. Nineteenth-century historicity masks the culture's evacuation of wonted historical meanings. But Foucault also sees in this stripping of historical meanings a process of redefinition in which historicity prepares to reassert itself in new, ambiguous forms.

> And the imaginative values then [the nineteenth century] assumed by the past, the whole lyrical halo that surrounded the consciousness of history at that period, the lively curiosity shown for documents or for traces left behind by time – all this is a surface expression of the simple fact that man found himself emptied of history, but that he was already beginning to recover in the depths of his own being, and among all the things that were still capable of reflecting his image (the others have fallen silent and folded back on themselves) a historicity linked essentially to man himself.
>
> (Foucault, 1989, p.369)

As a study of nineteenth-century historical representation the present work examines 'the imaginative values then assumed by the past', the period's sense of man being 'emptied of history' and its sense of the signs of man having 'fallen silent'. It will not tend to endorse the trace of humanist assertion, strange for Foucault and in context much qualified, in the notion of a new historicity emergent from 'the depths' of 'man himself'. Rather it is more in tune with the more characteristically Foucauldian formulation, in the very last words of the work quoted, which posit a future beyond humanist history in which 'man would be erased, like a face drawn in sand at the edge of the sea' (Foucault, 1989, p.387). What such an erasure of man and equally of the history of which he is the subject might mean has been sketched by Italo Calvino. This study examines the enactment within literature of an immense shift of meanings which he locates in the 1960s but which I see as of much longer gestation. His enumeration of its elements cites some essentially nineteenth-century cultural innovations.

> If we had to give a brief definition of this process, we could say that the notion of man as the subject of history is finished – the antagonist who has dethroned man must still be called man, but a man very different from what he was before. Which is to say, the human race of the 'big numbers' in exponential growth all over the planet; the explosion of the big cities; the ungovernability of

society and the economy, whatever system they belong to; the end of economic and ideological Eurocentrism; and the claiming of full rights by the outcasts, the repressed, the forgotten, and the inarticulate. All the parameters, categories, and antitheses that we once used to define, plan, and classify the world have been called into question. And not only those most closely linked to historical values, but even the ones that seemed to be stable anthropological categories – reason and myth, work and existence, male and female – and even the polarity of the most elementary combinations of words – affirmation and negation, above and below, subject and object.

(Calvino, 1989, 'Right and Wrong Political Uses
of Literature', pp.90–1)

WORLD-HISTORIC DERRING-DO

Despite this study's stated relegation of the genre my starting-point is a historical novel, Stendhal's *La Chartreuse de Parme* (1839), though one which gives a peculiarly ironic cast to that designation and in fact takes as its subject the possibility of a historical narrative. It is a work doubly justified to stand as the back-stop of our survey of nineteenth-century historical representation. It centres on that locus classicus of early nineteenth-century Western history, Waterloo, and subjects this event to an ironic, interrogative mode of representation, in effect a teasing refusal of representation, that has a vigorous later literary life. The adolescent hero, Italian aristocrat Fabrizio del Dongo, is a fanatical admirer of Napoleon and, on an impulsive personal initiative, makes a precarious solo journey from Milan to fight under his idol's direction at Waterloo. The stage is set for a historical encounter but the subsequent chapter titles – 'The Guns of Waterloo', 'An Army in Retreat', 'Cross-Country Flight' – arouse an expectation the narrative itself pointedly fails to satisfy: a vivid rendering of the Battle of Waterloo centring on Fabrizio's experience of combat and following recognisable contours of engagement, mutiny and retreat. In fact even the notion of Fabrizio's having experienced the battle at all is rendered thoroughly problematic. Fabrizio's expectations of combat are endlessly frustrated and deferred. The historical engagement he seeks proves an ignis fatuus. It would be difficult to find a more direct illustration of David Lodge's comment that in the nineteenth-century realist novel 'the main characters are alienated and their efforts to participate in history are mocked and frustrated' (Lodge, 1977, p.38).

Fabrizio's Waterloo is an untidy series of picaresque skirmishes and embarrassments and a tissue of unconfident interpretations and mis-readings. He is variously duped, victimised and befriended, continually loses his way, mistakes allies and enemies, muddles forays and retreats, and fails to identify Marshal Ney. Hegel said that to see Napoleon was to witness history on horseback, but Fabrizio misses his glimpse of this idol who is history, who gallops by unrecognised. Always either too early or too late for combat he encounters only its obscuring evidences – flying mud and veils of gun-smoke – or grim wastage – a horse thrashing in its own entrails, a stripped corpse with one staring eye. He shakes the corpse's hand for a dare and fires a single shot which may or may not have unhorsed a cavalryman. Adorno ridicules Hegel's view of history as 'world-historic derring-do' (Adorno, 1990, p.13) and it seems as if Fabrizio's Waterloo is another refutation of the Hegelian expectation that decisive actions and engagements are to be found at the centre of history. Fabrizio's engagement with history is, like shaking hands with a corpse, only the lifeless parody of an encounter. Knowing action only through inference Fabrizio experiences history negatively, through the evidence of its absence.

> Our hero stood looking at the road. A short time before, three or four thousand people had been hastening along it, packed to-gether like peasants in the tail of a procession. After the cry of 'Cossacks!' he saw precisely no one . . . He scanned the length of the road in both directions, and also the plain, but saw no trace of the Cossacks . . . He was absolutely alone in the middle of this plain which a short time back had been so crowded with people.
>
> (Stendhal, 1983, pp.76–7)

Fabrizio's characterisation reprises incomprehension – 'He could not make head or tail of what was happening', 'our hero who, to tell the truth, could not make head or tail of what she was saying', 'But what on earth's happening?' (Stendhal, 1983, p.59; p.72; p.67). He seems thus to illustrate the observation of Deleuze and Guattari that 'The novel has always been defined by the adventure of lost characters who no longer know their name, what they are looking for, or what they are doing, amnesiacs, ataxics, catatonics' (Deleuze and Guattari, 1988, p.173). In Stendhal this familiar puzzled disengagement has the experience of history as its enigmatic focus. In the very midst of the event Fabrizio repeatedly seeks verification that this is a battle and that he is in it. 'His chief sorrow was that he had not asked Corporal Aubry the question: "have I really taken part in a battle?" It seemed to him that he had, and he would have been supremely happy if he could have been certain of this.' '"Sir," he said at length to the sergeant, "this is the first time I have been present at a battle. But is this one a real battle?"' (Stendhal, 1983, p.77; p.60). Surely Waterloo is the very stage of history; if history is not encountered here, where is it?

Fabrizio is ever after embarrassed to be urged, and especially by women, to recount his Waterloo experience – his world-historic derring-do – since he is never quite sure that he actually had one. As Shakespeare's Roman patricians urge Coriolanus to acknowledge, the deeds of a soldier who will not suffer them to be recounted – Coriolanus calls this having his 'nothings monster'd' (II.ii.77) – might just as well be, perhaps are, nothings. An immense and immemorial tradition of epic narrative is decisively negated when a soldier in fiction will not have his deeds told. Fabrizio is an inept and insecure, and Coriolanus an impressively unwilling, literary version of the *Sprecher*. This is the conventional figure in Western painting and particularly post-Renaissance heroic depictions of historical events who, engaging the viewer with direct gaze, points to whatever battle or enthronement is depicted assuring through this visual address that 'I was there'. Or perhaps we might say that their discomfort as *Sprecher*s brings into sharper focus complexities and contradictions always implicit in that role. The *Sprecher* ostensibly canvasses assent to the truth of what is depicted which would explain a particular prominence in devotional art. In fact, by looking out from the canvas and acknowledging the viewer the *Sprecher* foregrounds the work's nature as a representation, while having its own apparently opposite intention, that of saying 'I am your witness and guarantor that this is real'. Pointing to the event, the *Sprecher* – like one of those faintly comic pointing hands once found in the margins of books – partly draws attention away from the action depicted/passage indicated to the process of its signification. The event is displaced – is this what Coriolanus feared? – by the act of signing which claims to be merely its supplement.

Something of the complexity of the *Sprecher*'s role inheres within the term *history* itself. Crucial to it – indeed making it unique within the language – is its particular duality of reference. It is both a form of study and that study's referent, both what Herodotos and Macaulay wrote and what they wrote about. It is both an event and the record of that event, an experience and a discourse predicated on that experience, the times and the sign of those times, action and the name of action. As a term it resists any separation, let alone ordering in priority, of being and discourse, of the signified and the sign. Thus in the context of our

Western intellectual traditions the term *history* carries an aura almost magical. By compounding these apparently opposed registers it suggests a promise of hidden synthesis, hints at a healing of the great rift dividing action and significance, matter and meaning. It is in these terms that, in the decade of Stendhal's novel, Hegel anatomises the word in *The Philosophy of History* (delivered as lectures, 1830–31).

> In our language the term *History* unites the objective with the subjective side and denotes quite as much the *historia rerum gestarum*, as the *res gestae* themselves: on the other hand it comprehends not less what has *happened*, than the *narration* of what has happened. This union of the two meanings we must regard as a higher order than mere outward accident; we must suppose historical narrations to have appeared contemporaneously with historical deeds and events. It is an internal vital principle common to both that produces them synchronously.
>
> (Hegel, 1956, p.60)

Lyotard in 1973 appears to make much the same point, if not with Hegel's admirable succinctness.

> We are used to positing the following sequence: there is the fact, then the witnesses' acccount, i.e. a narrative activity transforming the fact into a narrative . . . the work proper to historical science will be to undo what is done by narration, to set out from the linguistic datum of the narrative to reach, by critical analysis (of document, text, sources), the fact that is the raw material of this production . . . And yet it is obvious that the historian is himself no more than another director, his narrative another product, his work another narration, even if all this is assigned the index *meta-*: meta-diegesis, meta-narration, meta-narrative. History which talks about history, to be sure, but whose claim to reach this reference to the thing itself, the fact, to establish it and restore it, is no less crazy, all in all rather crazier, than the power of literary fiction freely deployed in the hundreds of discourses from which is born the huge legend of, for example, the *Odyssey*.
>
> (Lyotard, 1973, pp.180–1)

In fact we find Hegel here more radical than Lyotard. The latter does not actually deconstruct the 'sequence' he cites as the presumably erroneous popular conception. While suggesting that the historical fact as such is unrecoverable, Lyotard seems to leave untroubled the assumption that this occurs in some pure form and *precedes* its narration. Not so

Hegel who, in a measure of his genius, carefully weights the key terms 'contemporaneously', 'synchronously'. Of all the philosophy quoted in the present work nothing, I think, is as provocative as this assertion, a century and a half before post-structuralism, that events and their discourse (or is that discourse and its events?) are synchronous.

My own study is in some sense an analysis of this continuing problematic of 'writing the event' that troubles discourse at least from Hegel to Lyotard – as it should given Western thought's central preoccupation with the ongoing dialectical miracle of the transformation of matter into meaning, content into expression, the social process into a signifying system. That last is rather too glib a sentence, illustrating as it does how easy it is to slip into fomulations which solve the problem before even really posing it by assuming a pre-lingual primacy of process. But which really did come first, the chicken-deed or the egg-word? For Lacan, famous for regarding even the unconscious as a linguistic structure and thus apparently discrediting the very category of the pre-lingual, the beginning was the word.

> How, indeed, could speech exhaust the meaning of speech, or, to put it better, with the Oxford logical positivists, the meaning of meaning – except in the act that engenders it? Thus Goethe's reversal of its presence at the origin of things, 'In the beginning was the act', is itself reversed in its turn: it was certainly the Word (verbe) that was in the beginning.
>
> (Lacan, 1977 (1), p.61)

As a sign, the term *history* gives a peculiarly emphatic stress to a contradiction operating within every sign. A sign simultaneously evokes the presence of the signified it posits and acts as the evidence of its absence. Much more than a semantic quirk, this indeterminacy within the term is an indicator in little of the complexity of historical meaning. Is history an event or a discourse? Is there anything prior to discourse? What guarantees veracity if an event is inextricable from the surely never purely objective telling of that event? The term is its own little act of deconstruciton of perhaps the innermost presuppositon of Western thought – that being exists prior to, in a different state from, and should be privileged over, the conceptualising and discourse which is said to succeed it and be its supplement. Adorno points out the paradox within such a view. 'Being is the supreme concept – for on the lips of him who says "Being" is the word, not Being itself – and yet it is said to be privileged above all conceptuality' (Adorno, 1990, p.69). I think

Adorno's meaning is preserved if we substitute 'history' and 'discourse' for 'Being' and 'conceptuality' respectively.

Nineteenth-century fiction is a site of interrogation and dramatisation of these issues which this historiographically saturated century has thrown into focus. The ontological indeterminacy inscribed within the term history – is it matter, event or discourse? – lends a kind of intelligibility to the apparent lunacy of Dickens's Mr Dick in *David Copperfield* (1849–50). Oppressed by the belief that the 'trouble' in the head of Charles I was, upon his execution, transferred to his own, he endlessly writes out his 'Memorial', a personal statement into which Charles keeps intruding. He has made a kite out of its pages and, flying it on a long string, hopes to dissipate Charles and their shared trouble to the four winds. A historical event, a historical personage, the words which refer to them, his own mental oppression and physical matter which could be carried by the wind – to Mr Dick all these blur and converge in a weird mutation of unstable categories. Mr Dick, perhaps in this more representative of his century than eccentric to it, feels as a personal agony the weird instability of historical meaning. His confusion of categories has the honour of being Carlylean. Carlyle, another historical obsessive for whom great figures loom large, also confounds them, and the eras they exemplified, with script. 'Great Men are the inspired (speaking and acting) Texts of that divine BOOK OF REVELATIONS, whereof a Chapter is completed from epoch to epoch, and by some named HISTORY' (Carlyle, 1987, p.135). And for Nietzsche the French Revolution was 'the text [which] disappeared under the interpretation' (Nietzsche, 1966, p.49).

The frustrating indeterminacy of Fabrizio's Waterloo evokes a comparable complexity. In an elegant narrative manoeuvre of which we will encounter many variants in nineteenth-century writing Stendhal plays, like Dickens, on the ontological indeterminacy of the term *history* – experience or discourse? Uncertain of what, if anything, he has experienced, Fabrizio seeks to know it by reading about it.

> He had remained child upon one point only: Was what he had seen a real battle? And, if so, was that battle Waterloo?
> For the first time in his life he found some pleasure in reading; he was always trying to find in the newspapers, or in published accounts of the battle, some description or other which would enable him to identify the ground he had covered with Marshal Ney's escort, and later with the other general.
>
> (Stendhal, 1983, p.88)

Like Mr Dick, Fabrizio hopes that the trouble of history can be safely trammeled up in discourse. Stendhal asks the great nineteenth-century questions which, as novelists pose them, are the subject of my own work – Where is the standing-ground of history? Where does it take place? Literal topographic ground, the frustrating and indeterminate experience of an individual, subsequent journalistic or historical discourse and 'some description or other' – the historical event is somehow diffused amongst a whole range of ontological categories which are made to stand as evidence for each other. Something which was never exactly an experience is immediately displaced into discourse in such a way as to make any distinction between the terms problematic. Stendhal's implicit question 'Where does history take place?' is answered in the twentieth century by Adorno, 'language' – 'History does not merely touch on language, but takes place in it' (Adorno, 1974, p.219).

Recalling a childhood visit of 1824 to the site of the Battle of Waterloo, Ruskin is drawn to a more unselfconscious usage of the same strategy of Stendhal's whereby in evoking history experiential evidence is displaced by discursive.

> The defacing mound was not then built – it was only nine years since the fight; and each bank and hollow of the ground was still a true exponent of the course of charge or recoil. Fastened in my mind by later reading, that sight of the slope of battle remains to me entirely distinct, while the results of a late examination of it after the building of the mound, have faded mostly away.
>
> (Ruskin, 1989, p.94)

Where is that ground of history? – that 'fixed ground' which Foucault says is the gift that the concept of history brings to the human sciences in this period (Foucault, 1989, p.317). Ruskin's tell-tale phrase is 'fixed in my mind by later reading' in a statement so insistent upon material, experiential evidences. Even Ruskin, with none of Stendhal's scepticism and wry, ironic play over the appearances of power and history (which made him a favorite of Nietzsche's), finds himself drawn into a comparable recessive complication of ontological categories when describing historical evidences. Only the page before he has made an utterly characteristic statement of 'Another character of my perceptions I find curiously steady – that I was only interested by things near me, or at least clearly visible and present' (Ruskin, 1989, p.93), but he here acknowledges the experience whereby the 'clearly visible and present', the 'distinct' 'sight', is actually a function of 'later reading' so much so as even to displace the evidence of later seeing.

Ruskin, like Fabrizio, stands slightly perplexed at the empty site of a battle gone by, or rather *the* battle which *must* contain a clue to the meaning of the century to which it in effect gave birth and where the momentum of that essentially Enlightenment phenomenon, the French Revolution, finally hit the buffers. The century here inaugurated made historical thought its major intellectual concern and, as the acme of bourgeois power, was itself a historical conundrum. History here seemed to have achieved its apotheosis. As Hardy puts it, 'Everybody is thinking, even amid these art examples from various ages, that this present age is the ultimate climax and upshot of the previous ages, and not a link in a chain of them' (F.E. Hardy, 1986, p.191). To the victorious bourgeoisie the age must indeed have appeared the fulfilment of a long-withheld destiny or, in Hardy's slight studied awkwardness, 'the ultimate climax and upshot'. At the same time its entire industrial dynamic was invention, innovation, new wealth, the parvenu triumph of the modern. The tension of the age is thus enacted in Hardy's *A Laodicean* (1881) where Paula Power, a railway engineer's daughter and heiress of his new wealth owns and puzzles over the style – Gothic or Classical, faithfully restorative or boldly redesigning? – in which to revamp a castle so old that its origins – Saxon or Norman? – seem unrecoverable. In an age saturated with historicism and hence in which thought equates authority, authenticity and antiquity, where do these new conquerors stand? What is 'a true exponent' of the nineteenth century's own 'course of charge or recoil'? As Carlyle puts it,

> in this inquiring age, ask yourself, Whence came it, and Why and How? – and rest not, till, if no better may be, Fancy have shaped out an answer; and, either in the authentic lineaments of Fact, or the forged ones of Fiction, a complete picture and Genetical History of the Man and his spiritual Endeavour lies before you.
>
> (Carlyle, 1987, pp.58–9)

The promise of meaning tantalisingly held out by the historical event is a central imponderable of nineteenth-century discourse. Hegel had said that the *Weltgeist* chooses certain pivotal historical occurrences, such as the early death of Alexander, through which to articulate itself symbolically. They form what George Eliot calls 'a nodus, a ganglion, in the historical development of humanity' (G. Eliot, 1990, p.317). *War and Peace* (1869) attempts to puzzle out the intangible significance of the Napoleonic campaigns. Napoleon's emblem was the bee. What, asks Tolstoy, is the purpose of bees: to sting, to have their fill of nectar, to make honey, to reproduce, or to fertilise flowers? For all the exhaustive theorising, the bee escapes comprehension.

> Nevertheless the ultimate purpose of bees is not exhausted by any such purposes as the human mind may conceive of it. The higher the human intellect soars in its conception of possible purposes, the more does it realise that such purposes lie beyond its comprehension.
> Man cannot rise beyond a certain insight into the correlation of the bee's life with certain other phenomena of life. So also with the purposes for which historical personages and nations exist.
>
> (Tolstoy, 1979, pp.371–2)

Fabrizio's Waterloo, in which the *Weltgeist*'s self-disclosure is absurdly unrevealing, is a comically frustrated interrogation of one of these newly revered and yet seemingly inscrutable foci of meaning. Stendhal's earnest innocent in determined pursuit of historical engagement and of his historical idol is in some kind a representative nineteenth-century figure. Like him, the age attempts to read history after the Hegelian model of 'world-historic derring-do' or after the comparable Carlylean one, as a discourse 'On Heroes, Hero-Worship and the Heroic'. Perhaps the essence of his representativeness is his finding his pursuit of engagement with the historical event ever frustrated, deferred and displaced by discourse.

A QUESTION OF HISTORY

Foucault dubs the nineteenth century 'The Age of History', using the term as a sub-heading in the chapter of *The Order of Things* (1966), 'The Limits of Representation'. His subject here is precisely the relation he senses between the nineteenth century's fixation with historical meaning and its conception of representation as unprecedentedly oblique and problematic. Nineteenth-century historicism is the outcome of a process brewing in Western discourse since the Renaissance, essentially a great decay of reference and representation. Foucault elaborates here his famous model of epistemes, historically specific configurations of the elements of representation. The medieval episteme, up to the end of the sixteenth century, figured the cosmos as a divinely ordained pattern of resemblances, or, to use the period's own rich vocabulary of comparison, of Aemulatio, Analogia, Convenientia, Paritas, Similitas. Dramatic, pictorial and discursive representations are the mirrors of this nature and share in the universal process of imitation within this endlessly self-referential totality. There is a great fold running through nature whereby signs and phenomena touch and correspond in an immense patterning of similitude. 'The same remains the same, riveted onto itself' (Foucault, 1989, p.25).

With the Renaissance a new episteme is inaugurated as the rivets of universal sameness begin to work loose. *Don Quixote* (1605) dramatises this crisis. It is:

> a negative of the Renaissance world; writing has ceased to be the prose of the world; resemblances and signs have dissolved their former alliance; similitudes have become deceptive and verge upon the visionary or madness; things still remain stubbornly within their ironic identity: they are no longer anything but what they are; words wander off on their own, without content, without resemblance to fill their emptiness; they are no longer the marks of things; they lie sleeping between the pages of books and covered in dust.
>
> (Foucault, 1989, p.32)

So Don Quixote, champion of the medieval episteme, bibliophile of its quest literature and seeker of similitude, buckles on his armour and ventures out into the Renaissance world in a one-man attempt to buckle back together words and things, poetry and life. He refuses to acknowledge Sidney's distinction between the brazen world of reality and the golden one of poetry and resolutely reads the world as a marvellous Romance narrative, windmills as giants and a tin basin as a fabled golden helmet. He disowns the prevailing episteme in which 'The written word and things no longer resemble one another' (Foucault, 1989, p.48). He wraps the newly referenceless world back up in discourse.

The Classical episteme, beginning in the seventeenth century, is, Foucault argues, the first point where the binary model of signification, discrete pairings of a sign and a signified, becomes dominant. This is part of a shift in priorities Foucault sees exemplified in Descartes from a patterning of resemblances to a dispersal of identities and differences. In a formulation worth recalling in relation to the next chapter's examination of contrasting positions adopted by George Eliot and Hardy on questions of difference and similitude, Descartes is cited asserting the primacy of differentiation over comparison. 'It is a frequent habit when we discover several resemblances between two things, to attribute to both equally, even on points in which they are in reality different, that which we have recognised to be true of only one of them' (Foucault, 1989, p.51). Immanent resemblance is now only a faint cultural memory alluded to in new artistic forms in which the appearances of resemblance are exposed as illusory – *trompe-l'oeil* painting, comic illusions, the play which duplicates itself by representing another play – and in a poetic dimension of language now defined by metaphor, simile and allegory. The role of the sign itself has altered.

> The sign, in the Classical age, is charged no longer with the task of keeping the world close to itself and inherent in its own forms, but, on the contrary, with that of spreading it out, of juxtaposing it over an indefinitely open surface . . . . And it is by this means that it is offered simultaneously to analysis and to combination, and can be ordered from beginning to end.
>
> (Foucault, 1989, p.61)

There is now an essential coherence between the theory of representation and the theories of languages, of the natural orders, and of wealth and value, all of which are subject to the grid of knowledge the age is everywhere ordering in assiduous taxonomy and tabulation. Signs are more obviously seen as relating laterally to all the other signs ordered in the table of signs than to an absent referent, and all things can be read off from this grid of signs.

This is succeeded by the contemporary episteme, the outer limits of whose period of emergence Foucault puts at 1775 and 1825, which pushes the sign further into autonomy. Here 'the sign ceases to be a form of the world; and it ceases to be bound to what it marks by the solid and secret bonds of resemblance or affinity' (Foucault, 1989, p.67). There is now a decisive, unprecedented element. History erupts into the configuration of representation.

> the theory of representation disappears as the universal foundation of all possible orders; language as . . . the primary grid of things, as an indispensable link between representation and things, is eclipsed in its turn: a profound historicity penetrates into the heart of things, isolates and defines them in their own coherence, imposes upon them the forms of order implied by the continuity of time; the analysis of exchange and money gives way to the study of production, that of the organism takes precedence over the search for taxonomic characteristics, and, above all, language loses its privileged position and becomes, in its turn, a historical form coherent with the density of its own past . . . things become increasingly reflexive, seeking the principle of their

intelligibility only in their own development, and abandoning the space of representation.

(Foucault, 1989, p.xxiii)

'This event', Foucault argues, 'probably because we are still caught inside it, is largely beyond our comprehension' (Foucault, 1989, p.221) (this last statement seems unequivocally to state the current continuance of this episteme, other of his formulations imply that it is in the process of passing or has actually passed). 'The constitution of so many positive sciences, the appearance of literature, the folding back of philosophy upon its own development, the emergence of history as both knowledge and the mode of being of empiricity, are only so many signs of a deeper rupture'. After 1800 'words, classes, and wealth will acquire a mode of being no longer compatible with representation'. Here is inaugurated the age of 'Signs scattered through the space of knowledge' (Foucault, 1989, p.221; p.221; p.17).

Foucault's audacious and brilliant history of representation, or rather deconstructive teleology of representation's decay, is – especially as brutalised in my paraphrase – not immune to criticism. Derrida asks how one can write a history of epistemes when one's own discourse must be a function of its own episteme (*Writing and Difference*, 1978). He also questions Foucault's project of a history of madness in comparable terms. If 'madness' is that which has been defined as the unrepresentable thing excluded from the discourse of history, history's Other, how then can its history be written? Equally, if the writing of history is a form of representation, how can there be a history of the demise of representation? One might also feel uncomfortable that Foucault's historical model, if not exactly purposive, is securely progressive and teleological in the grand manner of the eighteenth- and nineteenth-century historical projects – Hegelian, Comtean, Darwinian, Marxist – which he presumably would classify as functions of a (possibly) antiquated episteme. Indeed, as a supposed deconstruction of historicism Foucault's model seems thoroughly structured by that historicism's most familiar forms. There is certainly something readily recognisable about a decadent historical model that measures the present's distance from some prior lost totality – Lukács's Epic era, the Greeks' own conception of the Golden Age – that was somehow fully present to itself, intelligible, self-identical. However, this caution registered, I find very valuable Foucault's characterisation of the nineteenth-century episteme as one in which history and representation enter into a problematic, indeed conflictual, configuration.

17

Foucault's characterisation of the contemporary episteme is worth expanding upon. The 'profound historicity' he claims for nineteenth-century discourse is easily demonstrated. Hegel and historicising run through the age like wine through water and his historical vision is one with which all subsequent historical thought has to engage, even if combatively. The era is everywhere cognisant of 'that Tissue of History, which inweaves all Being' (Carlyle, 1989, p.17). It is the 'enquiring age' the central issue of which is, as Carlyle formulates it, 'Whence came it, and Why, and How?' (Carlyle, 1989, p.58). 'Here', as Tolstoy is fond of saying, 'we have a question of history' (Tolstoy, 1979, p.446). 'The Past is the true fountain of knowledge . . . we do nothing but enact history, we say little but recite it: nay, rather, in that widest sense, our whole spiritual life is built thereon' (Carlyle, 1988, p.40). Here would be an instance of the nineteenth-century 'emergence of history as both knowledge and the mode of being of empiricity'. Carlyle recommends a dedicated historicity. 'Let us search more and more into the Past; let all men explore it, as the true fountain of knowledge; by whose light alone, consciously or unconsciously employed, can the Present and the Future be interpreted or guessed at' (Carlyle, 1988, p.40). Matthew Arnold acknowledges, more than hinting at weariness, his period's fulfilment of the Carlylean injunction.

> We scrutinise the dates
> Of long-past human things,
> The bounds of effaced states,
> The lines of deceased kings;
> We search out dead men's words, and works of dead men's hands.
>
> (*Empedocles on Etna*, lines 322–6)

It is the age into whose musty, bookish historicising, Baudelaire, self-proclaimed laureate of the new, complained of having to be born.

> The bookshelf loomed over my cradle
> Drear Babel of novels, history and verse
> Latin cinders and Greek dust
> There mingled . . .
>
> (Baudelaire, 1987, 'A Voice')

It is the era which regards itself, as Nietzsche says, 'as proud of its historical sense' (Nietzsche, 1990, p.178), where 'the historical sense reigns *without restraint*' but which he believes is in fact 'undermined by the study of history', 'ruined by history', 'overwhelmed and bewildered by history', living by 'cramming ourselves with the ages, customs, arts, philosophers, religions, discoveries of others'. We are 'walking encyclopaedias' misguidedly erecting a 'monumental history in full icon-like *veracity*' and revering a historical discourse – 'a Hegelian skeleton', history as 'disguised theology' – which serves only 'to stand guard over history to see that nothing comes of it except more history, and certainly no real events!'. He fulminates against the contemporary stitching of that Carlylean 'Tissue of History, which inweaves all being' which to him is 'The madly thoughtless shattering and dismantling of all foundations, their dissolution into a continual evolving that flows ceaselessly away, the tireless unspinning and historicising of all there has ever been by modern man, the great cross-spider at the node of the cosmic web' (Nietzsche, 1983, p.95; p.80; p.81; p.98; p.79; p.79; p.70; p.84; p.108).

Marx also sets himself the task of wresting history from Hegel – replacing the 'old, Hegelian junk' of 'sacred history – a history of ideas' with 'a profane history – a history of man' which is historical material-ism. An age which has lost faith in the transcendent must be persuaded to replace it with a faith in history, not Hegel's 'disguised theology' but the historical materialism which is 'the solution to the riddle of history' (Marx, 1977, p.89). Marx, like Carlyle, illustrates Foucault's conception that now history becomes both 'knowledge' and 'the mode of being of empiricity'. 'It is therefore the task of history, now the truth is no longer in the beyond, to establish the truth of the here and now' (Marx, 1977, p.89).

Lukács argues that for individuals history now enters into the marrow, it becomes something in which everyone participates and for the first time people actually feel themselves to be historical. 'It was the French Revolution, the revolutionary wars and the rise and fall of Napoleon, which for the first time made history a *mass experience*'. Now history is, and is generally felt to be, 'the bearer and realizer of human progress'. This complements the emergence of a conscious historicity in art. 'It is only during the last phase of the Enlightenment that the problem of the artistic reflection of past ages emerges as a central problem of literature'. Lukács finds the epitome of this movement in the hugely influential figure of Scott, the Hegel of historical representation. 'The typically human terms in which great historical trends become tangible had never before been so superbly, straighforwardly and pregnantly portrayed. And above all, never before had this kind of portrayal been consciously set at the centre of the representation of reality' (Lukács, 1962, p.20; p.25; p.18; pp.34–5).

My own argument – Stendhal rather than Scott, Foucault rather than Lukács, Adorno rather than Hegel – cannot concur with Lukács in finding typical of the nineteenth century a 'superb, straightforward and pregnant' portrayal of 'tangible' history, consciously centralised. Stendhal showing Fabrizio not able to find Waterloo – pivotal amongst the events Lukács regards as instrumental in making history a mass experience – seems a precise inversion of such a formulation. Lukács rightly identifies the concrete historical representation which is a crucial new *ambition* of discourse, but this is one nowhere realised, least of all 'superbly and straightforwardly'. I prefer Lukács's more cautious formulation that this now becomes a 'central problem of literature'. More telling is Nietzsche's conception of the whole issue as in crisis.

where has all the clarity, all the naturalness and purity of this relationship between life and history gone? In what restless and exaggerated confusion does the problem now swell before our eyes! Does the fault lie with us, who observe it? Or has the constellation of life and history really altered through the interposition of a mighty, hostile star between them?

(Nietzsche, 1983, p.77)

Nietzsche's fearsome rhetoric would hardly be exaggerated if, as Foucault suggests, the nineteenth century has impaled itself on the paradox whereby history is seen both as the very 'mode of being of empiricity' and as 'no longer compatible with representation'.

UNSPEAKABLE/UNHISTORIC

Foucault equates nineteenth-century historicism, and its continuing influence, with a referenceless discourse where signs, unhinged from things, are 'scattered through the space of knowledge'. The initial narrator of 'Heart of Darkness', florid eulogist of Tudor colonial adventuring, and hence prime rhetorical exponent of that historicism, pictures British history, in a Foucauldian formulation, as the play of splendidly autonomous 'names' 'like jewels flashing in the night of time' (Conrad, 1981, p.7). Marlow's narrative, famously fractured, crippled with intuitions of its own duplicity and inarticulacy, writhes within the dilemma of its own lack of reference and failure to represent. 'Kurtz . . . was just a word for me. I did not see the man in the name any more than you do. Do you see him? Do you see the story? Do you see anything?' (Conrad, 1981, p.39). Words as Kurtz himself uses them in his famed oral and written 'eloquence' glory in their autonomy from reference while history, thus obscured and muted, is rendered, like his unspecified crimes, an 'unspeakable act'. History here indeed 'abandons the space of representation' and, geographically and discursively, retreats into 'the heart of an immense darkness' (Conrad, 1981, p.111). In the form of Marlow's lie to the Intended, history is finally not represented, but misrepresented.

Conrad alerts us to how the newly unrepresentable nature of history coincides with, and is perhaps a function of, capitalism's modern colonialist phase. The sites of the colonial enterprise, the far-flung 'outposts of progress', are by definition at far geographical – and moral – remove from the centres of the discourses – legal, commercial, propagandist, historical and literary – required to endorse them. Colonial history is swathed both in the obfuscations of duplicitous discourse and geographically removed from scrutiny. This blind-spot of geography and discourse occludes a consequently all-licensed criminality. Such a blind-spot, another heart of darkness, is the setting of 'that remote novel' (Conrad, 1980 (1), p.8) *Nostromo*.

> Sky, land, and sea disappear together out of the world when the Placido – as the saying is – goes to sleep under its black poncho. The few stars left below the seaward frown of the vault shine feebly as into the mouth of a black cavern . . . The eye of God Himself – they add with grim profanity – could not find out what work a man's hand is doing in there; and you would be free to call the devil to your aid with impunity if even his malice were not defeated by such a blind darkness.
>
> (Conrad, 1986 (1), pp.41–2)

Conrad called *Nostromo* 'my largest canvas' (Conrad, 1980 (1), p.8) and as a pictorial representation it follows the law of perspective informing Western art since the fourteenth century: it is organised around a vanishing point. A novel everywhere structured by the unrepresented absence of historical observation, its central 'blind darkness', it gives a peculiarly apt illustration to Terry Eagleton's remark about Conrad that one has the sense of his 'sculpting a vacuum, shaping a void' (Eagleton, 1976, p.137). I am also reminded of the arguments of Toni Morrison on canonical 'whitemale' American fiction from Hawthorne to James. While apparently staggeringly incognisant of the omnipresent historical issue of their country and era, the African–American experience to which they hardly even allude, these novels are in fact everywhere shaped by this 'ornamental absence', this 'structuring absence' which they contort themselves to occlude. The African–American absence

21

from these works is the negative imprint of their momentous historical presence (Morrison, Trinity College Cambridge, Clark Lecture, 1990, unpublished).

In *Little Dorrit* (1855–7) Clennam comes to realise that his life, and the novel that enshrines it, has been organised around precisely the most crucial and yet least visible thing, the figure after whom the novel is named.

> Looking back upon his own poor story, she was its vanishing-point. Every thing in its perspective led to her innocent figure. He had travelled thousands of miles towards it; previous unquiet hopes and doubts had worked themselves out before it; it was the centre of the interest of his life; it was the termination of every-thing that was good and pleasant in it; beyond there was nothing but mere waste and darkened sky.
>
> (Dickens, 1983, pp.801–2)

Perhaps *Little Dorrit* and Morrison's 'whitemale' American novels are not the only instances of nineteenth-century discourse thoroughly structured by the existence – yet absence – of a crucial, unrepresentable meaning. This might be something of Adorno's admittedly enigmatic import when he says that the great realist novels 'derived their meaning precisely from the dissolution of coherent meaning' (Adorno, 1974, p.144). I am tempted to rephrase this: realist novels derive their representation precisely from their selective refusal of representation. *Middlemarch* (1871) circles the crisis of its own realist ambition threat-eningly evoked in the novel's own blind-spot in Dorothea's experience of Western history in Rome as unsurveyably chaotic and conflictual. Beyond realism's self-circumscribing sphere of representation, its 'sturdy, neutral delight in things as they were', this culture's oppressive historical truths – its 'Titanic . . . struggling', its 'deep degeneracy . . . degradation' – rest shrouded within 'the other side of silence'. The historical oppression which has facilitated the rise to power of the bourgeoisie and hence of its paradigmatic literary form, the realist novel, is the area where the clear eye of realism turns its obscuring 'disease of the retina' (G. Eliot, 1981, p.225; p.226).

Macaulay suggests that the period's historical discourse is compara-bly constructed. History is another pictorial representation organised around its vanishing point, defined by what it obscures. 'History has its foreground and its background . . . Some events must be represented on a large scale, others diminished; the great majority will be lost in the dimness of the horizon: and a general idea of the joint effect will be

22

given by a few slight touches' (Macaulay, 1860, p.340). So the 'Eye of History', to use Carlyle's term, also has its blind-spot, its diseased retina. As Macaulay readily admits, bourgeois historiography ensures precisely that 'the great majority will be lost in the dimness of the horizon'. In 'The Uses and Disadvantages of History for Life' Nietzsche freely admits and endorses the ambition of nineteenth-century historical discourse to obscure and occlude. Envious of animals' freedom from oppressive historical consciousness he advises a bovine forgetfulness and the firm drawing of that horizon of historical knowledge Macaulay describes.

> That which such a nature cannot subdue it knows how to forget; it no longer exists, the horizon is rounded and closed, and there is nothing left to suggest there are people, passions, teachings, goals lying beyond it. And this is a universal law: a living thing can be healthy, strong and fruitful only when bounded by a horizon; if it is incapable of drawing a horizon around itself, and at the same time too self-centred to enclose its own view within that of another, it will pine away slowly or hasten to its timely end.
>
> (Nietzsche, 1983, p.63)

We should forget because, as the victors who survive to remember history, we need to extinguish our own bad conscience. Nietzsche had declared, in a Marlowesque formulation, that 'It is not possible to live with truth' and pronounces the essence of art to be 'an interested, in the highest degree, and *ruthlessly* interested adjustment of things, a fundamental falsification' (quoted Lukács, 1962, pp.212–13). Thus is historical untruth enshrined as the only valid mode of discourse, with art as a privileged mode of such untruth. The falsification inherent in art should be exploited and literalised to aid the falsification of history. For Lukács 'This already is the philosophy of the lie as the necessary mode of reaction of a living human being to reality' (Lukács, 1962, p.213). Addressing the essay on history Lukács attacks Nietzsche's ethos of 'fundamental falsification'. On this issue Nietzsche is the exemplary bourgeois.

> He takes arms against academic history writing, against its isolation from life. However, the relation which he establishes between historical science and life is that of the conscious omission of unpleasant facts unfavourable to 'life'. Nietzsche relates history to life by invoking the following fact of life: 'All action requires the ability to forget'.

This already is a cynical philosophy of apologetics. What the university professors in the pay of the bourgeoisie, cowardly hiding behind the mask of objectivity, conceal with embarrassment, Nietzsche here pronounces openly and unashamedly. The historical necessity for the bourgeoisie of his time to falsify the facts of history, increasingly to omit them, appears to Nietzsche a 'profound', 'eternal', 'biological' truth of life.

What is extremely characteristic for the ideological development of this whole period is the way Nietzsche presents this philosophical justification of history . . . The philosopy of historical solecism is stated here, perhaps for the first time, in its most radical form . . . What it says in effect is that each unit, be it individual, race or nation can experience no more than itself. History exists only as a mirror of this ego, only as something to suit the special life needs of the latter. History is a chaos, in itself is of no concern to us, but to which everyone may attribute a 'meaning' which suits him, according to his needs.

(Lukács, 1962, pp.213–14)

As Brecht also laments in 'Questions from a Worker who Reads', such has always been the obscuring strategy of a triumphalist history. The worker who studies history finds no record of his own class, nor of any of history's defeated. Whose labour built the triumphal arches with which Rome bristles, and who were the vanquished whose defeat they record? Did Alexander conquer India singlehandedly, was Philip of Spain the only one to weep when the Armada went down?

> Every page a victory.
> Who cooked the feast for the victors?
>
> Every ten years a great man.
> Who paid the bill?
>
> So many reports.
> So many questions.
> (Brecht, 1976, p.253)

Here we recognise the spirit of Walter Benjamin also, for whom triumphal arches, and all cultural artefacts which survive because of their acquisition as loot, are objects of revulsion. The history of oppression is not written on the sides of monuments. The historical materialist needs to invert all the great images of authority, his task must be to 'brush history against the grain' (Benjamin, 1973, p.259). The very discipline of history reproduces the oppression which is its own hidden subject, not least in the century of Hegel who had done for history what Darwin was later to do for all geological time: placed aggression at the heart of its meaning. 'From the conflict of Master and Slave, [Hegel] deduced the entire subjective and objective progress of our history, revealing in these crises the synthesis to be found in the highest forms of the status of the person in the West, from the Stoic to the Christian, and even to the future citizen of the Universal State' (Lacan, 1977 (1), p.26).

Adorno develops his mentor Benjamin's position into a decisive rejection of history's purblind triumphalism.

> Benjamin said that history had hitherto been written from the standpoint of the victor, and needed to be written from that of the vanquished, we might add that knowledge must indeed present the fatally rectilinear succession of victory and defeat, but should also address itself to those things which were not embraced by this dynamic, which fell by the wayside – what might be called the waste products and blind spots that have escaped the dialectic. It is in the nature of the defeated to appear, in their impotence, irrelevant, eccentric, derisory. What transcends the ruling society is not only the potentiality it develops but also all that which did not fit properly into the laws of historical movement. Theory must needs deal with cross-grained, opaque, unassimilated material, which as such admittedly has from the start an anachronistic quality, but is not wholly obsolete since it has outwitted the historical dynamic. This can most readily be seen in art.
>
> (Adorno, 1974, p.151)

In a decisive rejection of Nietzschean 'fundamental falsification' Adorno argues, in for him a rare moment of affirmation, that it is art that sees into the blind-spot of written history. Hardy's aesthetic, dissenting from realist norms in its validation of, to use his own terms, 'irrelation','the accidents of inconsequence' and 'Time's Laughingstocks', values what Adorno here calls the historically 'irrelevant, eccentric, derisory'. Hardy turns his 'idiosyncratic mode of regard' on that 'great majority' Macaulay is untroubled to consign to recorded history's 'dim horizon'. 'Anne now felt herself close to and looking into the stream of recorded history, within whose banks the littlest things are great, and outside which she and the general bulk of the human race were content to live on as an unreckoned, unheeded superfluity' (Hardy, 1974, p.127). Hardy's novels repeatedly scrutinise this distorting perspective of 'recorded history', as when the protagonist of *A Laodicean* prefers to trust the evidence of touch to date Castle de Stancy in the face of documentation. He dates as Norman the supposedly Saxon survival thus uncovering conflict and the displacement of defeated historical meanings where the record faked a serene cultural continuity. Everywhere in 'recorded history' Hardy uncovers the distortions and strategies of exclusion evoked here in relation to Anne Garland. He is the great anatomist of the nineteenth-century's hectic activity of historical fabrications and appropriations – an age apparently revering historical authenticity in which people 'build ruins on maiden estates and cast antiques in Birmingham' (Hardy, 1975, p.152) and in which those who wield power, like Alec 'd'Urberville', do so by virtue of their appropriation of historical meanings and their construction of themselves as historical hoaxes.

George Eliot also turns her attention to unhistoric superfluities, which include her heroines. 'Her full nature, like that river of which Cyrus broke the strength, spent itself in channels which had no great name on the earth. But the effect of her being on those around her was incalculably diffusive: for the growing good of the world is partly dependent on unhistoric acts' (G. Eliot, 1981, Finale, p.896). Unhistoric Dorothea here is related only by an oblique analogy to Cyrus and 'recorded history'. Nothing is more typical of Eliot than a laborious patterning of historical and literary analogy that attempts to rescue her characters from their provincial, unhistoric obscurity. She thus attempts to revoke her characters' disinheritance from their 'share in the hard-won treasures of thought' (G. Eliot, 1983, p.381). Yet, perhaps increasingly in her work, the structure of analogy is tinged with the sense that the history which has excluded them – 'alien', 'struggling' 'degenerate', like Dorothea's oppressive experience of Rome – is better rejected than evoked as the oblique and untrustworthy guarantor of their meaning. She increasingly distances herself and her own novelistic practice from historicism. Thus she moves on from the historically oppressed *Romola*, the novel as researched and written by a historian, to *Middlemarch*'s distancing and problematising of contemporary historicism in the figure of Casaubon: a characterisation resonating with Nietzsche's contemporary attack on the work of nineteenth-century historians from which the 'fresh life of the present . . . withers away' so that 'scholarliness continues without it and rotates in egotistical self-satisfaction around its own axis' (Nietzsche, 1983, p.75). *Daniel Deronda* (1876) offers a profoundly ambivalent historical image. It apparently endorses Mordecai's and Daniel's historical mission, though the representation of this is pushed beyond the scope of the novel, it is itself swathed in obfuscating rhetoric and, being a Jewish mission, suggests rather a revisionist historiography of history's excluded than the realisation of conventional historical movements. This is then brilliantly counterpointed in the Gwendolen plot with an intimate rendering of a feeling emerging to dominance in the period, sensed doubly by women, of having to live divorced from a historical role. Eliot's career can be read as the gradual, painfully self-critical, even self-cancelling, process of erasing what she admits to being the 'Casaubon-tints . . . not quite foreign to my own disposition' (G. Eliot, 1954–5, vol. 5, p.322).

THE KALEIDOSCOPE MUST BE SMASHED

The implications of my argument are that George Eliot, Hardy and Conrad represent different stages of commentary on an essentially coherent process of historical thought and mis/representation, a process which continues into modernism. I will use the convenient term 'modernism', but wish to resist the implication of radical innovation and discontinuity within that designation. The form of representation characteristic of modernism, specifically its famously fraught and oblique presentation of history – what Lukács has unhelpfully but seminally castigated as its 'negation of history', its conception of man as 'an ahistorical being' (Lukács, 1969, p.167) – can be clearly deduced from the tortuous forms historicity adopts in these pre-modernist writers. Modernist 'ahistoricity', in other words, has a nineteenth-century history.

The novelistic careers of George Eliot, Hardy and Conrad span the years 1859 to 1925. This is a period in which the very definition of history undergoes a sea-change which Raymond Williams describes in *Keywords* (1976). The modern usage, emergent in this period, introduces an unprecedented sense of menace. A word previously redolent with achievement or promise becomes instead 'an argument against hope' and the indicator of 'a general pattern of frustration and defeat'. 'In its earliest uses *history* was a narrative account of events' (Williams, 1976, p.120; p.119) and derived from a root shared with 'story' meaning 'knowledge'. In early English use 'history' and 'story' were interchangeable and applied equally to accounts of imaginary events or of events supposed to be true, but from the fifteenth century on the terms diverge to refer to real and imagined events respectively. Foucault's argument of the long post-medieval process of the emergence of historical discourse as in some sense the antithesis of representation is perhaps supported by this long decline of the previously intimate relation between 'history' and 'story'.

Historicism, as it has been used in mC20, has a neutral sense (I) of a method of study which relies on the facts of the past and traces precedents of current events, but also a controversial sense (II), meant to discredit the general sense of *history* as a continuing process with definite implications for the future; (it has been most often used in attacks on Marxism but it would be relevant also to the Enlightenment and Idealist uses). It is not always easy to distinguish the attack on *historicism*, which centres mainly on the concept of a necessary or probable future, from a related attack on the notion of any *future* (in its specialised sense of a better, a more developed life) which uses the *lessons of history*, in a quite generalised sense, as an argument especially against hope. Though it is not always recognised or acknowledged as such, this latter use of *history* is probably a specific C20 form of *history* as this general process, though now used, in contrast with the sense of achievement or promise of the earlier and still active versions, to indicate a general pattern of frustration and defeat.

(Williams, 1976, p.119)

The idea that in the twentieth century the term history suffered this reversal in fortunes is registered almost as a consensus across that extraordinarily broad spectrum of political intents and practices we homogenise as modernist writing. The conception of history as 'a general pattern of frustration and defeat' finds echo in T.S. Eliot's formulation, commenting on what he feels Joyce has wisely excluded from *Ulysses* (1922), 'the vast panorama of anarchy and futility which is contemporary history' (T.S. Eliot, 1975, '*Ulysses*, Order, Myth', p.102). Modernism kicks hard against history. Its twin opposing temporal categories are the moment and eternity, permutated in strange combinations throughout its texts. These quite fill the narrative space which, in the nineteenth-century realist novel, had been the ostensible site of dramatisation of that now apparently excluded middle term, historical time.

History is explicitly a topic of *Ulysses*, but one characteristically aborted or redirected. The 'History' chapter, 'Nestor', begins with Stephen's listless attempt to teach a history lesson which degenerates into fragmentary recitation of *Lycidas*, calls for sir to tell a ghoststory, a posing of the riddle about the fox who buried his grandmother under a hollybush, and an eager mass exit to hockey. Williams's authoritative and pedagogic 'lessons of history' degenerate to lament, death-riddle, ghoststory, game. The abandoned topic was Pyrrhus, but this particular lesson of history has not been well studied – Armstrong thinks Pyrrhus is Latin for pier. The Pyrrhic victory is the perfect figure for Williams's gloss on the twentieth-century usage of history whereby an expected 'sense of achievement' actually confronts a 'general pattern of frustration and defeat'. Joyce pictures history as the lesson no one has learned, as the battle no one has won, and anticipates Benjamin's dictum that the strengths of the oppressed will forever call in question every victory that has ever fallen to the ruler. In the same chapter Stephen gives his famous definition of history as a personally oppressive 'pattern of frustration and defeat' – 'History, Stephen said, is a nightmare from which I am trying to awake'. He is being detained by Catholic anti-semite Mr Deasy who expounds his conviction that 'All human history moves towards one great goal, the manifestation of God'. History is thus one of those 'big words' Stephen fears 'which make us so unhappy'. So is it also for Leopold Bloom, butt of anti-semitic jibes and slights, and Hungarian–Jewish 'waste product', to use Adorno's term, of the Christian historical teleology lauded by Mr Deasy. 'Irrelevant, eccentric, derisory', he hates to be drawn into pub conversations of history and ventures to demur, 'But it's no use . . . Force, hatred, history, all that. That's not life for men and women, insult and hatred. And everybody knows that it's the very opposite of that that is really life' (Joyce, 1986, p.28; p.28; p.26; p.273).

Stephen has intuitions, apparently untinged by regret, of the conflagration of the whole historical edifice. 'I hear the ruin of all space, shattered glass and toppling masonry, and time one livid final flame'. The shattering of that glass reverberates throughout modernism, for which history is the ruin of representation. Stephen's image for Ireland's cultural achievement is 'the cracked lookingglass of a servant' (Joyce, 1986, p.20; p.6). *The Waste Land* (1922) pictures itself as 'A heap of broken images' (T.S. Eliot, 1984, p.63) and Pound's 'Near Perigord' as 'A broken bundle of mirrors!' (Pound, 1988, p.63). As Virginia Woolf puts it, 'And so the smashing and the crashing began. This it is that we hear all round us, in poems and novels and biographies, even in newspaper articles and essays, the sound of breaking and falling, crashing and destruction. It is the prevailing sound of the Georgian age' (Woolf 1980, 'Mr Bennett and Mrs Brown', pp. 333–4).

Adorno and Horkheimer choose as an exemplary figure of the twentieth century's fraught relation with history the emigrant, urged by his fellows to aid his survival by forgetting his personal, and his country's historical, past (Adorno and Horkheimer, 1989, p.216). Lukács offers a comparable characterisation of the typical protagonist of modernism, though he couches it as a criticism of the deficiences of this unfavoured literary method rather than the registering of an actually existing, indeed ubiquitous, mode of being. In contemptuous reference to Heidegger's concept of 'thrownness-into-being' (*Geworfenheit ins Dasein*) he dismisses modernism's depiction of 'an ahistorical being' – 'the hero himself is without personal history. He is "thrown-into-the-world": meaninglessly, unfathomably' (Lukács, 1969, p.170). This is the situation of Kafka's protagonist Karl in that inexplicably neglected novel *Amerika* (1927), a hopeful but bewildered middle-European immigrant to New York. As early as *The Philosophy of History* Hegel had characterised America as the emigrant's escape from history. 'It is a land of desire for all those who are weary of the historical lumber-room of old Europe . . . It is for America to abandon the ground on which hitherto the History of the World has developed itself' (Hegel, 1956, pp.86–7).

It is precisely as a negation of the old historical categories that Kafka depicts America and Karl's vision of it is a paradigm of the scattered, atomistic, unassimilable seeing of modernism. Joyce's shattered glass of historical collapse sounds in the streets of New York, in this historically stripped, ever-mutating and self-renewing scene which has, to use Hegel's term, dizzyingly 'abandoned the ground'.

> From morning to evening and far into the dreaming night that street was the channel for a constant stream of traffic which, seen from above, looked like an inextricable confusion, for ever newly improvised, of foreshortened human figures and the roofs of all kinds of vehicles, sending into the upper air another confusion, more riotous and complicated, of noises, dust and smells, all of it enveloped and penetrated by a flood of light which the multi-tudinous objects in the street scattered, carried off and again busily brought back, with an effect as palpable to the dazzled eye as if a glass roof stretched over the street were being violently smashed into fragments at every moment.
>
> (Kafka, 1988, *America*, p.465)

Here is representation's *Kristallnacht*. For Lukács, one aspect of the 'descriptive' malaise characteristic of the novel under capitalism is that it attempts to obscure the all-determining fact of history with a 'false contemporaneity'. This results in a form of representation which Kafka has amply illustrated – 'the false contemporaneity of description trans-forms the novel into a kaleidoscopic chaos' (Lukács, 1970, p.122). The streets of New York, the dazzling image of contemporaneity, are that kaleidoscopic chaos. We could compare also Marlow's form of seeing in *Lord Jim* (1900), similarly dazzled, atomistic and kaleidoscopic. 'There was, as I walked along, the clear sunshine, a brilliance too passionate to be consoling, the streets full of jumbled bits of colour like a damaged kaleidoscope: yellow, green, blue, dazzling white' (Conrad, 1980 (2), p.122).

Poe, and of course his instances are American, describes the kaleidoscopic as the bourgeois mode of seeing par excellence. The very form of interior design favoured in bourgeois households constructs their habitat as a kaleidoscope world. In a phrase intriguing in its evocation of a self-deconstructing mimesis he condemns this decor characterised by 'The exaggerated employment of mirrors'. He goes on to condemn the great engine of kaleidoscopic seeing fuelled by bourgeois economics and technology.

> As for those antique floor-cloths still occasionally seen in the dwellings of the rabble – cloths of huge, sprawling, and radiating devises, stripe-interspersed, and glorious with all hues, among which no ground is intelligible – these are but the wicked invention of a race of time-servers and money-lovers – children of Baal and worshippers of Mammon – Benthams, who, to spare thought and economize fancy, first cruelly invented the Kaleidoscope, and then established joint-stock companies to twirl it by steam.
>
> (Poe, 1986, 'The Philosophy of Furniture', p.416)

A Beckett protagonist wishes only for the destruction of the world shaped by 'the exaggerated employment of mirrors', for a luddite attack on the kaleidoscopic engine, 'this old body to which nothing ever happened, or so little, which never met with anything, loved anything, wished for anything, in its tarnished universe, except for the mirrors to shatter, the plane, the curved, the magnifying, the minifying, and to vanish in the havoc of its images' (Beckett, 1980, 'The Calmative', p.53).

Lukács will not acknowledge Kafka's insight, that twentieth-century capitalism, like its New York heartland here, itself refutes history, thrives by being 'ever newly improvised', mesmerises its observer with the spectacle of contemporaneity, dazzles him with an ever renewed violence and shattering of all formed images. It is the ahistoric kaleidoscope world. Kafka is reported to have said that 'To believe in progress is to believe that there has not yet been any'. Kafka has another marvellous image for this new American mode of being and discourse which he renders in his depiction of Karl's uncle's American mechanical writing-desk. This is an immense surreal mechanism ever mutating, discomposing and newly reforming itself after the controller's whim and

31

in which, self-deconstructively, surfaces collapse into depths and depths conflate into surfaces.

> In his room stood an American writing-desk of superior construction . . . it had a hundred different compartments of different sizes, in which the president of the Union himself could have found a fitting place for each of his state documents: there was also a regulator at one side and by turning a handle you could produce the most complicated combinations and permutations of the compartments to please yourself and suit your requirements. Thin panels sank slowly and formed the bottom of a new series or the top of existing drawers promoted from below; even after one turn of the handle the disposition of the whole was quite changed and the transformation took place slowly or at delirious speed according to the rate at which you wound the thing round. It was a very modern invention, yet it reminded Karl vividly of the traditional Christmas panorama which was shown to gaping children in the market-place at home, where he too, well wrapped in his winter clothes, had often stood enthralled, closely comparing the movement of the handle, which was turned by an old man, with the changes in the scene.
>
> (Kafka, 1988, *America*, pp.466–7)

A kind of kaleidoscope of script, a great engine of discourse, the desk is like America itself. It mesmerises with its continual self-revision, its mutation of all appearances, its combination of chaos and contrivance, ever collapsing and self-reconstructing. Capitalism is always neo-capitalism. Kafka envisages the modern world as an immense mechanism continually throwing up illusions of order out of its chaotic workings. Here are all the elements of Walter Benjamin's modernist conception of history as catastrophe.

> The course of history, as it presents itself under the conception of catastrophe, can really claim the thinker's attention no more than the kaleidoscope in the hand of the child, where all the patterns of order collapse into a new order with each turn. The image is thoroughly justified. The ideas of those in power have always been the mirrors thanks to which the picture of an 'order' came about – The kaleidoscope must be smashed.
>
> (Benjamin, 1974, 'Zentralpark', p.660) (own translation)

ALL THE WORLD'S NOT A STAGE

Fabrizio after Waterloo, unable to tell of the historical experience he is not sure he has had, has something of a twentieth-century counterpart in Walter Benjamin's depiction of the archetypal combatant of the First World War. But the Stendhalian humour has drained out of Benjamin's depiction of a soldier in a historical encounter which negates the category of individual experience and stubs out storytelling.

> With the [First] World War a process began to become apparent which has not halted since then. Was it not noticeable at the end of the war that men returned from the battlefield grown silent – not richer, but poorer in communicable experience? What ten years later was poured out in the flood of war books was anything but experience that goes from mouth to mouth. And there was nothing remarkable about that. For never has experience been contradicted more thoroughly than strategic experience by tactical warfare, economic experience by inflation, bodily experience by mechanical warfare, moral experience by those in power. A generation that had gone to school on a horse-drawn streetcar now stood under the open sky in a countryside in which nothing remained unchanged but the clouds, and beneath these clouds, in a field of force of destructive torrents and explosions, was the tiny, fragile human body.
>
> (Benjamin, 1973, p.84)

The very concept of history is, as I have suggested, predicated on that which Benjamin here says modern existence negates – 'communicable experience'. It is both experience and the communication of that experience. It presupposes the kind of experience which *can* be communicated, an empathy between doing and telling. Is history itself becoming obsolete in an age 'not richer, but poorer in communicable experience'? Benjamin's argument here is in the context of 'The Storyteller', his tribute to Leskov and obituary of the art of storytelling. Humanity's seemingly universal and inalienable artform and medium of its shared wisdom is in fact now becoming extinct, the victim of a history antipathetic to it.

> the art of storytelling is coming to an end. Less and less frequently do we encounter people with the ability to tell a story properly. More and more often there is embarrassment all around when the wish to hear a story is expressed. It is as if something that seemed inalienable to us, the securest among our possessions, were taken from us: the ability to exchange experiences.
>
> (Benjamin, 1973, p.83)

Modernist fiction readily illustrates the antipathetic relations of story-telling and contemporary history Benjamin sketches. The novel of Lawrence's which most obviously addresses the First World War – so often the determining absence in his work, obliquely evoked but not represented – is *Kangaroo* (1923). Awkward, querulous and historically disturbed, it appears an exemplary instance of the contemporary shattering of story under historical pressures. It is informed by Lawrence's experiences during this 'terrible, terrible' war, when, though medically exempt from combat, he was still called up for repeated degrading medical examinations, and both he and German-born Frieda were harassed and kept under surveillance by the police as suspected spies. These events erupt into a quite separate story about the protagonist's political entanglements in Australia as, in effect, incongruously interpolated embittered autobiography, in the very long chapter whose title echoes Stephen Dedalus's conception of history, 'The Nightmare'. Lawrence fulminates against the war in Benjaminesque terms. It is the eradication of that centrally honoured Lawrentian value, the individual's integral selfhood: 'The terrible, terrible war, made so fearful because in every country practically every man lost his head, and lost his . . . integrity, which alone keeps life real'. The story is suspended for long periods of invective feebly dramatised and evidently in Lawrence's own voice as if in illustration of the war's negation of narrative, a dereliction of novelistic duty the novel freely acknowledges: 'Chapter follows chapter and nothing doing'. The reader's impatience with such a paucity of storytelling is acknowledged by being dismissed: 'If you don't like the novel, don't read it'. One chapter, as if a paradigm both of modernist narrative form and of the shattered, atomistic historical experience it confronts, is called 'Bits'. Lawrence echoes Benjamin's characterisation of the individual as vulnerable, isolated and adrift 'in a field of force of destructive torrents and explosions, was the tiny, fragile human body' – 'He was loose like a single timber of some wrecked ship, drifting over the face of the earth'. The protagonist offers a telling summation of the modern experience of history, and a defence of the novel's own refusal of epic historical narration, '"I'm afraid, Jaz," said Somers, "that, like Nietzsche, I no longer believe in great events"' (Lawrence, 1988, p.236; p.312; p.313; p.287; p.180).

Kangaroo looks as if it could have been both a great account of the emotional consequences of the First World War and a prophecy of the emergence of nationalistic/fascistic politics, but somehow fails to be either and ends up rather an emphatic statement of the incompatibility of modern history and novelistic representation. As such, it illustrates the dilemma identified by Adorno. *'All the world's not a stage* – The coming extinction of art is prefigured in the increasing impossibility of representing historical events. That there is no adequate drama about Fascism is not due to lack of talent; talent is withering through the insolubility of the writer's most urgent task' (Adorno, 1974, p.143).

The Second World War only redoubles the crisis of the unrepresentable nature of modern conflicts and their eradiction of the category of experience that Benjamin identified in relation to the First.

> The total obliteration of the war by information, propaganda, commentaries, with camera-men in the first ranks and war reporters dying heroic deaths, the mish-mash of enlightened manipulation of public opinion and oblivious activity: all this is another expression for the withering of experience, the vacuum between men and their fate, in which their real fate lies. It is as if the reified, hardened plaster-cast of events takes the place of events themselves. Men are reduced to walk-on parts in a monster documentary film which has no spectators, since the least of them has his bit to do on the screen. It is just this aspect that underlies the much-maligned designation 'phoney war'.
>
> (Adorno, 1974, p.55)

My reading of *Nostromo*, particularly, resonates with Adorno's formulation that, under modern conditions, 'It is as if the reified, hardened plaster-cast of events takes the place of events themselves'. A novel apparently dramatising revolutionary and counter-revolutionary turmoil in a Central American state appears almost to render history as stasis. A viscous narrative curls sluggishly around the congealed masses of dense and stately descriptive set-pieces, themselves characteristically mesmerised by lowering images of stasis; a mountain, an unmoving figure, a statue, an urn, a corpse, an impenetrably black night on a still gulf. People and emotions are transfixed within the immanent reification of this Medusan world, men are like monuments, a woman's heart is like a wall of silver bricks. Echoing Adorno's vocabulary, Sulacan women are powdered 'till they looked like white plaster casts with beautiful living eyes' (Conrad, 1986 (1), p.73).

Acutely Conradian also is a wariness like Adorno's of the 'information, propaganda, commentaries' which, under a technologically advanced capitalism in its colonialist phase, form the medium of all life and expression. Conrad is everywhere cognisant of the immanence of propagandist, discursive strategies which, since they are the medium of his times and hence his own expressiveness, the novelist cannot hope

fully to evade. Colonialist discourse is a basin in which words swill
brackishly. Conrad dramatises the painful sense of his own texts as
tainted and duplicitous, as collusions with contemporary constructions
of the history of capitalist and colonialist adventuring: Captain Mitchell
with his ideologically obscuring epic narrative of Sulacan history – more
'world-historic derring-do' – hijacks long stretches of the narration of
Nostromo; Marlow has to wrest the telling of 'Heart of Darkness' from
its initial narrator, a Kiplingesque eulogist of Britain's colonial projects.
Conrad refused Roger Casement's invitation to contribute to his notorious report, based substantially on photographic evidence, on the
Belgian regime's atrocities in the Congo which Conrad had witnessed
and which are the subject of 'Heart of Darkness'. In *Nostromo* an
enigmatic figure somehow representing the future and disliked by the
narrator, but who intrigues Nostromo himself, is a photographer.
Conrad registers a sense of his period as Deleuze and Guattari
characterise it, as one when the writer's medium of words and books is
being superseded as the pre-eminent channel of knowledge by the
information technologies to which Adorno refers. Conrad struggles to
render the truth of history within a discursive medium everywhere
tainted with ideological duplicities, and which is itself losing its primacy
as the conveyer of historical meanings and drifting into irrelevance. Or,
recalling Adorno's dictum that history does not merely touch on
language, but takes place within it, we should perhaps rather say, which
is losing its primacy as the site where history is constructed.

Adorno tends to stress the newness of the conditions he describes
and their predication upon specifically twentieth-century historical
phenomena. My practice is to push his analyses back into the nineteenth
century and relate them to the conditions which made possible later
historical manifestations. I feel justified given that, for example,
Nietzsche in 1874 sounds like a nineteenth-century Adorno on just this
crux: a creeping inauthenticity of historical experience, even of wars,
which is immediately decanted into a discourse which renders –
'exhibits' it – as spectacle and diversion.

> modern man . . . allows his artists in history to go on preparing a
> world exhibition for him; he has become a strolling spectator and
> has arrived at a condition in which even great wars and revolutions
> are able to influence him for hardly more than a moment. The war
> is not even over before it is turned into a hundred thousand
> printed pages and set before the tired palates of the history-
> hungry as the latest delicacy. It seems that the instrument is almost
> incapable of producing a strong and full note, no matter how

vigorously it is played: its tones at once die away and in a moment have faded to a tender historical echo.

(Nietzsche, 1983, p.83)

The fact that Nietzsche is here in effect repeating an observation of George Eliot's – these thinkers are not readily aligned – suggests that they are both justly observing a deep-rooted nineteenth-century phenomenon. 'It is doubtful whether our soldiers would be maintained if there were not pacific people at home who fancy themselves soldiers. War, like other dramatic spectacles, might possibly cease for want of a "public"' (G. Eliot, 1983, p.250).

There is a clear congruence of thought on these issues between Nietzsche, Adorno and Benjamin. For Nietzsche the result of nineteenth-century commentary on the French Revolution was that 'the text finally disappeared under the interpretation'. Adorno on the Second World War talks of 'the total obliteration of the war by information, propaganda, commentaries'. Benjamin says of the First World War that it stubbed out storytelling while 'What was poured out in the flood of war books was anything but experience that goes from mouth to mouth'. The central historical events of modern history dissolve into voluminous discourse, negate personal experience and invalidate the literary forms based upon the communication of that experience. They negate the very category of history, are themselves unhistoric acts.

> But the Second World War is as totally divorced from experience as is the functioning of a machine from the movements of the body, which only begins to resemble it in pathological states. Just as the war lacks continuity, history, an 'epic' element, but seems rather to start anew from the beginning in each phase, so it will leave behind no permanent, unconsciously preserved image in the memory. Everywhere, with each explosion, it has breached the barrier against stimuli beneath which experience, the lag between healing oblivion and healing recollection, forms. Life has changed into a timeless succession of shocks, interspersed with empty, paralysed intervals.
>
> (Adorno, 1974, p.125)

The last sentence describes time as characteristically rendered in a Beckett play and indeed Adorno honours Beckett elsewhere as modern history's laureate. He is the poet of the Holocaust, the central, paradigmatic 'unspeakable act' of twentieth-century history which everywhere informs him but which he never names. 'Beckett has given us the only fitting reaction to the situation of the concentration camps – a situation he never calls by name, as if it were subject to an image ban' (Adorno, 1990, p.380). Beckett renders Adorno's account of the Second World War as the voice for which history is both the suffocating medium of existence and an absence, both a monumental accretion under which one is crushed and an unknowable, unnamable negation. Here is Adorno's history which is stripped of the consolations of successive time, with neither memory nor anticipation, shivered into innumerable instants, which is the negation of history.

> the question may be asked, off the record, why time doesn't pass, doesn't pass, from you, why it piles up all about you, instant on instant, on all sides, deeper and deeper, thicker and thicker, your time, other's time, the time of the ancient dead and the dead yet unborn, why it buries you grain by grain neither dead nor alive, with no memory of anything, no hope of anything, no knowledge of anything, no history and no prospects, buried under the seconds.
>
> (Beckett, 1979, *The Unnamable*, p.358)

It is the emergence of history under this guise which is the subject of this work – not Lukács's nostalgically conjectural 'superbly, straightforwardly and pregnantly portrayed' historicity and its reassurance of 'the old epic self-activity of man, the old epic directness of social life, its public spontaneity' (Lukács, 1962, p.35). Rather, as Adorno and Horkheimer describe it, it is the negation of all these humanistic categories.

> The disturbed relationship with the dead – forgotten and embalmed – is one of the symptoms of the sickness of experience today. One might almost say that the notion of human life as the unity in the history of an individual has been abolished: the life of the individual is defined only by its opposite, destruction, but all harmony and all continuity of conscious and involuntary memory have lost their meaning. Individuals are reduced to a mere sequence of instantaneous experiences which leave no trace, or rather whose trace is hated as irrational, superfluous, and 'overtaken' in the literal sense of the word. Just as every book which has not been published recently is suspect, and the idea of history outside the specific sphere of historical science makes modern man nervous, so the past becomes a source of anger. What a man was and experienced in the past is as nothing when set against what he now is and has and what he can be used for. The well-meaning if threatening advice given

frequently to emigrants to forget all their past because it cannot be transferred, and to begin a completely new life, simply represents a forcible reminder to the newcomer of something which he has long since learned for himself. History is eliminated in oneself and others out of a fear that it may remind the individual of the degeneration of his own existence – which itself continues.

(Adorno and Horkheimer, 1989, p.216)

THE CENTRE OF NOTHING

My argument is that the central, explicit topic of twentieth-century artistic discourse is its own inability to represent historical events and furthermore that this is the implicit – emergent, unacknowledged, repressed – topic of nineteenth-century discourse. In *Hitler: The Führer and the People* (1975) J. P. Stern has made an excellent study of the discursive context of Nazism, particularly the German literary, philosophical and propagandist precedents, some of them nineteenth-century, to the enflaming Götterdämmerung rhetoric of *Mein Kampf* and of the oratory so carefully staged amidst the 'solemn kitsch' of the Nuremberg rallies. Hitler's accounts of his First World War service both in letters from the front and later in *Mein Kampf* itself share an identical and anonymous style as if collapsing the distinction between private and public address and erasing the very category of the personal. It is surely telling that in the recent scam over the spurious Hitler diaries this prose has proved so easily fakeable. As a style it perfectly illustrates Benjamin's observations about how this conflict promulgated a discourse impoverished in the communication of experience and from which the category of the individual has been expunged. 'What ten years later was poured out in the flood of war books was anything but experience that goes from mouth to mouth.'

> In every detail and down to the choice of verbal forms and syntax, they read like the reports of the enthusiastic chauvinistic journalists of the time . . . they reproduce exactly the inhuman jargon of the 'popular' as well as the 'serious' German and Austrian Press . . . all described in the hectic yet dead language of a writer who seems to have no private feelings but is experiencing events through the prefabricated medium of the public convention.
>
> (Stern, 1990, p.159)

The corresponding dimension to this crisis within discourse is evidenced in the inability of literature adequately to depict Hitler. Some historians have ventured to suggest that, because of the banality of

Hitler's own views and the derivativeness and contradictions of his rule, Nazi Germany was uncentred, 'a vast network of interlocking organizations with a ghostly Nothing at its core' (Stern, 1990, p.4). The notion of the 'ghostly Nothing' has further been enshrined by a failure of the literary imagination to encompass this historical subject. Stern quotes the Viennese satirist Karl Kraus in 1933, 'Mir fällt zu Hitler nichts ein' ('As to Hitler, I have no comments to make').

> And although this is followed by an essay of more than 300 pages which constitutes one of the greatest political and cultural polemics ever written, there is poetic truth in Kraus's famous dictum. The satirist whose incomparable wit and articulate indignation had commented on the follies and outrages of thirty years of Central European history now acknowledges that what is happening in 'the New Germany' is beyond the reach of satire, beyond the meaning that literature can encompass. And, apart from a few pages by Richard Hughes and Günter Grass, creative literature has failed to illuminate the central figure of German and European history in the first third of the twentieth century. Here again, then, we seem to be left with a phantom, a centre of Nothing. Yet this relative failure is characteristic of the travail of literature in many other areas of the modern world – the world which is what it is partly as the result of Hitler's acts of destruction.
>
> (Stern, 1990, p.5)

Stern's argument cannot but itself act as an unwitting illustration of the knotty impossibility of this issue of the representation of such historical figures and events. What would the adequate depiction look like, what would its models be? He gives short shrift to *The Great Dictator* (1940) and *The Resistible Rise of Arturo Ui* (1941): 'The true nature of the man is trivialised and obscured rather than illuminated by the antics of Charles Chaplin and the deeply unfunny comedy of Bertolt Brecht' (Stern, 1990, p.2). The logic is awry. Is a satire possible that does not in some essential sense trivialise? Chaplin is dismissed as too playful and funny; Brecht, perversely, as not funny enough. And when the subject is Hitler, is the sort of psychologising implied by 'illuminating' 'The true nature of the man' adequate, desirable, or even possible? For Adorno the history of fascism had itself rendered 'aesthetically obsolete' and discreditable the very psychological representation Stern advocates (and which, incidentally, Chaplin and Brecht can be seen as devising new forms precisely to occlude).

That there is no adequate drama about Fascism is not due to lack
of talent: talent is withering through the insolubility of the writer's
most urgent task. He has to choose between two principles, both
equally inappropriate to the subject: psychology and infantilism.
The former, now aesthetically obsolete, has been used by significant artists only as a trick and with a bad conscience . . .

(Adorno, 1974, p.143)

Hitler, if anyone – the utter impersonality of whose literary voice Stern
has himself expertly analysed – should give us reason to pause over the
invocation of humanist categories such as the 'true nature' of personal
identity. Stern's nostalgia is carefully couched, but it is nostalgia none
the less, a Lukácsian longing for a lost world of realist/humanist
representation.

Tolstoy's historico-philosophical epilogue, in which he argues for
the notion of impersonal historical forces does not invalidate the
bulk of *War and Peace*, a panorama of living persons. If there were
no other differences between Hitler and Napoleon, the existence
of *War and Peace* and Beethoven's Third Symphony alone would
make any significant comparison problematic. But even though it
may be impossible to represent it through a panorama of living
persons, the Hitler phenomenon – its reality and its myth –
remains the most important single phenomenon of its age.

(Stern, 1990, p.5)

What a terrible irony there is in invoking a literary model of 'a panorama
of living persons' in the context of mass slaughter. On these issues there
seems to be no position free of offence, taint or duplicity. To claim and
theorise a historical manifestation's inaccessibility to representation is in
some sense to collude with its silencing. This seems doubly pernicious
in relation to Nazism, about which there was nothing silent or discreet.
George Steiner points to a peculiarly chilling fact: the fastidious over-
elaboration of representation which was a component of Nazi violences.
Horrors were articulated, recorded, annotated, photographed and
filmed with teutonic assiduousness.

It is nauseating and nearly unbearable to recall what was wrought
and spoken, but one must. In the Gestapo cellars, stenographers
(usually women) took down carefully the noises of fear and agony
wrenched, burned or beaten out of the human voice. The tortures
and experiments carried out on live beings at Belsen and
Matthausen were exactly recorded. The regulations governing the

41

number of blows to be meted out on the flogging blocks at Dachau were set down in writing. When Polish rabbis were compelled to shovel out open latrines with their hands and mouths, there were German officers there to record the fact, to photograph it, and to label the photographs. When the SS elite guards separated mothers from children at the entrance to the death camps, they did not proceed in silence. They proclaimed the imminent horrors in loud cheers: 'Heida, heida, juchheisassa, Scheissjuden in den Schornstein!' ('Hey, hey, hooray, Jewish shits up the chimney!')

The unspeakable being said, over and over, for twelve years. The unthinkable being written down, indexed, filed for reference.
(Steiner, 1969, 'The Hollow Miracle', p.141)

Surely all representation is in some sense tainted after such usages. It will never again be possible to posit as axiomatic, as Burke does in 1757, the transforming power of representations, even and especially of human suffering, on the grounds that we feel 'a simple pain in the reality, yet a delight in the representation' (Burke, 1990, p.44). Conrad seemed to be intuiting the emergence of these issues, and their bleak implications for his own art, at the very beginning of the century. In 'Heart of Darkness' the Company accountant in the Congo is a precursor of the coming bureaucratisation of violence. Within sight of the grove of death he makes 'correct entries of perfectly correct transactions' and keeps the Company's books in 'apple-pie order'. 'When one has to get to make correct entries, one comes to hate these savages – hate them to death' (Conrad, 1981, p.27). Conrad is also an artist I am reminded of by the formulation of Stern's whereby Hitler offers literature a subject with 'a centre of Nothing' and so functions as the phantasmal metonym of the impalpability to art of the defining events of twentieth-century history. Conrad wrote in 'Heart of Darkness', *Nostromo* and *The Shadow-Line* (1917) the first great, paradigmatic twentieth-century literary texts conscious of being quelled and hushed by history. It has been said of him that he is an artist in whom one has the sense of his 'sculpting a vacuum, shaping a void' (Eagleton, 1976, p.137) and that 'the secret casket of his genius contained a vapour rather than a jewel' (Forster, 1936, p.135). F.R. Leavis has written that 'the reverberation of *Nostromo* has something hollow about it; with the colour and life there is a suggestion of a certain emptiness' (Leavis, 1980, pp.229–30) and through Marlow Conrad famously located the fugitive meanings of his own narratives as 'not inside, like a kernel' but outside as a 'misty halo' (Conrad, 1981, p.8). For me Beckett is our other great laureate of the decay of historical representation and of the resonant vacuity of the historical discourse which takes as its impossible subject the 'centre of Nothing'.

> who may tell the tale
> of the old man?
> weigh absence in a scale?
> mete want with a span?
> the sum assess
> of the world's woes?
> nothingness
> in words enclose?
>   (Beckett, 1988, p.247)

Dramatist Joshua Sobel gives a strangely arresting formulation of the crisis in his statement about his play *Ghetto* (first performed 1989) that he finally forced himself to grasp what had previously seemed to him to be 'a frightening, repulsive kind of "noli me tangere" subject' (Sobel, 1989, p.9), the genocide of the European Jews. Christ's words after the resurrection make an extraordinary but exquisite source for a Jewish articulation of the Holocaust. 'Untouchable | you were not' says Geoffrey Hill of a child victim of the gassings in 'September Song' (Hill, 1985, p.67), a maximally ambiguous phrase oscillating between despairing and hopeful meanings, rather as Sobel's biblical allusion was in its context an apparent negating imperative yet pregnant with the promise of transcendence ('for I have not yet ascended . . .'). Hill's poem attempts to bring the touch of recognition to one of the untouchable caste whose murderous manhandling has proved the untouchable subject. Dare one conclude that in even its most negative formulations on the most devastating subjects language seems to contain an irreducible residue of assertion, what Adorno's Frankfurt School colleague Bloch called 'The Hypothesis of Hope'? Hill's lyric is so chronically reticent as almost to erase itself and has something of its own 'centre of Nothing' in the pathetic little implosion of the central stanza.

> (I have made
> an elegy for myself it
> is true)
>   (Hill, 1985, p.67)

The poem here itself admits the burden of Adorno's conclusion about 'the coming extinction of art' and the most famous of his formulations that 'To write lyric poetry after Auschwitz is barbaric' (Adorno, 1983, p.34). But even Adorno's monumental pessimism seems to admit the hypothesis of hope in his assessment of what language can and cannot touch, or be touched by – 'history does not merely touch on language, but takes place in it' (Adorno, 1974, p.219).

But the issue cannot be left there, given that in twentieth-century history there is always something more and worse, something to further out-top extremity. J.G. Ballard has pointed out that the Second World War ended with the nuclear bombings which were the down-payment on the coming cataclysm of the Third. In the nuclear age language truly faces its nemesis. Martin Amis has talked of the contemptuous strategies of deceit characteristic of our language of nuclear conditions which is either euphemistic – 'conflict control' is a military term for nuclear war – or infantile – the 'Star Wars' programme is named after an adolescents' adventure film, the bombs dropped on Hiroshima and Nagasaki were called, as if cartoon characters, 'little boy' and 'fat man' (Amis and Ballard in conversation on Open University television programme 'Literature and History', first broadcast BBC 2, 2 October 1991). Here is the 'infantilism' Adorno identifies as one amongst the shrivelled repertoire of responses we have to our history. According to how one reads Ballard's *Empire of the Sun* (1984) the 'Boy's Own' robustness of its style – reminiscent of Conrad's late, exhausted adventure mode – either foregrounds and problematises or merely capitulates to and reproduces this babyish banalising of historical discourse. Conversely the bomb itself is an eloquent inscriber. An explosion which leaves only permanent shadows of its victims has a gruesome poetry of its own in scripting the face of the earth with evidences of innumerable obliterated 'centres of Nothing'.

Staggeringly, in the 1980s, even this horror became superseded, partially displaced by the apparently imminent prospect of the end of nature through an ecological cataclysm. The 'coming extinction of art' comes to seem small beer. Hardy, a nineteenth-century artist for whom consequently an articulate tragic mode was still just available, advocated a bracing 'full look at the Worst' in 'In Tenebris: II'. But Hardy, who emerges in the next chapter as the artist par excellence of the 'centre of Nothing', could not anticipate that the grotesque new grammar of the twentieth century would admit of no such absolute terms as 'worst', only an endless succession of its intensifiers.

2

'A HISTORY OF THE LIGHTS AND SHADOWS'

Aspects of history, myth and realism in Hardy and George Eliot

A DOCUMENT OF CIVILISATION

What is 'a history of the lights and shadows'? To the narrator of *Middlemarch* that question would be meaningless since the term refers to that which cannot be articulated. Not famous for self-doubt, the narrator uses it as part of a striking admission of failure on behalf of Dorothea and him/herself in the extraordinary Chapter 20. Dorothea is enduring her excruciating honeymoon in Rome and after two pages of magnificent prose evoking the jarring of the city's 'stupendous fragmentariness' against her 'young sense' the narrator suggests that actually the experience defeats the descriptive powers of them both. 'However, Dorothea was crying, and if she had been required to state the cause, she could only have done so in some such general words as I have already used: to have been driven to be more particular would have been like trying to give a history of the lights and shadows' (G. Eliot, 1981, p.226).

In this chapter, and particularly its remarkably rich opening paragraphs, vulnerabilities beyond Dorothea's own are being exposed. The chapter is dotted with comments acknowledging areas of experience, such as Dorothea's 'most unaccountable, darkly-feminine manner' (G. Eliot, 1981, p.232), beyond what it can represent and explain. These serve to indicate that it, like the heroine it describes as alienated alike from Rome's culture and her new husband's mind, is concerned with the limitations of its own understanding. In the paragraph before the one referring to the history of lights and shadows there is the famous reference to 'the roar that lies on the other side of silence' that we are mercifully spared from hearing. This mysterious 'history of lights and shadows', we might suggest, represents whatever lies on the penumbral 'other side' of George Eliot's own silence. Could this be that 'other side' which Hardy intended to make articulate – 'Perhaps I can do a volume of poems consisting of the *other side* of common emotions'?

(F.E. Hardy, 1986, p.58) (original emphasis). We might call it the 'shaded side', to borrow from Hardy's own description of *Tess of the d'Urbervilles* (1891) as 'the shaded side of a well-known catastrophe' (T. Hardy, 1985, 'Preface to the Fifth and Later Editions', p.37). In a sense 'the history of the lights and shadows' is realism's term for what its own method defines as beyond representation, its 'Other'. Hardy's fiction, and *Tess* in particular, takes as a point of departure the sort of problems of representation Eliot dramatises in this chapter. As is hinted by his describing his novel as offering to show the 'shaded side' of what is familiar, his work explores the nature of such a history and thus offers us the form of representation beyond realism that George Eliot's narrator imagines impossible, or intolerable.

As a revelation of the tensions in George Eliot's own practice, Chapter 20 of *Middlemarch* is as much an essay on realism as the famous Chapter 16 of *Adam Bede* (1859) (which follows a chapter called 'Links', a term whose significance we will have cause to consider) but one suggesting a much more fraught and vulnerable status for her method. Dorothea's oppression and disturbance in Rome where, like a more troubled Alice, she has been 'tumbled out among incongruities', threaten to tumble the novel's own realist method into confusion. Chapter 19 had ended with the narrator speculating, prompted by Ladislaw, that 'There are characters which are continually creating collisions and nodes for themselves in dramas which nobody is prepared to act with them. Their susceptibilities will clash against objects that remain innocently quiet'. Dorothea's experience of Rome realises, in terms for which the narrator proposes the definition 'tragedy', what is here approached with knowing poise – the notion of a susceptibility in painful collision with a world of unresponsive, unassimilable objects (G. Eliot, 1981, p.226; p.223; p.226).

Matthew Arnold gave a significant gloss on the intentions of realism when he defined culture as 'the endeavour to see things as they are, to draw towards a knowledge of the universal order which seems to be intended and aimed at in the world' (Arnold, 1988, p.46). The first part of his definition is echoed by Ladislaw who relishes Rome and upbraids Dorothea for 'her want of sturdy neutral delight in things as they were' (G. Eliot, 1981, p.325) (a phrase pregnant with contradictions which run to the heart of realism – how can 'delight' be 'neutral'?). But dismally failing this Arnoldian injunction, Dorothea's tortured version of sightseeing is precisely an experience of clash and collision between her sensibility and the unintelligible objects of culture, and her form of vision is unforgettably likened to a retinal disease. The result is a powerful intimation of the alienation latent within the realist ethic and aesthetic and the whole sub-structure of beliefs about the legitimacy and intelligibility of culture that underpin it, crystallised in the image of Dorothea anxiously scanning the showcase of the West's cultural treasures only to meet in return the reified 'marble eyes' of an 'alien world'.

after the brief narrow experience of her girlhood she was beholding Rome, the city of visible history, where the past of a whole hemisphere seems moving in funeral procession with strange ancestral images and trophies gathered from afar.
But this stupendous fragmentariness heightened the dreamlike strangeness of her bridal life . . . the oppressive masquerade of ages, in which her own life too seemed to become a masque with enigmatical costumes.
To those that have looked at Rome with the quickening power of a knowledge which breathes a growing soul into all historic shapes, and traces out the suppressed transitions which unite all contrasts, Rome may still be the spiritual centre and interpreter of the world . . . The weight of unintelligible Rome might lie easily on bright nymphs to whom it formed a background for the brilliant picnic of Anglo-foreign society; but Dorothea had no such defence against deep impressions. Ruins and basilicas, palaces and colossi, set in the midst of a sordid present, where all that was living and warm-blooded seemed sunk in the deep degeneracy of a superstition divorced from reverence; the dimmer but yet eager Titanic life gazing and struggling on walls and ceilings; the long vistas of white forms whose marble eyes seemed to hold the monotonous light of an alien world: all this vast wreck of ambitious ideals, sensuous and spiritual, mixed confusedly with the signs of breathing forgetfulness and degradation, at first jarred her as with an electric shock, and then urged themselves on her with that ache belonging to a glut of confused ideas which check the flow of emotion. Forms both pale and glowing took possession of her young sense, and fixed themselves in her memory even when she was not thinking of them, preparing strange associations which remained through her after-years. Our moods are apt to bring with them images which succeed each other like the magic-lantern pictures of a doze; and in certain states of dull forlornness Dorothea all her life continued to see the vastness of St Peter's, the huge bronze canopy, the excited intention in the attitudes and garments of the prophets and evangelists in the mosaics above,

and the red drapery which was being hung for Christmas spreading itself everywhere like a disease of the retina.

(G. Eliot, 1981, pp.224–6)

This famous passage has a notable literary ancestor, and a descendant, but is distanced from both in the untempered severity of its mood. In this evocation of 'the weight of unintelligible Rome' Eliot has drained her Wordsworthian source of the consolation the flagging poet imbibes surveying the ruins of Tintern Abbey who experiences 'that blessed mood'

> In which the heavy and the weary weight
> Of all this unintelligible world,
> Is lightened . . .
> ('Lines Composed above Tintern Abbey', ll.39–41)

Henry James has to sweeten the experience of the Roman ruins in making it that of the 'bright nymph' Isabel Archer who 'had long before taken old Rome into her confidence, for in a world of ruins the ruin of her happiness seemed a less unnatural catastrophe. She rested her weariness upon things that had crumbled for centuries and yet were still upright' (James, 1984, p.564). For Eliot ruins do not hold the promise of psychic restoration, the consolation of identification they do for Wordsworth and James, a point we will recall in discussing the issues of antiquity, ruination and gender as they intersect in *Romola*, a novel whose heroine is, like Dorothea here, alienated amid antiquarian artefacts. In fact the response to Rome Eliot here registers seems rather to rhyme with that of Hardy who is also oppressed by this 'history-haunted' site – though I will want later to develop this point of comparison into a point of contrast. 'After some days spent in the Holy City Hardy began to feel, he frequently said, its measureless layers of history to lie upon him like a physical weight'. He finds the 'altae moenia Romae' 'gaunt to the vision' and 'depressing to the mind' and after his visit of 1887 is not reluctant to leave 'Time's Central City'. 'It was with a sense of having grasped very little of its history that he left the city, though with some relief, which may have been partly physical and partly mental' (T. Hardy, 1984, p.105; F.E. Hardy, 1986, p.188; T. Hardy, 1984, p.103; F.E. Hardy, 1986, p.191). One recalls Marx, 'The tradition of all the dead generations weighs like a nightmare on the brain of the living' (Marx 1977, p.300).

According to Arnold, the kind of oppressive unintelligibility of spectacle Dorothea experiences expresses a quintessentially nineteenth-century crisis. In 'On the Modern Element in Literature' he diagnoses as the most pressing need of his age that of 'intellectual deliverance' from the pressure of mere information, from that 'vast multitude of facts awaiting and inviting comprehension' (Arnold, 1960, 1, p.20). Another occasion for Dorothea's anxiety in this chapter is that Casaubon begins to order and write up his ever-accumulating notes for the *Key to all Mythologies*, so Arnold's metaphor of the age's intellectual crisis being its inability to deal with a 'vast multitude of facts awaiting and inviting comprehension' is again strikingly close to Eliot's own. Such a deliverance is achieved, Arnold argues, 'When we have acquired that harmonious acquiescence of mind which we feel in contemplating a grand spectacle that is intelligible to us; when we have lost that impatient irritation of mind which we feel in the presence of an immense, moving, confused spectacle which, while it perpetually excites our curiosity, perpetually baffles our comprehension' (Arnold, 1960, 1, p.20). The echoing of Arnold's and Eliot's vocabulary is exact: his 'Immense, moving, confused . . . baffles our comprehension'; her 'vast', 'moving', 'confused', 'unintelligible'. Dorothea's disturbance of mind and perception could hardly be further from the 'harmonious acquiescence' Arnold calls for between the spectator and the objects of his vision which he posits as the prerequisite of the realist ambition of 'seeing things as they are'. The heaped-up disparity that Eliot keeps finding new terms to evoke here and in adjoining paragraphs – 'stupendous fragmentariness', 'vast wreck', 'mixed confusedly', 'incongruities', 'endless minutiae', 'confusion', 'tumultuous' – recalls the terms of Arnold's objection to the poetry of Browning with its sadly symptomatic expression of the contemporary malaise in its 'confused multitudinousness'. 'Visible history' seems to be as 'unintelligible' as its chiaroscuro counterpart of my title, being in addition, 'enigmatical', 'oppressive', and 'monotonous', while the narrator gestures inconclusively in compensation towards the supposedly deeper-seated harmonies of 'the suppressed transitions which unite all contrasts'. In Rome's 'vast wreck' of 'ideals', its 'strange', 'shocking' and 'alien' art, religion and architecture, those crucial polarities of Victorian discourse, culture and anarchy, collapse into each other as if their dichotomy were a fiction. The passage renders compellingly problematic both the cherished cultural principles and fetish of objectivity Arnold presents in *Culture and Anarchy* (1869) as interdependent ideals.

I would suggest that at the root of Dorothea's alienation and disturbance here is precisely the 'collision' of presupposed ideal Arnoldian categories – 'the suppressed transitions which unite all contrasts' – with a culture in fact characterised by division, discontinuity and acquisitive

49

conflict and bearing the ghostly inscription of such conflict in its very showpiece artefacts which are themselves engaged in perpetual 'Titanic . . . struggling' and the endeavour to 'take possession' of their spectators. Eliot has brilliantly intuited the centrality to the Western art tradition of the concept of possession, and given it an eerie twist. Lévi-Strauss argues that Western art is all about provoking in the spectator the desire to possess both the artefact and that which it depicts. 'It is this avid and ambitious desire to take possession of the object for the benefit of the owner or even of the spectator which seems to me to constitute one of the outstandingly original features of the art of Western Civilisation' (quoted without reference Berger, 1972, p.84). For Dorothea it is this art which now, as if avenging its status as the object of ownership, 'takes possession' of its spectator.

The vision of the West's history this passage sketches is not that of the 'cooperation of successive generations, the source to which the gradual growth of civilisation is to be traced' that Comte argued characterised human history, the essential feature of which is 'continuity' (Comte, 1865, p.404) and of which the narrator's 'suppressed transitions' would seem to be a cautious version. Its wearying weight of unintelligible contrasts and of juxtaposed opulence and degradation is closer to the conflictual history Marx posits and his rejection of such idealising teleological distortions as Comte's when he argues that 'History is nothing but the succession of the separate generations, each of which exploits the materials, the capital funds, the productive forces handed down to it by all preceding generations, and thus, on the one hand, continues the traditional activity in completely changed circumstances with a completely changed activity' (Marx, 1965, p.60).

Dorothea's metaphors and sentiments about Rome's 'funeral procession with strange ancestral images and trophies gathered from afar' 'in the midst of a sordid present' are exactly those Walter Benjamin uses in discussing the 'cautious detachment', or even 'horror', that the spectator of cultural treasures must feel if he or she is alive to the history of struggle, conquest and acquisition they flaunt.

> Whoever has emerged victorious participates to this day in the triumphal procession in which the present rulers step over those who are lying prostrate. According to traditional practice, the spoils are carried along in the procession. They are called cultural treasures, and a historical materialist views them with cautious detachment. For without exception the cultural treasures he surveys have an origin which he cannot contemplate without horror. They owe their existence not only to the great minds and

talents who have created them, but also to the anonymous toil of their contemporaries. There is no document of civilisation which is not at the same time a document of barbarism.
(Benjamin, 1973, 'Theses on the Philosophy of History', p.238)

Benjamin's famous final sentence makes explicit Western history's confounding of Arnold's polarities, culture and anarchy, and throws an ominous shadow over *Middlemarch*'s acknowledged status as a supreme 'document of civilisation'.

THE CONCEALED TOTALITY OF LIFE

Victorian honeymoons, in art and actuality, are famously grisly, confrontational and depressingly sexless affairs. This discovery is made by Tess and Angel Clare, Heathcliff and Isabella Linton, and Miss Havisham who never even gets to hers. This last bride, eternally arrested as if by a malicious enchantment on the threshold of consummation, is a nineteenth-century figure to consider, the frustrations of a Fabrizio feminised. One thinks also of Ruskin's disastrous and unconsummated wedding-night which, like Dorothea, he experienced as a strange amalgam of anxieties from artistic, antiquarian and sexual sources. He balked at the sight of female pubic hair, the existence of which he had not been prepared for by his studies in classical statuary. He could never again bear to approach this distressingly unstatuesque woman and there was an eventual annulment. This is an instance to recall in relation to the nineteenth century's perhaps fraught equation of women and statuary of which *Romola* and *Daniel Deronda* are brilliant expositions. In Hardy's poem 'Honeymoon Time at an Inn', an already inexplicably gloomladen couple are startled as 'Something fell sheer, and crashed, and from the floor / Lay glittering at the pair with a shattered gaze' (T. Hardy, 1984, p.515). An old pier-glass has fallen from the wall and the 'Spirits Ironic' delight in presaging 'Long years of sorrow'. The 'Spirits of Pity' take a minimal consolation from the fact that this sounds more like the usual fate of married couples than it does a particular doom. Life imitated the art of Dorothea's misery in Eliot's own honeymoon with John Cross in Venice in 1880. With an intriguing gender reversal it was then the young groom of the revered older authoress who suffered 'a sudden mental derangement' (Haight, 1985, p.544) and flung himself from the hotel balcony into the Grand Canal and had to be fished out by passing gondoliers.

But why always Dorothea? Sexual/marital frustrations aside, I suggested earlier that she has a double source of misery in this chapter –

repulsion from Rome's ruins and distress at the lack of urgency shown by Casaubon in relation to the ever-deferred completion of the *Key to all Mythologies*, another depressingly unconsummated project. Eliot's counterpointing of these multiple but related sources of repulsion and frustration – cultural, sexual, historical, intellectual – provides a rich play of ideas and the role of Casaubon's unrealisable project is a crucial one. Casaubon's theory and (minimal) practice as a mythographer is simply stated. He is assembling a vast collection of diverse 'mythical fragments' which he intends to demonstrate are all corrupted derivations from a single lost Ur-myth about the sun. These 'tremendous fragments of meaning' (I am thinking of Paul Klee's term for his art in *On Modern Art* (1924)) once formed a splendidly intelligible mythic whole.

> he had undertaken to show (what indeed had been attempted before, but not with that thoroughness, justice of comparison, and effectiveness of arrangement at which Mr Casaubon aimed) that all the mythical systems or erratic mythical fragments in the world were corruptions of a tradition originally revealed. Having once mastered the true position and taken a firm footing there, the vast field of mythical constructions became intelligible, nay, luminous with the reflected light of correspondences.
>
> (G. Eliot, 1981, p.46)

The parallels with the novel's other instances of grand male artistic and intellectual projects are marked. Ladislaw's artist friend Naumann is an apostle of the Pre-Pre-Raphaelite 'Nazarene' school seeking an uncorrupted authenticity of art in its originating medieval forms. Ladislaw calls him 'one of the chief renovators of Christian art' (G. Eliot, 1981, p.245) where he means 'reviver' rather than 'restorer'/'repairer', but perhaps the distinction is not really that marked. Lydgate struggles with pathological experiments inspired by Bichat intended to uncover the 'primitive tissue' (G. Eliot, 1981, p.178) from which diverse animal tissue forms, he supposes, derive. He seeks, as Lukács claims the novel as a genre does, 'the concealed totality of life' (Lukács, 1978, p.71). The Platonic presuppositions of a Lydgatesque scientific project based on the suppression of difference and the positing of a concealed totality have been witheringly discredited by Nietzsche.

> Just as it is certain that one leaf is never quite like another, so it is certain that the concept leaf is constructed by an arbitrary dropping of individual differences, through a forgetting of what differentiates; and this awakens the idea that there is something in

52

nature besides leaves which would be 'leaf', that is to say an original form, according to which all leaves are woven, drawn, circumscribed, coloured, curled, painted, but by clumsy hands, so that no example emerges correctly and reliably as a true copy of the original form.

(Nietzsche, 1980, Vol.I, 'Über Wahrheit und Lüge in aussermoralische Sinne', pp.879–80)

Nietzsche has with characteristic insight crystallised the whole mode, not only of scientific enquiry but of enquiry itself, against which he sets himself: the denial of difference and diversity, the dismissal of actual appearances, the veneration of abstract and conjectural original forms. A precisely comparable argument to this of Nietzsche's is offered by Lévi-Strauss about his and Casaubon's object of study, myths. Myths, says Lévi-Strauss, are the most unsuitable phenomena to choose to boil down into archetypes, sources and original forms. They simply refuse such reduction to essences: their heterogeneity is their essence, form and function. In the 'Overture' to *The Raw and the Cooked: Introduction to a Science of Mythology, I* (1964) Lévi-Strauss states the purpose of the book as the exposition of a single Bororo myth. This he calls, in a term that recalls Casaubon's methodology, 'the key myth'. However he is quick to disown the Casaubonian presuppositions we might see in the term and states that, although his project restricts itself to the exposition of this single myth 'yet to achieve even partial success, it must assimilate the subject matter of two-hundred others' (Lévi-Strauss, 1970, p.4). So Lévi-Strauss's project moves in the opposite direction to Casaubon's, unravelling the one into the many instead of trying to bind the many back up into the one. Lévi-Strauss recognises that it is in the nature of his mythic subject that it tends to fray or, as he puts it, nebulise. 'However it is approached, it spreads out like a nebula, without ever bringing together in any lasting or systematic way the sum total of the elements from which it blindly derives its substance' (Lévi-Strauss, 1970, p.2). As the term 'Overture' suggests, Lévi-Strauss pursues an analogy between myth and music. Neither, he argues, can be approached as if they had the qualities of objects: outline, location, centredness, presence. Rather they are shadowy anti-objects, never fully present, that disturb the category of the actual.

If it is now asked where the real centre of the work is to be found, the answer is that this is impossible to determine. Music and mythology bring man face to face with potential objects of which only the shadows are actualized, with conscious approximations (a musical score and a myth cannot be more) of inevitably unconscious truths, which follow from them.

(Lévi-Strauss, 1970, pp.17–18)

Myths are never complete, so knowledge of them can never be finished. The mythographer can never be, as Hardy calls Matthew Arnold, 'a finished writer' (T. Hardy, 1982 (1), p.437) because 'the analysis of myths is an endless task . . . The evidence is never complete'. Here is an aid to understanding the chronic resistance to completion of the *Key to all Mythologies*. Casaubon projects a completion that can never be realised because the very object of his study resists it.

> But I do not hope to reach a stage at which the subject matter of mythology, after being broken down by analysis, will crystallise again into a whole with the general appearance of a stable and well-defined structure . . . The ambition to achieve such knowledge is meaningless, since we are dealing with a shifting reality, perpetually exposed to the attacks of a past that destroys it and of a future that changes it.

(Lévi-Strauss, 1970, p.3)

Nietzsche had implied that nature defies Plato. For Lévi-Strauss myth defies Descartes.

> The study of myths raises a methodological problem, in that it cannot be carried out according to the Cartesian principle of breaking down the difficulty into as many parts as may be necessary for finding the solution. There is no real end to mythological analysis, no hidden unity to be grasped once the breaking-down process has been completed. Themes can be split up *ad infinitum*. Just when you think you have disentangled and separated them, you realise that they are knitting together again in response to the operation of unexpected affinities. Consequently the unity of the myth is never more than tendential and projective and cannot reflect a state or a particular moment of the myth. It is a phenomenon of the imagination, resulting from the attempt at interpretation; and its function is to endow the myth with synthetic form and to prevent its disintegration into a confusion of opposites. The science of myths might therefore be termed 'anaclastic', if we take this old term in the broader etymological sense which includes the study of both reflected rays and broken rays. But unlike philosophical reflection, which aims to go back to its own source, the reflections we are dealing with here concern

rays whose only source is hypothetical. Divergence of sequences and themes is a fundamental characteristic of mythological thought, which manifests itself as an irradiation.

(Lévi-Strauss, 1970, p.5)

The web of *Middlemarch* is ravelled – and I here mean to exploit the full contradictoriness of the term 'ravel' whose semantic curiosity evidently appealed to the author of *Silas Marner: The Weaver of Raveloe* (1861). 'Ravel' means the same as 'unravel'. It means itself and its own opposite, synthesis and deconstruction combined. Thus in *Middlemarch* we have a novel which in its own avowed positing of 'the suppressed transitions which unite all contrasts' seems to accord with Lukács's ambition for the genre that it 'uncover or construct the concealed totality of life'. At the same time it actually centres on a character's failure to realise a similarly reconstructive project addressing a subject, mythology, which in fact reveals 'no hidden unity'. Lévi-Strauss on myth provides crucial insights from which post-structuralism can be seen to have emerged. Derrida is an admirer of his mythography and discusses it at length in 'Structure, Sign and Play in the Discourse of the Human Sciences' in *Writing and Difference*. For Derrida it is only a short step from Lévi-Strauss's analyses to his own central contribution to post-structuralist thought; the conception of the primacy within all discourse, mythic and other-wise, of structure, deferral and difference.

There is no unity or absolute source of the myth. The focus or the source of the myth are always shadows and virtualities which are elusive, unactualizable, and non-existent in the first place. Every-thing begins with structure, configuration or relationship. The discourse on the ancentric structure that myth itself is, cannot itself have an absolute subject or an absolute centre.

(Derrida, 1978, p.286)

Of course Casaubon's 'small monumental records' – how characteristic of him that his work should be simultaneously small and monumental – never do gell and his work remains more like the scattered, mimetic anarchy of Hardy's shattered pier-glass than his own conjectured mirror-surface where myths become 'intelligible, nay, luminous with the reflected light of correspondences'. Casaubon has unwittingly written a masterly demonstration of post-structuralist premises. His work's chronic resistance to synthesis and completion is an exemplary instance of the persistence of difference and deferral.

THE ACCIDENTS OF INCONSEQUENCE

We have noticed a certain similarity in the responses of Eliot and Hardy to Rome's monuments. We might, however, further note that Hardy, in possible contrast to Eliot, is keenly interested to depict cultural monuments in ways that contradict the desire to read in them the evidences of Comtean 'continuity' and 'cooperation'. In a curious scene given great weight in *A Laodicean* the hero Somerset exposes his architect rival as a fraud because the latter has dated as Saxon what Somerset concludes to be the Norman Castle De Stancy. The accurate examiner of culture finds evidence not of survival and continuity but of conquest and rupture. In *Jude the Obscure* (1896) the villagers of Marygreen are exemplary illustrations of Marx's view of history in 'exploiting the materials . . . handed down . . . by . . . preceding generations . . . with a completely changed activity'. They are dismantling the old church to make pig-sties and rockeries. As an architect of ecclesiastical 'restorations' Hardy had participated, if with later regret, in nearly equivalently drastic remodellings.

With these Hardyesque emphases in mind, we might usefully compare Jocelyn Pierston's experience of Rome in *The Well-Beloved* (1897) with Dorothea's.

> To those who have looked at Rome with the quickening power of a knowledge which breathes a growing soul into all historic shapes, and traces out the suppressed transitions that unite all contrasts, Rome may still be the spiritual centre and interpreter of the world.
>
> (G. Eliot, 1981, p.225)

> Being in Rome, as aforesaid, Pierston returned one evening to his hotel to dine, after spending the afternoon among the busts in the long gallery of the Vatican. The unconscious habit, common to so many people, of tracing likes in unlikes had often led him to discern, or to fancy he discerned, in the Roman atmosphere, in its light and shades, and particularly in its reflected or secondary lights, something resembling the atmosphere of his native promontory.
>
> (T. Hardy, 1986, pp.101–2)

It is typical of a George Eliot sentence actually to assert a great deal less than at first appears, like a guarantee threaded with qualifications. Who are 'those', do they actually exist, and are their abilities to divine immanent connection and meaning such as to inspire awe or incredulity? She seems to be able to express scepticism and yearning simultaneously towards an object that is more contradictory the more one examines it. Is Eliot using 'and' where she should use 'or' and yoking mutually exclusive elements? Her tendency appears to be the opposite of that she ascribes to Tom Tulliver who was 'prone to see an opposition between statements that were really quite accordant' (G. Eliot, 1983, p.103). If you are revitalising 'historic shapes' are you not rather highlighting than eliminating 'contrasts'? Is Rome's being a 'spiritual centre' or focus of meaning not the opposite of its being the 'interpreter of the world' and therefore a footnote to something more important? We get the impression that Eliot is gingerly handling some cherished ideologies that threaten to crack open into contradiction. 'The suppressed transitions which unite all contrasts' speaks volumes about the fundamental priorities of realism. Using a chapter title 'Links' before her famous defence of realism in *Adam Bede* gives a clue to the reliance of the realist method on belief in the immanence of meaningful connections and relations, the 'web' of circumstances and correspondences as Eliot likes to picture it. The narrator of *Middlemarch* calls them 'suppressed transitions' as if suggesting that they offer an alternative to the 'stupendous fragmentariness' that here appears to characterise culture, and the narrator of *Daniel Deronda*, as if elevating the concept to the status of a physical law, 'hidden affinity' (G. Eliot, 1984 (2), p.380). Binding, connections and relations become key terms for narrator and protagonist alike; Dorothea craves 'a binding theory which could bring her own life and doctrine into strict connection with that amazing past' and envies Ladislaw his response to Rome which 'saved you from seeing the world's ages as a set of box-like partitions without vital connection' (G. Eliot, 1981, p.112; p.244). Daniel is inspired by Judaism's 'binding history', craves 'insight into the principles which form the vital connections of knowledge' and feels 'the imaginative need of some far-reaching relation'; rather as his narrator likes to 'connect the course of individual lives with the historical stream' and scorns 'small social drama' not 'penetrated by a feeling of wider relations' (G. Eliot, 1984 (2), p.417; p.220; p.815; pp.121–2; pp.185–6). Assessing the tradition of critical realism of nineteenth-century fiction Lukács offers a formulation which sounds close to these narrators' and protagonists' concerns: 'The novel seeks, by giving form, to uncover and construct the concealed totality of life' (Lukács, 1978, p.71). Even Lukács's use of 'and' is Eliot-like in its specious yoking of opposites and exposes a comparable ideological crux – is the realist artist discovering or inventing 'concealed totality'?

Hardy's depiction of Jocelyn's visit to the Vatican's long sculpture gallery (where at the end of Eliot's chapter Dorothea is discovered in a pose that attracts the attention of Naumann as if herself a piece of Rome's statuary) so precisely addresses the problems Eliot uses Dorothea's experience of Rome to articulate, that one is tempted to think it is a conscious riposte. It occurs a few chapters beyond one entitled 'Juxtapositions' as if in reply to Eliot's similar prioritising of 'Links', which, as we shall see, is appropriate to the tendencies of Hardy's aesthetic at this time. The reference to 'the unconscious habit, common to so many people, of tracing likes in unlikes' seems a direct hit at the aesthetic of Eliot's narrator. Notice the exactness of Hardy's choice of vocabulary and how he ironically places the term 'tracing' that both Eliot and Comte's 1865 translator reached for to depict their notion of the uncovering of connections – one that very neatly equivocates between the functions of discovering and inventing. Hardy relentlessly contextualises such a vision as his protagonist's utterly subjective impression, 'often led him to discern, or fancy he discerned'. Eliot offers the possibility of Rome as the 'spiritual centre'. Hardy's prose plays here with the avoidance of centrality, the very syntax of the sentence continually slides off from primary statement. Nearly the whole assertion dissolves into qualifying parentheses, its long-anticipated climax coming as the mealy-mouthed 'something resembling' that in fact deflects us further from Rome itself by means of a comparison. Here is an aesthetic of deferral par excellence. Moreover, Rome does not exist for Jocelyn as a real and present entity, let alone as a 'centre' for anything else. It is only to be observed in its 'atmosphere', which we might at first take to mean 'pervading ambience' as in a room's atmosphere, but in fact has its other meaning of 'a surrounding yet remote haze' as in the earth's atmosphere. Ever postponed and deflected, like an elusive object surrounded by mirrors and dissolving into a field of reflection and re-reflection, the reality of Rome for Jocelyn would appear to be like the meaning of a story for the Marlow of 'Heart of Darkness', 'not inside like a kernel but outside, enveloping the tale which brought it out only as a glow brings out a haze, in the likeness of one of those misty halos that sometimes are made visible by the spectral illumination of moonshine' (Conrad, 1981, p.8). The heart of Rome's darkness towards which we thought we were travelling turns out not to be Rome itself at all, but something about it that somewhat resembles something else. It is not a darkness that possesses a heart, but a heart composed of darkness and negation – a casket containing not a jewel but a vapour, a centre of nothing. George Eliot, however, with her Rome as possibly 'spiritual centre and interpreter of the world' has the best of both versions of the world, so to speak: kernel and halo, jewel and vapour. It is both an ultimate source of meaning and one of an endless field of correspondences and interpretations with no absolute origin other than the 'world' i.e. everything. Her Rome is simultaneously the Ur-text and a footnote to something else.

Another instance of Hardy's castigation of 'the habit common to so many people, of tracing likes in unlikes' is elaborated in 1922 in the 'Apology' to *Late Lyrics and Earlier*. A scornful appraisal of his critics in these terms expands into a statement of aesthetic principle introducing some striking terms of approbation; 'chance little shocks', 'juxtaposition', 'discordant', 'irrelation', 'the accidents of inconsequence'.

> To add a few more words to what has already taken up too many, there is a contingency liable to miscellanies of verse that I have never seen mentioned, so far as I can remember; I mean the chance little shocks that may be caused over a book of various character like the present by the juxtaposition of unrelated, even discordant, effusions; poems perhaps years apart in the making, yet facing each other. An odd result of this has been that dramatic anecdotes of a satirical and humorous intention following verse in graver voice, have been read as misfires because they raise the smile they were intended to raise, the journalist, deaf to the sudden change of key, being unconscious that he is laughing with the author and not at him. I admit that I did not foresee such contingencies as I ought to have done, and that people might not perceive when the tone altered. But the difficulties of arranging the themes in a graduated kinship of moods would have been so great that irrelation was almost unavoidable with efforts so diverse. I must trust for right note-catching to those finely-touched spirits who can divine without half a whisper, whose intuitiveness is proof against all the accidents of inconsequence.
>
> (T. Hardy, 1984, 'Apology' to *Late Lyrics and Earlier*, p.559)

Hardy's critics in their searching-out of 'likes in unlikes' must have been brought up on the preface to the second edition of *Lyrical Ballads* (first edition 1798) where Wordsworth states as axiomatic 'the pleasure which the mind derives from the perception of similitude in dissimilitude' (Wordsworth, 1985, p.740). Hardy's characterising of his work with that resonant term 'the accidents of inconsequence' is particularly revealing in that it precisely reverses the connotations of a formula he had previously favoured when describing his work, 'the true sequence'.

In the meagre theoretical statements we can glean from novels' prefaces this formula undergoes significant revisions of meaning indicating that his concept of what constitutes 'truth' is decisively shifting. To trace these permutations is to sketch the development of an aesthetic in clear opposition to one of 'suppressed transitions' and for which 'Juxtapositions' rather than 'Links' become defining characteristics. In the 1895 preface to *The Trumpet-Major* an aesthetic is assumed that both idealises a hard-won formal coherence in the artwork and presupposes that such coherence acts as the mirror of an equivalently coherent reality. 'Those who have attempted to construct a coherent narrative of past times from the fragmentary information furnished by survivors, are aware of the difficulty of ascertaining the true sequence of events indiscriminately recalled' (T. Hardy, 1974, p.37). 'Fragments' need to be marshalled into the construction of a 'coherent narrative' and 'indiscriminately recalled events' forged into, using the key Hardy formula, 'the true sequence'. 'True' here seems to mean both objectively occurring, like the experience of the survivors of Waterloo to whom he here refers, and also true in a more abstract sense that supposes the representation of all truth to take the form of coherent sequence, as in the architectural usage with which Hardy would be familiar where something is true if it falls into strict alignment.

When the phrase had occurred four years earlier in the 1891 preface to *Tess* meanings were quite differently weighted. 'The story is sent out in all sincerity of purpose, as an attempt to give artistic form to a true sequence of things' (T. Hardy, 1985, 'Explanatory Note to the First Edition', p.35). Here the sense of 'true' as formally aligned is not evoked, only the artistic reworking of events gives, or 'attempts' to give, form to a previously meaningless sequence. If we recall Lukács's definition of the novel's function these two prefaces appear to adopt opposed positions as to whether the artistic function is one of 'uncovering' or 'construction'. The Hardy of *Tess of the d'Urbervilles* makes rather than finds form and truth, whereas the Hardy of *The Trumpet-Major* had seemed to expect to discover and reproduce it.

Thirty-one years after the 1891 preface in the 'Apology' to *Late Lyrics and Earlier* that resonant term 'accidents of inconsequence' which he uses to describe his work precisely reverses the meanings of the previously favoured formula, replacing 'truth' with 'accidents' and 'sequence' with 'inconsequence', and thus decisively undermines the pretensions to truth of either uncovering or constructing 'the true sequence of things'. When Hardy here ridicules his critics' spurious 'intuitiveness' which is proof against 'the accidents of inconsequence', he seems almost to be ironically recalling the aesthetic priorities of the early years of his own career, as twenty-seven years earlier in the preface to *The Trumpet-Major* he was troubling over 'the difficulty of ascertaining the true sequence'. Hardy's shift to lyric collections from novels would seem to be a natural outcome of an aesthetic ever more attracted to accident, irrelation and inconsequence.

WHAT DIFFERENCE, THEN?

Given the opposed versions of repetition we have seen voiced in the narrator of *Middlemarch*'s ideal of a 'knowledge which . . . traces out the suppressed transitions which unite all contrasts' and Hardy's rejection of such a 'knowledge' in his critics who impose such transitions upon his work despite its nature as 'the juxtaposition of unrelated, even discordant, effusions', it is relevant to compare Gilles Deleuze on the two alternative theories of repetition he finds structuring Western thought and discourse.

> Let us consider two formulations: 'only that which resembles itself differs', 'only differences resemble one another'. It is a question of two readings of the world in the sense that one asks us to think of difference on the basis of pre-established similitude or identity while the other invites us on the contrary to think of similitude and even identity as the product of a fundamental disparity. The first exactly defines the world of copies or of representations; it establishes the world as icon. The second, against the first, defines a world of simulacra. It presents the world of phantasm.
>
> (Deleuze, 1969, p.302)

Deleuze identifies the perspective which thinks of difference 'on the basis of a pre-established similitude' as Platonic and that which sees similitude 'as the product of a fundamental disparity' as Nietzschean. Compare *The Joyful Wisdom*, 'to perceive resemblance everywhere, making everything alike, is a sign of weak eyesight' (Nietzsche, 1910, p.87). In this sense George Eliot's conception can be identified with the Platonic mode, Hardy's with the Nietzschean, as is suggested by a discussion of this passage of Deleuze from J. Hillis Miller's *Fiction and Repetition* (1982).

> What Deleuze calls 'Platonic' repetition is grounded in a solid archetypal model which is untouched by the effects of repetition . . . The assumption of such a world gives rise to the notion of a

metaphoric expression based on genuine participative similarity or even on identity, as when Gerard Manley Hopkins says he becomes Christ, an 'after Christ' . . . A similar presupposition, as Deleuze recognises, underlies the concept of imitation in literature. The validity of the mimetic copy is established by its truth of correspondence to what it copies. This is, so it seems, the reigning presupposition of realist fiction and of its critics in nineteenth- and even twentieth-century England.

(Hillis Miller, 1982, p.6)

If Hopkins believes himself an 'after Christ', the heroine of *Middlemarch* is introduced to the reader as an illustration that even in the nineteenth century 'Here and there is born a Saint Theresa' (G. Eliot, 1981, 'Prelude', p.26), an 'after Theresa'. Hillis Miller's reference to the presuppositions of realist-minded critics recalls the 'finely-touched spirits' Hardy's 'discordant effusions' encountered. Hillis Miller rightly asserts of this Platonic/mimetic conception of repetition that 'to many it seems the normative one'. The very term 'realism' underlines this normative assumption. In continuing his account, Hillis Miller actually refers to Hardy to illustrate the other, Nietzschean form of repetition, which posits a world based on difference.

Each thing, this other theory would assume, is unique, intrinsically different from every other thing. Similarity arises against the background of this 'disparité du fond' (fundamental disparity). It is a world not of copies but of what Deleuze calls 'simulacra' or 'phantasms'. These are ungrounded doublings which arise from differential interrelations among elements which are all on the same plane. This lack of ground in some paradigm or archetype means that there is something ghostly about the effects of this second type of repetition. It seems that X repeats Y, but in fact it does not, or at least not in the firmly anchored way of the first sort of repetition. An example would be the way Henchard in *The Mayor of Casterbridge* thinks, during his wanderings at the end of his life, that he returns to the spot where he sold his wife in the scene which opens the novel. In fact, as the narrator tells us, with Hardy's characteristic insouciant ironic cruelty, he has not correctly identified the place.

(Hillis Miller, 1982, p.6)

Realism offers what Hardy rejects, 'a world of copies'. Copies, tracings, returns, repetitions: these are realism's indispensable motifs and strategies. A study of their literary significance in the nineteenth century could take as its starting-point their insistent presence in *David Copperfield*. *Copperfield* is copy-filled. The novel keenly permutates the term 're/tracing' which has such a vigorous nineteenth-century life and which appears here in almost the whole gamut of its various, or compounded, meanings: reading, writing, recalling, recounting, copying a picture, indicating the outline of an object, following an established route, pursuing to an origin (see usages: Dickens, 1985, p.770; p.772; p.886; p.902; p.944). The characters themselves are equivalently assiduous copyists. Traddles never quite shakes his childhood habit of chalking all available surfaces with skeletons, appropriately moribund figures, and finds a wife with complementary leanings. She trains herself as a copy-writer, even basing the firm, legalistic hand with which she fills her copy-books on a model. David is also employed re-iterating an authoritative discourse; he works in the House of Commons transcribing parliamentary speeches. Mr Dick – here again a typical rather than eccentric figure – is 'incessantly occupying himself in copying everything he could lay his hands on' (Dickens, 1985, p.908).

Lacan has excellently defined the 'real' as 'that which always comes back to the same place' (Lacan, 1977 (2), p.42). This simply adds the notion of circular movement to Foucault's definition of the medieval episteme in which 'The same remains the same, riveted onto itself' (Foucault, 1989, p.25). The era of the great realist novels and the Gothic revival in architecture and its associated medievalisms are broadly contemporaneous cultural phenomena. Of course, Hardy had substantial dealings with both and, possibly, distanced himself from both. Perhaps the two projects are united in nostalgia for the Lacanian 'real', a lost world of correspondences, repetitions and returns. If a realist art is thus concerned to perfect the circularity of its returns it sounds rather like the 'mad art' which attempts 'the inconceivable' of the demented innocent Stevie in Conrad's *The Secret Agent* (1907). As assiduous as Mr Dick at his copying, Stevie hunches fixedly over his pencil and compass and endlessly inscribes 'circles, circles; innumerable circles, concentric, eccentric; a coruscating whirl of circles' (Conrad, 1980 (1), pp.45–6).

Of course, as Hillis Miller has pointed out, coming back to the same place is what Hardy's characters so pointedly fail to do. This is a crucial aspect of their 'unreal' modernity. Their 'returns', like that of the Native, are never quite to the same spot. The location of Tess's rape/seduction is not, which would have afforded a cruelly chiming 'poetic justice', The Vale of the White Hart, the immemorial site of analogous huntings-down, but the one next to it. Michael Henchard journeys in a doomed attempt to re-establish relations. He makes the guilt-laden trip back to

63

the spot – in fact mistaking it – where he once sold his wife. Tess also begins her novel with a journey supposed to re-establish relation and whose end is tragedy. She reluctantly seeks out a relation who turns out to be a usurper. Thus she seeks the familial/familiar in the unfamiliar, and finds only the unfamiliar disguised as the familiar. Henchard's and Tess's journeys thus exemplify a crucial aspect of the modern as Klee describes it in *On Modern Art*: its un-Wordsworthian determination not to satisfy the seekers of the familiar. Klee ridicules those who insist on divining a 'familiar face' in one of his canvasses, or complain 'That isn't a bit like uncle'. 'To hell with uncle' says the modern artist. He has renounced the wonted artistic function of conjuring the presence of the familial/familiar (Klee, 1989, p.33; p.31).

Hardy chooses to frustrate readers of the strange and in some instances cruel satisfactions of relation, likeness, repetition and return. Of course the cruelty can sometimes be in the frustration. The distinctive grief-magic of *Poems of 1912–13* derives from the poet's own rehearsal of such failed repetitions. He obsessively circles, returns, retraces, repeats, remembers, revisits places and events associated with Emma; but such returns are now scorched by the terrible difference of her absence. See 'Where the Picnic Was' in which he returns alone to the site – now marked by a 'burnt circle' – of last year's outing, or the poignant and exactly entitled 'A Circular'. Apparent repetitions are riven with tragic difference.

> I walked up there today
> Just in the former way;
>   Surveyed around
>   The familiar ground
>   By myself again:
>   What difference, then?
> Only that underlying sense
> Of the look of a room on returning thence.
> (T. Hardy, 1984, 'The Walk', ll.9–16, p.340)

TERRIBLE ITERATION

To take these Deleuzian connections a stage further we can observe that Hardy is the artist of the simulacrum par excellence. Tess, who 'was in a dream wherein familiar objects appeared as having light and shade and position, but no particular outline' (Hillis Miller goes on to identify the reliance of dream experience on 'ungrounded doublings' with the Nietzschean mode) and occupied a world 'peopled by phantoms and voices antipathetic to her'; Jocelyn, whose 'life seemed no longer a professional man's experience, but a ghost story'; Sue, whom Jude describes as 'a phantasmal bodiless creature'; Jude, who describes himself as 'spectre-seeing always' and Hardy himself, who entitles a collection of poems *Human Shows, Far Phantasies, Songs and Trifles,* all seem occupants of a world, not of crisp realist copies, but of 'ghostly' 'simulacra' and 'phantasms' (T. Hardy: 1985, p.232, p.135; 1986, p.140; 1981, p.279, p.302).

Hardy's is a haunted art. Scattered observations from journals recorded in the *Life* sketch an aesthetic consciously opposed to realism ('"realism" is not art') and proposing a great inversion of prevailing aesthetics so that material reality is displaced as the goal of representation by shadowy and spectral anti-realities – one is reminded of Lévi-Strauss's conception of myth – materiality itself now partaking of this newly prioritised shadowyness. 'The Realities to be the true realities of life, hitherto called abstractions. The old material realities to be placed behind the former, as shadowy accessories.' That such innovative conceptions are not readily articulable within the prevailing discourse is suggested by the peculiarly self-cancelling term Hardy uses for them, 'abstract realisms' (F.E. Hardy, 1986, p.229; p.177; p.177). *Tess of the d'Urbervilles* is 'the shaded side of a well-known catastrophe' and in Hardy's hands 'shaded' contains all the Deleuzian meanings – lacking outline, penumbral, haunted, ghostly, nuanced in the registration of difference. Hillis Miller's assessment of that Nietzschean perception that 'Each thing is intrinsically different from every other thing. Similarity arises against the background of this 'disparité du fond' exactly paraphrases Clare's statement of shock, during a honeymoon for Tess the awfulness of which outDorotheas Dorothea's, that she does not share and embody his mimetic vision of correspondences. 'Could it be possible, he continued, that eyes which as they gazed never expressed any divergence from what the tongue was telling, were yet ever seeing another world behind her ostensible one, discordant and contrasting' (T. Hardy, 1985, p.305).

Both Dorothea and Tess suffer the experience of alienation from the objectivity of the world. Consider the similarity of their characterisation. Dorothea endures 'a nightmare in which every object was withering and shrinking away from her' (G. Eliot, 1981, p.308) while for Tess 'All material objects around announced their irresponsibility with terrible iteration' (T. Hardy, 1985, p.305). But while both experience the world as 'discordant and contrasting', Tess is shown both rightly to perceive and actually to embody a 'world of phantasm' whose only law is lawless 'disparité du fond', whose 'simulacra' are 'unrelated', 'discordant' and 'contrasting' while George Eliot plays on the possibility of Dorothea's apparently equivalent vision being diseased.

With characteristic George Eliot ambivalence, the description of Dorothea's experience of Rome at first conjures up the possibility of exactly such a world of fundamental disparity, simulacra and phantasms where, sounding like Tess's 'dream', 'forms both pale and glowing took possession of her young sense, and fixed themselves in her memory even when she was not thinking of them'. 'Unintelligible Rome' and its 'stupendous fragmentariness heightened the dream-like strangeness of her bridal life' and threatened to make her own life 'a masque with enigmatical costumes'. But with a characteristically near imperceptible modulation in her sense to a more normative perspective, after saying how all this disparity 'jarred her as with an electric shock', Eliot continues 'and then urged themselves upon her with that ache belonging to a glut of confused ideas which check the flow of emotion'. We might be tempted to equate that 'ache' with that of 'modernism' as the famous phrase has it in *Tess*, were it not that Eliot asserts its source to be 'confused' ideas with that term's Platonic/mimetic presupposition of a prior clarity and connectedness. After the possibility has been held out that the 'incongruities' amongst which she has been 'tumbled' are the attributes of an incongruous world, the passage goes on to suppress that possibility when it states that 'in certain states of dull forlornness Dorothea all her life continued to see . . . the red drapery which was being hung for Christmas spreading itself everywhere like a disease of the retina' (G. Eliot, 1981, p.226). That image precisely places – or displaces – Dorothea's disordered vision as a product of certain despondent moods, or a symptom of ophthalmic disorder, or at least as utterly subjective – a pessimistic reversal of the escapist connotations of 'seeing the world through rose-tinted spectacles'. And yet also, to give the richness of the image its full play, note that the vision of Dorothea here is of everywhere-spreading uniformity rather than of heaped-up disparity, a nightmare realisation of what was hailed at the beginning of the same paragraph as an elusive ideal, the tracing of the transitions uniting all contrasts. It is as if in nervous reaction to the vision of 'disparité du fond' this paragraph has so persuasively conjured up – so in opposition to the Platonic/mimetic grounding of George Eliot's ethic and aesthetic – she reverses the problem at the last minute, choosing as the lesser of two evils the more easily contemplated one, for the Platonic imagination anyway, of too much uniformity, an embarrassment of resemblance. It is as if Dorothea's eyes are becoming infected with the same disease that has long reified the eyes and vision of the statuary that so oppress her, 'the long vistas of white forms whose marble eyes seemed to hold the monotonous light of an alien world'.

Eliot is a highly ambivalent artist of repetition. She registers alternately the reassurances and the oppressions of the return to Same which, using the Lacanian and Deleuzian definitions, is realism's unerring trajectory. The 'montonous' is here a cause of revulsion to Dorothea but had been an object of nostalgia for the narrator of *The Mill on the Floss*. 'What novelty is worth that sweet monotony where everything is known and *loved* because it is known?' (original emphasis) (G. Eliot, 1983, p.94). Silas Marner at his weaving however, like Conrad's Stevie or, indeed, like the conception of the realist artist we are here considering, is fixed in contemplation of a more soured monotony 'his eyes bent close down on the slow growth of sameness' (G. Eliot, 1973, p.69).

The image of the diseased retina – whether imposing inaccurate disparity or connectedness – presupposes the possibility of an ideal mental and perceptual health that Matthew Arnold does in *Culture and Anarchy*.

> For as there is a curiosity about intellectual matters which is futile and merely a disease, so there is certainly a curiosity, – a desire after the things of the mind simply for their own sake and for the pleasures of seeing them as they are, – which is, in an intelligent being, natural and laudable. Nay, and the very desire to see things as they are, implies a balance and regulation of mind which is not often attained without fruitful effort, and which is the very opposite of the blind and diseased impulse of mind which is what we mean to blame when we blame curiosity.
>
> (Arnold, 1988, p.44)

It is intriguing that although the thrust of the assertion is behind a Platonic/mimetic world of 'things as they are', the very argument that 'the very desire to see things as they are, implies a balance and regulation of mind' as a prerequisite to an ordered perception, seems inadvertently to admit that the very 'balance and regulation' are in the mind and then eye, of the beholder, not immanent in a world of regular copies. We make, then impose, the regulation – note the vocabulary of dominion – we do not find.

We can now begin to gauge how far Hardy is from positing a Platonic/Arnoldian normative and mimetic vision of 'things as they are' governed by 'balance and regulation' when he contrasts his own 'idiosyncratic mode of regard' (F.E. Hardy, 1986, p.225) to 'the views of life prevalent at the end of the nineteenth century' (T. Hardy, 1985, 'Preface to the Fifth and Later Editions', p.38). Surely what Hardy means by his 'idiosyncratic mode of regard' is comparable to Tess's vision of a world 'discordant and contrasting' beyond Clare's merely 'ostensible' one. In the opening of *Tess* the narrator opposes the present to the period 'before the habit of taking long views had reduced emotions to a monotonous average' (T. Hardy, 1985, p.45). Such a condemnation of the nineteenth-century proponents of Platonic repetition embraces in censure Arnold's call for 'regulation' of mind and vision, the homogenising impulse of Hardy's critics, George Eliot's optimistic invocation of 'uniting all contrasts' and the degeneration of all these, as Hardy might see it, into the numbing uniformity of 'long vistas of white forms whose marble eyes seemed to hold the monotonous light of an alien world'. In George Eliot's image the 'solid archetypal model which is untouched by the effects of repetition' that Hillis Miller describes as the product of the Platonic/mimetic mode of repetition and representation, becomes literal as a row of statues, a nightmare of proliferating copies, precisely a 'long vista' or 'long view' reducing human difference and change to 'monotonous average'.

For me the most impressive feature of George Eliot's art is its willingness to expose its own limitations, its readiness to be haunted by the oppressions latent within its own method. 'The Lifted Veil' (1879) – grisly, unsettling and unreal – is the dark inversion of her realism, the unconscious of her method. Latimer's vision of Prague takes responses like those of Dorothea in Rome one step further into enemy territory in evoking the full grimness of the Platonic world, a world populated by statues, reified into memory and locked into repetition.

> a city under the broad sunshine, that seemed to me as if it were the summer sunshine of a long-past century arrested in its course . . . scorching the dusty, weary, time-eaten grandeur of a people doomed to live on in the stale repetition of memories, like deposed and superannuated kings in their regal gold-inwoven tatters. The city looked so thirsty that the broad river seemed to me a sheet of metal; and the blackened statues, as I passed under their blank gaze, along the unending bridge, with their ancient garments and their saintly crowns, seemed to me the real inhabitants and owners of this place . . .
>
> (G. Eliot, 1985, p.11)

Of the inhabitants he concludes 'It is such grim, stony beings as these, I thought, who are the fathers of ancient faded children' (G. Eliot, 1985, p.12). Hardy's Jude, himself the father of an ancient, faded child, is haunted by the line of Shelley's that evokes a comparable oppression. Sue quotes 'Shapes like ourselves hideously multiplied' and he responds 'What a terrible line of poetry! . . . Though I have felt it myself about my fellow creatures, at morbid times' (T. Hardy, 1981, pp.305–6). Hardy has obviously felt it also and offers another version of it as the assertion of the antiquarian Parson – amateur exponent of the Victorian long view in his hobby of 'hunting up pedigrees' – that the d'Urbervilles are 'extinct . . . gone down – gone under' and now lie 'At Kingsbere-sub-Greenhill: rows and rows of you in your vaults, with your effigies under Purbeck-marble canopies' (T. Hardy, 1985, p.45).

Such is the vision Tess herself struggles to resist. When Clare questions her on her fears 'she thought that he meant what were the aspect of things to her' and replies 'you seem to see numbers of tomorrows just all in a line, the first of them the biggest and clearest, the others getting smaller and smaller as they stand further away; but they all seem very fierce and cruel and as if they said "I'm coming! Beware of me! Beware of me!"'. Also in the same chapter she similarly resists Clare's attempt to assimilate her – seeing her as he does from 'the unmeasureable, Andean altitude of his' – into a series of mythical, literary and historical feminine archetypes. He tries to make her identify with the heriones of the novels, myths and histories he urges her to read, to see herself not merely as the 'after Theresa' her Christian name already makes her, but after Eve, after Artemis, after Demeter, 'a visionary essence of woman – a whole sex condensed into one typical form' (T. Hardy, 1985, p.180; p.181; p.187). As also indeed, the context in which the narrator places her is clogged with allusion to mythic, folk and historical archetype. Her protest recalls the 'row upon row' of ancestral images.

> 'Because what's the use of learning that I am one of a long row only – finding out that there is set down in some old book somebody just like me, and to know that I shall only act her part; making me sad, that's all. The best is not to remember that your nature and your past doings have been just like thousands' and thousands', and that your coming life and doings'll be like thousands' and thousands'.'
>
> (T. Hardy, 1985, p.182)

Jude echoes her concerns and vocabulary of assimilation into a 'row', when he claims, '*I* am not to be one of "The soldier saints who, row on row / Burn upward each to his point of bliss"' (T. Hardy, 1981, p.258).

'Call me Tess' she begs (rather than, we might think, 'After Theresa' like Dorothea) and Hardy obliges in his title, but then compromises that individuality by imposing the historical perspective of the rows of 'the d'Urbervilles'. She attempts by that name to achieve and preserve identity but ironically recalls the fate of the tessera, the mosaic fragment that is merely a tiny unit of a far larger pattern of tessellation, its own colour and outline sunk into the design. Her life threatens to resolve into a repetition of repetitions, 'terrible iteration' indeed.

STATUARY AND SIMULACRA

An extraordinary statement of the 'Platonic' aesthetic in terms of approbation and echoing this pervasive imagery of the 'vista' of 'statuary' is Arnold's 'Preface' to his *Poems* of 1853. Arnold praises the objectivity of Greek drama and contrasts it with the subjective dialogue of the mind with itself – or with a world of phantasm – of modern literature.

> The action itself, the situation of Orestes, or Merope, or Alcamaeon, was to stand the central point of interest, unforgotten, absorbing, principal . . . The terrible old mythic story on which the drama was founded stood, before he entered the theatre, traced in its bare outlines upon the spectator's mind; it stood in his memory, as a group of statuary, faintly seen, at the end of a long and dark vista: then came the poet, embodying outlines, developing situations, not a word wasted, not a sentiment capriciously thrown in: stroke upon stroke, the drama proceeded: the light deepened upon the group; more and more it revealed itself to the riveted gaze of the spectator; until at last, when the final words were spoken, it stood before him in broad sunlight, a model of immortal beauty.
>
> (Arnold, 1987, 'Preface to the First Edition of *Poems*', p.660)

Arnold's stage which is in effect merely a statue's pedestal could hardly better illustrate Adorno's formulation about the reified world brought about by nineteenth-century industrial capitalism in which 'All phenomena rigidify, become insignias of the absolute rule of that which is' (Adorno, 1983, p.34). Arnold's perverse conception of drama as the reifier of archetypes seems an anxious and anal denial of what appears patently much truer of it – that it is a promiscuous form, or anti-form, which refracts textual authority and authenticity, playfully dispersing them through layers of performance and interpretation that are ever-changing and re-staged. One might say this was doubly true of Greek tragedy. Far from faithfully reproducing mythic archetypes these dramatists were concerned to stage radical and even irreverent variants of the mythic narratives and figures. One could speculate that it was precisely this imperative which allowed for the emergence of the tragic drama proper from its ritualistic/religious origins. Whether or not this is the case, a refusal of archetype is surely evidenced in the widely differing characters and fates of the multiple Medeas, Electras and Iphigenias dispersed through Aeschylus, Sophocles and Euripides or in the way that each of these dramatists created their own variant of the Orestes myth in *The Oresteia* and the latter's respective *Electras*. Arnold's view of myth is determinedly Casaubonian. Casaubon looks in myth for 'a tradition originally revealed' and works in the expectation of seeing the object of his study become 'intelligible, nay, luminous' before him. So too for Arnold the 'model of immortal beauty' is to be illuminated until 'it stood before him in broad daylight'. There is no room here for the myth as Lévi-Strauss understands it – a thing of shadows, nebulising, never fully present, where all one encounters 'face to face' are 'potential objects of which only the shadows are actualized'.

According to Arnold's mimetic perspective, the spectator's cultural memory internalises the mythic plots, carries the mental tracing of the vista of statuary. Notice the recurrence of that term 'tracing' to convey the Platonic conception – as when Ruskin voices a precisely comparable aesthetic of the reproduction of psychologically embedded archetypes when he talks of contemporary revivalist architecture 'tracing out this grey, shadowy, many-pinnacled image of the Gothic spirit within us' (Ruskin, 1904, p.660). The dramatist's function is merely to illuminate the latest manifestation of the series, to give it the 'outline' the narrator of *Daniel Deronda* posits as the first requisite of cognition. 'The beginning of an acquaintance whether with persons or things is to get a definite outline for our ignorance' (G. Eliot, 1984 (2), p.145). Tess, of course, 'was in a dream wherein familiar objects appeared as having light and shade and position but no particular outline'. The representations that might have given her life coherence do not progress from Arnold's initial state of being merely 'faintly seen'; they remain as shadowy simulacra rather than emerging into the light as crisp copies.

The Arnoldian artist retrieves the archetypes from the past or from their ethereal realm and his artwork is the act of illuminating a static 'model' or 'icon' (to use Deleuze's terms) to which the spectator's gaze, itself equally static and passive, is 'riveted'. Notice how all Arnold's concern for drama as action has petrified into the static image of lighting up statuary. The objective, realist view embodies this deadness of the 'object'. If art merely imitates given archetypes, the deadness, stasis and monotony evoked in Eliot's, Arnold's and Hardy's imagery of the oppressive vista of statuary – Hardy pointedly makes them funeral ones – is decisively appropriate. There is a resonant contrast here between Arnold's conception of art as the modifying of objects by light and Hardy's rapturous reception of the late, critically scorned, luminous and near-abstract Turners he saw in the 1889 exhibition and his appreciative assessment that 'What he paints chiefly is *light as modified by objects*' (F.E. Hardy, 1986, p.216) (original emphasis). This is a remarkable assertion because it so overturns the normative mimetic assumption that the object must be primary. In Hardy's statement the 'object', the supposedly given, objective icon of representation loses its 'objectivity', here meaning both its claim to be real and external and its status as the rightful goal of perception. It loses the outline that preserves that status, as Rome does for Jocelyn, as objects do for Tess. Her 'dream wherein familiar objects had light and shade and position but no particular outline' precisely evokes the luminous strangeness of those shimmeringly near-abstract, 'mad' canvases.

Notice how much more reductive and enforced a version 'the riveted gaze of the spectator' offers of 'that harmonious acquiescence of mind which we feel in contemplating a grand spectacle that is intelligible to us: when we have lost the impatient irritation of mind which we feel in the presence of an immense, moving, confused spectacle which, while it perpetually excites our curiosity, perpetually baffles our comprehension'. There is nothing to comprehend in the fully revealed 'model of immortal beauty', certainly nothing 'moving'. In this last word the play between transitive and intransitive, emotional and kinetic connotations embodies all the possibilities of non-objective interplay between spectator and artwork Arnold's 'Preface' suppresses. Contemplation of a static, immortal archetype petrifies the spectator as much as what he or she perceives. The gaze is 'riveted', and that word conveys a repulsive sense of enforced stasis and connection, being squarely a product of Arnold's industrial present rather than the supposedly 'immortal' classical past. It as if the spectator here, too, were a mere 'statue' whose 'marble eyes hold the monotonous light of an alien world'. Arnold's and Eliot's imagery is in danger of representing the encounter with culture as a meeting of medusan gazes.

A pointedly relevant attack upon this debilitating, reifying element within the realist ambition is Lukács' classic essay 'Narrate or Describe'. Lukács argues that the 'descriptive' method characteristic of nineteenth-century literary realism, and particularly evident in Flaubert and Zola, is a result and reflection of the intensely alienated experience of life under industrial capitalism. In its painstakingly detailed endeavour to depict the Arnoldian standard of 'things as they are', realist writing in fact ends up with an essentially static *description* of the world as an object, instead of a *narration* of process into which author and reader enter as participants. This form of realism denies the reader the liberating and empowering vision of the world and its history as an unconcluded process, seen, as it were, from within and without with the supposed dividing line blurred. The descriptive method freezes the status quo, according to its oppressive but transient reality an absolute and universal status – to use Deleuze's terms, it erects 'an icon of eternal truth', or Arnold's 'model of immortal beauty'. It robs human life of any possibility of change as it attempts to efface the 'constructed' rather than 'uncovered' nature both equally of history and the literary text. The politically quietist connotations of Ladislaw's remark about taking a 'sturdy neutral delight in things as they were' (revealingly ironic in relation to his supposedly reformist politics) hint at the debilitating tendencies within realism Lukács criticises.

Arnold craves 'objectivity', while the reified experience of art he describes would seem to be symptomatic of what Marx means by the 'objectification' he sees as endemic under industrial capitalism. Recalling the 'background' of 'disparité du fond' envisaged by the 'Nietzschean' form of vision and representation that Hardy uncannily echoes in Tess's vision of 'another world beyond her ostensible one, discordant and contrasting', Marx argues that the alienation and objectification he sees as characteristic of life under industrial capitalism derive from a material and economic version of just such a fundamental disparity. Marx argues that alienation is founded upon the disparity between the productive power of labour, which becomes increasingly great with the expansion of capitalism, and the lack of control which the worker is able to exert over the objects which he produces. A result of this disparity is that for the worker his own labour becomes an object and that 'it exists outside him, independent and alien, and becomes a self-sufficient power opposite him, that the life he has lent to the object affronts him, hostile and alien' (Marx, 1977, p.79). The term of Marx's which we translate as 'objectification', or 'commodification', *Vergegenständlichung*, must be one of the most expressive terms of the nineteenth century and conveys the whole of Marx's meaning with a compacted fullness. The word for an object, 'Gegenstand', suggests that which stands (stand) opposite (gegen). But the state of being 'opposite' is more than spatial in that it evokes a state of antagonism as 'gegen' means 'contrary' and 'Gegner' an opponent. Thus the term contains within itself the whole of Marx's meaning and preserves his metaphor when he says that 'the life he has lent to the object affronts him, hostile and alien'. The way the spectator is confronted by the artwork in Arnold's imagery, 'it stood before him', 'the central point of interest, unforgotten, absorbing, principal . . . terrible' precisely evokes the debilitating fetishisation of the object Marx diagnoses. One could hardly imagine more direct statements of *Vergegenständlichung* as a felt experience than Dorothea's apprehension of 'every object withering and shrinking away from her' and that of Tess whereby 'all material objects announced their irresponsibility with terrible iteration'.

This context helps clarify why achieving the form of perception that lends an ideal fixity to objects is a troubling concern of Victorian writing. J.S. Mill regards it as a moral imperative and like Arnold he uses the imagery of accurate visual perception to suggest an ultimate intelligibility and rightness to be uncovered in all things. 'A man of clear ideas errs grievously if he imagines that whatever is seen confusedly does not exist: it belongs to him, when he meets with such a thing, to dispel the mist, and fix the outlines of the vague form which is looming through it' (Mill, 1980, 'Bentham', p.61). George Eliot also craves a world of defined objects, and a passage from her journal of 1856 gives an intriguing insight into the conjunction of scientific investigation, taxonomy and acts of naming that she hopes, at least at this point at the very start of her novelistic career, will achieve it. She describes her obsession to know the names of all the plants she discovers on a naturalising expedition to Ilfracombe.

> I never before longed so much to know the names of things as during this visit to Ilfracombe. The desire is part of the tendency that is now constantly growing in me to escape from all vagueness and inaccuracy into the daylight of distinct, vivid ideas. The mere fact of naming an object tends to give definiteness to our conception of it – we have then a sign that at once calls up in our minds the distinctive qualities which mark out for us that particular object from all others.
>
> (G. Eliot, 1954–5, vol. 2, 8 May–26 June 1856, p.250)

The objectivity of scientific procedure is intriguingly blended with echoes of Arnold's aesthetic in an image of drawing objects from the realm of vagueness and inaccuracy into the daylight where they stand revealed as definite, vivid and particular. Such emphases as these of

Arnold, Mill and Eliot lend resonance to concern with the 'vagueness' or 'fixity' of forms expressed in the handling of description in fiction. *Daniel Deronda* both makes a clear statement of a solidifying aesthetic – 'Here undoubtedly lies the chief poetic energy: – in the force of imagination that pierces and exalts the solid fact, instead of floating among cloud-pictures' – and realises it in its eminently solid descriptive forms. 'No youthful figure there was comparable to Gwendolen's as she passed through the long suite of rooms adorned with light and flowers, and, visible at first as a slim figure floating along in white drapery, approached through one wide doorway after another into fuller illumination and definiteness' (G. Eliot, 1984 (2), p.431; p.73). We can add the bringing of objects and characters 'into fuller illumination and definiteness' (remember Arnold's artist illuminating his statuary and 'embodying outlines') to 'a definite outline for our ignorance', 'a sturdy neutral delight in things as they were' and an eye for 'the suppressed transitions which unite all contrasts' as ideals of the realist perspective. *David Copperfield* intends to conjure the 'distinct presence' of this object-world. Its second chapter begins 'The first objects that assume a distinct presence before me . . .' (Dickens, 1985, p.61). To cite Arnold, 'What is *not* interesting, is that which does not add to our knowledge of any kind; that which is vaguely conceived and loosely drawn; a representation which is general, indeterminate and faint, instead of being particular, precise and firm' (original emphasis) (Arnold, 1987, 'Preface to the First Edition of *Poems*', p.655).

In Hardy and Eliot their respective choice of titles gives a sketch of the different positions their aesthetics adopt on this matter of the precise, the located, the particular. Eliot's titles name either a location or an individual. Before one has even opened *Felix Holt* (1866), *Daniel Deronda*, *The Mill on the Floss* or *Middlemarch* one has sensed an affirmation of the self-identity of people and of places: or rather not quite, since *Middlemarch* at least teases brilliantly on these issues. 'Middle' evokes the securely, indeed squarely located but 'march' is an antiquated term for a boundary, for example between parishes, or for a disputed no-man's-land between territories, and thus suggests the marginal, the ambivalently located or even unlocated. Fusing the terms creates a nonsense, a place-name that half evokes displacement (this last further stressed by the subtitle *A Study of Provincial Life*). More evident in Eliot, however, is the strand, if a submerged one, that finds satisfying the otherwise oppressive sense of fixity of individuals and locations and their conjunction suggested, for example, in the chapter title 'Romola in her Place'. There is a certain gratifying, rounded, self-enclosure of identity suggested in the titles *Adam Bede, Silas Marner* and *Daniel Deronda* where little patternings – alphabetical, cadential or alliterative – make first and surnames complement each other. Had Eliot named *Romola* with the heroine's married name it would be called *Romola Melema* where the near-echoing of the terms approaches the phonetic over-determination of the tongue-twister. Conversely Hardy's titles disturb the self-identity of people and of places. None of his novels names places except the early *Under the Greenwood Tree* (1872) which is perhaps located in the Eliot manner but *Far from the Madding Crowd* (1874) and *The Return of the Native* (1878) suggest a displacement from the centre, a distance, a dislocation, a circling. *The Trumpet-Major* and *The Mayor of Casterbridge* (1886) name ranks and titles rather than the individuals who hold them but so also in a sense do *Tess of the d'Urbervilles* and *Jude the Obscure* where an initial informal proper name is yoked awkwardly to a quasi-formal title. As names/titles *Tess of the d'Urbervilles* is scored through by conflicting class registers ('Poor wounded name . . .') and *Jude the Obscure* is curiously self-erasing, an anti-title.

Hardy's descriptive strategies are in tune with these emphases on displacement and the perturbation of presence and self-identity. He seems particularly to relish reversing the movement towards a 'fuller illumination and definiteness' in representation. Repeatedly in Hardy an object's halo of luminosity prevails in perception over the object itself so that with Hardy as with Turner 'What he paints chiefly is *light as modified by objects*'. Consider, for instance, the exquisite Turneresque rendering of Jude's first sighting of Christminster where the keynotes are refraction, reflection, mirage and chimaera.

> Some way within the limits of the stretch of landscape, points of light like topaz gleamed. The air increased in transparency with the lapse of minutes, till the topaz points showed themselves to be the vanes, windows, wet roof slates, and other shining spots upon the spires, domes, freestone-work, and varied outlines that were faintly revealed. It was Christminster, unquestionably; either directly seen, or miraged in the peculiar atmosphere.
>
> The spectator gazed on and on till the windows and vanes lost their shine, going out suddenly like extinguished candles. The vague city became veiled in mist. Turning to the west, he saw that the sun had disappeared. The foreground of the scene had grown funereally dark, and near objects put on the hues and shapes of chimaeras.
>
> (T. Hardy, 1981, p.41)

No individual light was visible, only a halo or glow-fog overarching the place against the black heavens behind it . . .

(T. Hardy, 1981, p.42)

There is a 'ribbed cloud' in *Jude* 'through which the moon showed its
position rather than its shape, and one or two of the larger stars made
themselves visible as faint nebulae only' (T. Hardy, 1981, pp.196–7).
There are the drunkards in *Tess* where he describes how 'around the
shadow of each one's head' showed 'a circle of opalised light, formed by
the moon's rays upon the glistening sheet of dew' (T. Hardy, 1985,
p.113), or, of course, Jocelyn's view of Rome as that of its 'atmosphere',
its 'lights and shades' and 'particularly its reflected or secondary lights'.

Hardy remarks twice in the 'Notes' quoted in the *Life* his appreciation of the 'fine conception' of the artist Gérôme in depicting, or rather
avoiding depicting, the crucifixion, 'The *shadows only* of the three
crucified ones seen' (original emphasis). He recalls the painting when
stimulated by the 'new forms and original aspects' of religion expressed
by the occupants of a temperance hotel. 'They open fresh views of
Christianity by turning it in reverse positions, as Gérôme the painter did
by painting the *shadow* of the Crucifixion instead of the Crucifixion
itself as former painters had done' (original emphasis) (F.E. Hardy,
1986, p.76; p.206). In other words, Gérôme is another artist attracted by
'the shaded side of a well-known catastrophe'.

A FOLD IN THE SURFACE OF SIGNS

A dangerous yet thrilling eruption of infinite possibilities – and inconsis-
tencies – can be seen as a product of Hardy's historical moment. In an
essay describing the changes in Western thought associated with Marx,
Freud and Nietzsche, Foucault has argued that the work of these
thinkers represents the latest stage in the destruction of the Renaissance
technique of interpretation based on a belief in the universal resemblance of things. He characterises the dominant epistemological
mode of the nineteenth century as one whereby things are understood
temporally according to their history or according to how they can be
traced to an origin that is at one and the same time seen as their essence
and yet also as fundamentally 'Other' to them. The common hermeneu-
tic Foucault finds in Marx, Freud and Nietzsche rejects this
presupposition of origin or 'depth' in which truth or meaning is
concealed in favour of a pure exteriority that shows depth to be illusory
and merely a fold in the surface of signs. In these circumstances,
interpretation becomes an infinite task, moving into a shadowy region in

which both interpretation and interpreter are threatened with rupture and madness. All interpretation is, like mythography, infinite. 'Interpretation finally becomes an infinite task . . . from the nineteenth century on signs enchained themselves in an inexhaustible network, itself also infinite, not because they rest on a resemblance without edges but because there is an irreducible gulf and opening' (Foucault, 1967, p.190). Foucault relates this opening up of an abyss of interpretation to these thinkers' shared refusal of the concept of origination. All three regard it as impossible to go back to an unequivocal starting-point, the apparently authoritative source refers elliptically to something still further back and so on ad infinitum in shadowy reflection and re-reflection. The radical nature of this as the rejection of a world of crisp copies of an archetype, of fixed and self-evidently intelligible forms, is clear. The shadowy process of interpretation replaces the self-confident one of imitation. As Deleuze's use of the term 'Platonic' indicates, the mimetic conception these thinkers reject is a pure form of metaphysics. The ambition of the metaphysician, as Derrida describes it, is that of,

> returning 'strategically', ideally, to an origin or to a 'priority' held to be simple, intact, normal, pure, standard, self-identical, in order *then* to think in terms of derivation, complication, deterioration, accident etc. All metaphysicians, from Plato to Rousseau, Descartes to Husserl, have proceeded in this way, conceiving good to be before evil, the positive before the negative, the pure before the impure, the simple before the complex, the essential before the accidental, the imitated before the imitation, etc. And this is not just *one* metaphysical gesture among others, it is *the* metaphysical exigency, that which has been the most constant, most profound and most potent.
>
> (Derrida, 1970, p.236)

The category of the root, the origin, is patently a category of dominion privileging the autochthon over the immigrant, the settler over the migrant, the scion over the usurper. It is political through and through as will become clear in the next chapter's acknowledgement of the urgency of nineteenth-century – and even current – contentions over whether 'Western' culture had an ethnically pure source in an autochthonous ancient Greece or was at this supposed point of origin already a Semitic and Afroasiatic derivative. Martin Bernal in *Black Athena: The Afroasiatic Roots of Classical Civilisation*, vol. I (1987) has demonstrated how this great Ur-topic – which was to have evolutionary theory with its all-determining structure of genealogy, kinship, descent and filiation as its complement and supra-historical context – structured all nineteenth-century historical thought and representation. Anxious and self-serving constructions of genealogy are at the heart of nineteenth-century ideology. As Bernal also stresses, the crucial and most deeply pernicious ideological innovation of the latter half of the nineteenth century must be the emergence to academic and political legitimacy of conceptions of racial purity. The pursuit to pure origins is the central mode of this culture's self-legitimation. 'The origin – seductive because it will not be appeased by the derivative, by ideology – is itself an ideological principle' (Adorno, 1990, p.155).

It is worth pondering that Tess's shaded history is that of being sent to re-establish the authority of aristocratic connections and her d'Urberville origins, only to find her family 'relations' are fake 'irrelations' and 'the true sequence' of her succession, an 'accident' of the sheerest 'inconsequence'. Hardy's story of a violated but still pure woman refuses to represent woman's history as that of 'the pure before the impure'.

Hardy's first poem, or at least the poem retrospectively accorded that status in the *Life*, is 'Domicilium'. As such it stands as the first entry in the New Wessex edition of the collected poems, as if their epigraph, alongside a drawing by Hardy of the birthplace cottage it describes. A work emphatically in Hardy's Victorian rather than Modern mode, the poem skirts sentimentality in its over-determined equation of birth, location, familial settlement, naming and nature. The poet's paternal grandmother describes the cottage at the time of the family's first establishment there fifty years before, the building has since become tousled with 'hardy flowers' and the final line concentrates the poem's quiet hymning of domestication and territorial settlement, 'So wild it was when first we settled here'.

'Domicilium' has a ghostly negative in Hardy's oeuvre in the poem I want to study here, 'The Pedigree'. This arresting lyric of 1916 is a masterly compendium, and demonstration of the interdependence, of the elements of the 'Platonic' paradigm – the mirror, the tree, the tracing, the long perspective, lineage, the intimidating sight demanding observation, the oppressive succession of Same. But the poem renders all these figures strange – quite literally, they become freakish and sinister – and attempts to invert and oppose them, to make its somewhat desperate declaration of independence from them. The poem stages the struggle for emergence of a vulnerable modernity and its wary back-glance at the conspiracy of mimesis and tradition it resists. The poet is sitting up at night poring over his family tree. The moon, hedged with 'green-rheumed clouds', looks weird and sickly and the pedigree takes on freakish life.

> So, scanning my sire-sown tree,
> And the hieroglyphs of this spouse tied to that,
> With offspring mapped below in lineage,
> Till the tangles troubled me,
> The branches seemed to twist into a seared and cynic face
> Which winked and tokened towards the window like a Mage
> Enchanting me to gaze thereat.

Here the Hardy flowers fester. The window he is urged to contemplate is 'a mirror now'. The poet is disturbed to see 'every heave and coil and move I was' here prefigured in the recessive succession of likenesses. Hardy, like Tess, is the victim of fearful genealogies. The poet registers with horror – could Poe be an unexpected influence? – his necessary containment within the repetoire of eversameness and, with equal urgency, his refusal of such assimilation.

> Said I then, sunk in tone,
> 'I am the merest mimicker and counterfeit! –
> Though thinking, *I am I*,
> *And what I do I do myself alone.*'
> – The cynic twist of the page thereat unknit
> Back to its normal figure, having wrought its purport wry . . .

Origination, mimesis, relation, dominion: this poem exactly articulates the interdependence of these elements of the 'Platonic' paradigm. The family tree the poet contemplates with such disquiet exemplifies what Deleuze and Guattari call the 'arborescent model' they find sprouting everywhere in traditional Western thought and representation. Indeed Western thought is a veritable forest of such structures, and the deconstructive project of Deleuze and Guattari is in effect a bout of deforestation. The tree – whether spreading in genealogy, philosophy, linguistics or psychoanalysis – is a mimetic model centrally concerned with tracing the status quo.

It is our view that genetic axis and profound structure are above all infinitely reproducible principles of *tracing*. All of tree logic is a logic of tracing and reproduction. In linguistics as in psycho-analysis, its object is an unconscious that is itself representative, crystallised into codified complexes, laid out along a genetic axis and distributed within a syntagmic structure. Its goal is to describe a de facto state, to maintain balance in intersubjective relations, or to explore an unconscious which is already there from the start, lurking in the dark recesses of memory and language. It consists of tracing, on the basis of an overcoding structure or supporting axis, something that comes ready-made. The tree articulates and hierarchizes tracings; tracings are like the leaves of a tree.

(Deleuze and Guattari, 1988, p.12)

A 'turning in reverse positions' (to borrow Hardy's term) of this metaphysical aborescent conception seems to be the possibility Carlyle evokes in an extraordinary image in the essay 'The Niebelungen Lied' where, speculating on the murky origins of these Germanic songs, he suggests alternative images one could use for discussing history and culture. The first he uses, but implicitly rejects, is quintessentially nineteenth-century in positing the aetiological, arborescent model Foucault and Deleuze and Guattari identify, 'Thus though Tradition may have but one root, it grows like a Banian, into a whole overarching labyrinth of trees'. But Carlyle continues:

> Or rather, we might say, it is a Hall of Mirrors, where in pale light each mirror reflects, convexley or concavely, not only some real Object, but the Shadows of this in other mirrors; which again do the like for it: till in such reflection and re-reflection the whole immensity is filled with dimmer and dimmer shapes; and no firm scene lies round us, but a dislocated, distorted chaos, fading away on all hands, in the distance, into utter night.

(Carlyle, 1896, vol. 3, pp.114–15)

This exquisite image articulates a vision of history George Eliot in the phrase 'a history of the lights and shadows' had represented as an impossibility. Such is the chaotic chiaroscuro hidden on the other side of her silence. Here realism's mirroring ambition has turned uncontrollably wrong with the mirrors dislocating and distorting what they should copy and mirroring each other as much as they do it. Here is the shattered, scattered gaze of the fallen pier-glass. Not only does the image as a whole recall the subdividing, 'reflected' lights and shades of Jocelyn's centreless Rome, but each element of it echoes an element of the characterisation of Tess and her vision, her 'dream wherein familiar objects had light and shade and position but no particular outline' as well as the world she sees beyond the 'ostensible' one, 'discordant and contrasting'.

I said earlier that this is not merely Tess's perspective, but that she actually embodies it, and this is rendered quite literally in the beautiful

81

description in similarly refractive terms of her 'large tender eyes' which were 'neither black nor blue nor grey nor violet; rather all these shades together, and a hundred others, which could be seen if one looked into their irises – shade behind shade – tint beyond tint – around pupils that had no bottom'. Tess's eyes have the iridescent 'tint beyond tint' of Turner's colouring. The description, with a typical Hardyesque elliptical sliding off from repetition, goes on to describe her with a precise ambivalence as 'an almost standard woman' (T. Hardy, 1985, pp.140–1), leaving the reader to decide which term to stress, the standardness or its incompletion. The chapter had begun with a sunrise and grants the sun a penetrating gaze 'demanding the masculine pronoun for its adequate expression' and Tess's eyes are clearly contrasted to the riveting and appropriative Arnoldian male gaze. Here Hardy goes one further than George Eliot in her eloquent call in 'The Natural History of German Life' for a language characterised by a 'fitful shimmer of many-hued significance' by actually enacting that 'fitful shimmer' rather than merely stating it – as 'shade' means both 'hue' and 'shadow', colour and its negation, so 'shade behind shade' flickers between various possible meanings, 'tint behind shadow', 'shadow behind shadow', and so on, or all iridescently overlaid.

Like Carlyle's distortedly reflecting mirrors, Tess's eyes refer you to no unequivocal object or centre, their brilliant mercurial play of colours and reflections evoking potentialities quite other than 'the monotonous light of an alien world'. The shifting significances of colour and language here evoke a form of perception antithetical to that disturbingly dominant in Arnold and Eliot, freed from mirror copies, the veneration of objects, origins, fixity and the repetitious precedential 'doings' of thousands and thousands. Like Bottom's dream, which also 'hath no bottom', they posit no final grounding in the real.

3

MORE MONUMENTS AND MAIDENS
George Eliot and history

I
'A REPORT OF UNKNOWN OBJECTS':
Silas Marner

If men no longer had to equate themselves with things, they would
need neither a superstructure of things nor an invariant picture of
themselves, after the model of things.

Adorno, *Negative Dialectics*

Thus all physical and intellectual senses have been replaced by the
simple alienation of all these senses, the sense of having. Man's
essence had to be reduced to this absolute poverty, so that it might
bring forth out of itself its own inner riches.

Marx, *Economic and Philosophical Manuscripts of 1844*

Describing *Silas Marner* to Blackwood during its composition in 1861
Eliot commented that 'it sets in strong light the remedial influences of
pure, natural human relations' (G. Eliot, 1954–5, vol. 4, p.87). Many
natural things set in strong light are merely seen to wither, but let that
pass. She could not have addressed a more pertinent issue nor undertaken a more urgent literary task. A great topic in British letters for at
least the preceding two decades had been the contemporary extirpation
of precisely the 'pure, natural human relations' that *Silas* is, in this
statement at least, intended to assert. *Dombey and Son* (1848) is a
thwarted *Silas Marner* in which the emotionally enervated Mr Dombey,
unlike Eliot's protagonist, tragically misses his opportunity for redemp-
tion through a relationship with a loving daughter. In line with this
crucial negation, the novel poses the issues of 'pure, natural human
relations' more sceptically. 'Was Mr Dombey's master-vice, that ruled
him so inexorably, an unnatural characteristic? It might be worthwhile,
sometimes, to inquire what Nature is, and how men work to change her,

and whether, in the enforced distortions so produced, it is not natural to be unnatural' (Dickens, 1984, p.737). Here is the great question posed by Dickens's oeuvre, and one which could not be more relevant to nineteenth-century experience: whether it is not now 'natural to be unnatural'. *Silas Marner* poses a comparable question on its opening page as the inhabitants of Raveloe ponder 'how was a man to be explained' and the novel constitutes Eliot's answer.

In approaching a novel so evidently engaging with a contemporary construction of identity in its new, bourgeois form it might be well to take soundings from the prevailing discourse, and its critics. In the same year *Dombey and Son* asks whether it is not now natural to be unnatural, Marx and Engels in *The Communist Manifesto* (1848) pour scorn on those twin bourgeois illusions, 'Human Nature' and the 'individual'. The former 'belongs to no class, has no reality, and exists only in the misty realm of philosophical fantasy' and the latter only really means the middle-class owner of property (male, of course, married women owned no property) and even his individuality is, under capitalism, an illusion. 'In bourgeois society capital is independent and has individuality, while the living person is dependent and has no individuality' (Marx, 1977, p.241; p.233).

As Engels had put it in the chapter of *The Condition of the Working Class in England* (1844) 'The Great Towns', the contemporary social formation is exemplified by crowded urban streets where people hurry past

> as though they had nothing in common, nothing to do with one another . . . while it occurs to no man to honour another with so much as a glance. The brutal indifference, the unfeeling isolation of each in his private interest becomes the more repellent and offensive, the more these individuals are crowded together, within a limited space. And, however much one is aware that this isolation of the individual, this narrow self-seeking, is the fundamental principle of our society everywhere, it is nowhere so shamelessly barefaced, so self-conscious as just here in the crowding of the great city. The dissolution of mankind into monads, of which each one has a separate essence, and a separate purpose, the world of atoms, is here carried out to its utmost extreme.
>
> (Engels, 1987, p.69)

It was the 'shock' of such arbitrary and alienating urban encounters which Benjamin found in Baudelaire and regarded as the exemplary modern experience (Benjamin, 1975). These alienated and alienating conditions are momentarily glimpsed in *Silas Marner* as an apprehensive

Silas and Eppie return to the 'great industrial town' attempting to locate the religious community of Silas's youth but encountering only 'the noise, the movement, and the multitude of strange indifferent faces' (G. Eliot, 1973, p.239). In *A Tale of Two Cities* (1859) Dickens equates with devastating absoluteness the urban scene, a recessive, monadic individuality and death.

> My friend is dead, my neighbour is dead, my love, the darling of my soul, is dead; it is the inexorable consolidation and perpetuation of the secret that was always in that individuality, and which I shall carry in mine to my life's end. In any of the burial-places of this city through which I pass, is there a sleeper more inscrutable than its busy inhabitants are, in their innermost personality, to me, or than I am to them?
>
> (Dickens, 1990, p.44)

In such nineteenth-century townscapes is formed the individuality which is a synonym of alienation posited by Adorno: 'The individual owes his crystallisation to the forms of political economy, particularly those of the urban market . . . If today the trace of humanity seems to persist only in the individual in his decline, it admonishes us to make an end of the fatality which individualises men only to break them in their isolation' (Adorno, 1974, p.148 and p.150).

The immediate discursive context for *Silas Marner* (1861) is the particular urgency with which bourgeois writing at the end of the 1850s and beginning of the 1860s sets out to effect this 'crystallisation', to engineer this 'fatality which individualises men'. A number of key non-fiction texts appear at this juncture. J.S. Mill's *On Liberty* (1859) is a sacred text of nineteenth-century bourgeois individualism and his intellectually scrupulous project – Hardy called him 'personified earnestness' – is, in essence, the intellectual big brother – more reflective, less brazen – of that year's other best-selling entrepreneurial handbook, Samuel Smiles's *Self-Help*. Given these works' explicit individualism it is easy to imagine that such a context made it possible for bourgeois readers to assimilate Darwin's *The Origin of Species* (1859) to the prevailing competitive ethic even before the formulation of the inevitable banalisation 'social Darwinism'. Burckhardt's *The Civilisation of the Renaissance in Italy* (1860, English translation 1878) famously discovers in the Renaissance the birth of the individual which 'led the individual to the most zealous and thorough study of himself under all forms and under all conditions' (Burckhardt, 1990, p.198).

Mill's work is at least honest enough to writhe within its own self-cancelling contradiction as a bourgeois critique of a bourgeois reality. In the famous chapter 'On Individuality as one of the Elements of Well-Being' he calls for a humanising regeneration of a society characterised by individualist competition through increased individualism. 'It is not by wearing down into uniformity all that is individual in themselves, but by cultivating it and calling it forth, within the limits imposed by the rights and interests of others, that human beings become a noble and beautiful object of contemplation' (Mill, 1987, p.127). A devastating analysis did Mill but know it: human subjects under capitalism are rendered, like Arnold's statuary, impotent, alienated, objectified and are furthermore fooled, by analyses such as Mill's, into an aesthetic appreciation of their own degraded condition as 'a noble and beautiful object of contemplation'. The shift from plural to singular is telling. While arguing for a healthily multiplying plurality of subjects Mill's own prose works grammatically to an opposed end, resolving 'human beings' into the smooth totality of the lone 'object'. One can at least respect Mill's impotent humanist protest at the dehumanising tendency of contemporary labour, however muddled it is in hailing the problem as its own solution. 'Human nature is not a machine to be built after a model, and set to do exactly the work prescribed for it, but a tree, which requires to grow and develop itself on all sides, according to the tendency of the inward forces which make it a living thing' (Mill, 1987, p.123). Hardy's admiration for Mill was immense and he had a complex relation to this key chapter. In the *Life* he tells how, like all students of the 1860s, he knew the piece almost by heart and that he re-read it throughout his life in moments of despondency. But when Sue in *Jude the Obscure* quotes Mill's words to Phillotson, it is in terms of a negation. She would so love to live out its vision of individual free-growth, but cannot. 'Why can't you act upon them? I wish to always' (T. Hardy, 1974, p.244).

There were harsher voices than Mill's. Ruskin had anticipated his concerns over the dehumanising subjection of workers to the processes of industrial labour in *The Stones of Venice* (1851). After extensive complaint on apparently purely aesthetic grounds – mass-produced products are drearily uniform – he finally exposes the self-serving politics behind bourgeois concern over the degrading mechanisation of labour.

> It is verily this degradation of the operative into a machine, which, more than any other evil of the times, is leading the mass of the nations everywhere into vain, incoherent, destructive struggling . . . the foundations of society were never yet shaken as they are at this day. It is not that men are ill fed, but that they have no pleasure

in the work by which they make their bread, and therefore look to wealth as the only means of pleasure.

(Ruskin, 1904, 'The Nature of Gothic', p.194)

So from a bourgeois perspective the dehumanisation of labour is more urgently a political danger than it is a humanitarian/ethical concern. The revolutionary potential within this alienation was the subject of the period's most penetrating analysis, but one that was to remain long silent. In the *Economic and Philosophical Manuscripts of 1844*, unpublished until 1932, Marx details the ways in which the modern industrial worker's alienated relation to the products of manufacture result in his own objectification. Silas, the misanthropic weaver who becomes a function of his labour rather than vice versa, alienated from his Raveloe community, filled with a strange distrust of the natural world, shrivelled and distorted to the status of an object, is clearly a fellow of the alienated, commodified worker of Marx's analysis. Feuerbach's humanism was still a powerful influence on Marx at this early point in his writings and for those sceptical about this posited congruence between Marx and Eliot one can at least suggest that she too, who in 1854 had translated *Das Wesen des Christenthums*, was working through her own relation to these influences. Their characterisations are really strikingly congruent, as is best illustrated by simply placing passages side by side.

The worker is distorted and devalued in proportion to the form and value he gives to the product:

Marx: the more values he creates the more valueless and worthless he becomes, the more formed the product the more deformed the worker . . . (1977, p.79)

Eliot: His gold, as he hung over it and saw it grow, gathered his power of loving together into a hard isolation like its own. (1973, p.92)

Eliot: Strangely Marner's face and figure shrank and bent themselves into a constant mechanical relation to the objects of his life, so that he produced the same sort of impression as a handle or a crooked tube, which has no meaning standing apart. (1973, p.69)

His labour objectifies, commodifies him:

Marx: The depreciation of the human world progresses in direct proportion to the increase in value of the world of things.

Labour does not only produce commodities; it produces itself and the labourer as a commodity and that to the extent to which it produces commodities in general. (1977, p.78)

Eliot: The light of his faith quite put out, and his affections made desolate, he had clung with all the force of his nature to his work and his money; and like all objects to which a man devotes himself, they had fashioned him into correspondence with themselves. His loom, as he wrought in it without ceasing, had in its turn wrought on him . . . (1973, p.92)

He is alienated from the natural world:

Marx: The relationship of the worker . . . to the sensuous exterior world and to natural objects [is] as to an alien and hostile world opposed to him. (1977, p.81)

Eliot: his inherited delight to wander through the fields in search of foxgloves and dandelion and coltsfoot, began to wear to him the character of a temptation. (1973, p.57)

Eliot: his steps never wandered to the hedge-banks and the land-side in search of the once familiar herbs; these too belonged to the past, from which his life had shrunk away . . . (1973, p.70)

He is further alienated from his fellows, and even from himself:

Marx: An immediate consequence of man's alienation from the product of his work, his vital activity and his species-being, is the alienation of man from man. When man is opposed to himself, it is another man that is opposed to him . . . one man is alienated from another as each of them is alienated from the human essence. (1977, p.83)

Eliot: he listened docilely, that he might come to understand better what this life was, from which, for fifteen years, he had stood aloof as from a strange thing, wherewith he could have no communion . . . (1973, p.190)

Eliot: So, year after year, Silas Marner had lived in this solitude, his guineas rising in the iron pot, and his life narrowing and hardening itself more and more into a mere pulsation of desire and satisfaction that had no relation to any other being. (1973, p.68)

Of course *Silas Marner* effects Silas's disenchantment from alienation, but the socialised alternative the novel offers is not unequivocally appealing. His guide is the spinner of nauseatingly acquiescent homespun wisdom and repressive 'good sense', Dolly Winthrop, whose counsel Silas at first finds incomprehensible. 'Her simple view of life and its comforts, by which she had tried to cheer him, was only like a report of unknown objects which his imagination could not fashion' (G. Eliot, 1973, p.68). Dolly's homely philosophy perpetuates the dual forms of tyranny and subservience; she advocates punishing children by locking them in the coal-hole and reveres as 'good words' because she has seen them in church, the letters, IHS, she prints on all her baking but cannot herself read. James Kavanagh applies Jane Gallop's term 'phallic mother' to Nelly Dean in *Wuthering Heights* (1848), 'the [female] figure who wields the phallic tools of the symbolic order, of language and culture . . . she becomes an agent of patriarchal law' (Kavanagh, 1985, pp.39–40). Dolly Winthrop would be a less equivocal candidate. Her labour, like Silas's, is inscribed with the uncomprehended signs of authority which not only her baking but her discourse endlessly disseminates and prepares for consumption. Her catch-phrase is 'I wouldn't speak ill o'this world, seeing as them puts us in it knows best' and, like Ladislaw counselling Dorothea into 'a sturdy neutral delight in things as they were', she ushers Silas into the acquiescent conservatism which this culture extracts as the price of admission: 'a humble sort of acquiesence in what was held to be good, had become a strong habit of that new self which had been developed in him . . . he had come to appropriate the forms of custom and belief which were the mould of Raveloe life . . .' (G. Eliot, 1973, p.201).

Objectification is certainly the theme of a novel which is essentially a long permutation on the term 'object': alienated amidst a world of 'unknown objects' Silas at first suffers, in the loss of his gold, 'a bewildering separation from a supremely loved object' to be blessed with a human replacement in the shape of Eppie, 'an object compacted of changes and hopes' (G. Eliot, 1973, p.201; p.166). Silas's relations to objects are intense. His beloved water pot, which in an odd incident he accidentally breaks but keeps the reassembled pieces, exemplifies the object which, its use-value and sympathy to human purposes shattered, takes on a purely symbolic, fetishistic status.

It had been his companion for twelve years . . . always lending its handle to him . . . its form had an expression of willing helpfulness . . . Silas picked up the pieces and carried them home with grief in his heart. The brown pot could never be of use to him any more, but he stuck the bits together and propped the ruin in its old place for a memorial.

(G. Eliot, 1973, p.184)

Essentially a funerary artefact, the 'memorial' pot is the mourning sign of a lost intimacy between man and the object. Let us register for future reference the historical resonances of that term 'ruin'. Silas is not alone in Eliot's oeuvre as the anal hoarder of death-tainted, fetishised objects detached from use-value. The Dodson sisters outdo each other in obsessive fussing over the quality of their respective trousseaux – linen, china and furniture which become a source of anxiety to Mrs Tulliver greater than her husband's paralysis. Sister Glegg has an expensive, once-worn bonnet as the particular object of her commodity fetishism which, unswathed from its tissue shroud, is displayed to envious relatives in a scene of 'funereal solemnity'. A more literal death-taint lingers over Nancy Cass's drawer full of baby clothes, 'all unworn and untouched', which she has preserved for fourteen years after a still-birth. She has been wont to visit the little collection in a poignant reworking of the image of Silas daily poring over his gold but where the hoard represents absence rather than plenitude. Mr Transome in *Felix Holt* tends his collection of 'dried insects' and mineralogical specimens in shallow drawers, occupying himself in continual schemes for their rearrangement. Romola's father Bardo collects antiquities and ancient manuscripts, 'lifeless objects' – most antiquities that survive to be collected are tomb-furnishings – which oppress Romola with a 'sad dreariness', 'the parchment backs, the unchanging mutilated marble, the bits of obsolete bronze and clay' (G. Eliot, 1984 (3), p.98). Casaubon hoards the 'small monumental records' which are the results of his mytho-historical researches. Dead-letters, they endlessly accumulate as his 'lifeless embalmment of knowledge', the 'shattered mummies' supposed to endorse a theory 'already withered in the birth like an elfin child' (G. Eliot, 1981, p.229; p.519). Eliot makes an explicit analogy between Silas's life-withering accumulation of capital and equivalently miserly and death-tainted intellectual projects.

His life had reduced itself to the mere functions of weaving and hoarding . . . The same sort of process has perhaps been undergone by wiser men, when they have been cut off from faith and love – only, instead of a loom and heap of guineas, they have some erudite research, some ingenious project, or some well-knit theory.

(G. Eliot, 1973, pp.68–9)

Middlemarch is a compendium of such research, projects and theories: Lydgate's experiments on his pickled animal specimens in pursuit of the 'primitive tissue', Mr Farebrother's entomological collection and Mr Brooke's disordered 'documents' and cultural memorabilia would be instances. Silas's money, the Dodson sisters' and Nancy's domestic goods and clothes, Bardo's and Mr Brooke's manuscripts and cultural artefacts, Lydgate's, Farebrother's and Transome's pickled and pinned specimens and even Casaubon's knowledge and, by implication, the very myth and history it processes seem all equally assimilated to a prevailing fetishism of the object. No aspect of reality seems immune from being accumulated into little hoards of death-objects, corpse-collections turned capital. In confirmation of a comment of Macherey's that the nineteenth-century bourgeoisie turn history into their private property or, as Marx puts it, history is currently rendered 'a collection of dead facts' (Marx, 1977, p.165), even history is here accumulated as one such death-hoard. In fact the whole of Western culture had appeared to Dorothea under precisely this guise, as a stash of corpse-capital, a 'funeral procession with strange ancestral images and trophies gathered from afar'.

This centrality to the nineteenth century of the notion of collecting of which *Silas Marner* particularly is an analysis and a prophecy is worth pausing over. In a withering attack on Lukács for using his study of nineteenth-century fiction to indulge his own fetishism of the object, Brecht indicates the centrality of such fetishism for the nineteenth century and its determining role in the construction of identity. Lukács had been stating his admiration for Balzac; Brecht points out that Balzac was himself an obsessive collector and that his narratives 'follow possessions (fetishism of objects) through generations of families and their transference from one to the other'. Collecting and competition are primary means of the nineteenth century's construction of identity.

In the primeval forest of early capitalism individuals fought against individuals, and against groups of individuals; basically they fought against 'the whole of society'. This was precisely what determined their individuality. Now we are advised to go on creating individuals, to recreate them, or rather to create new ones, who will naturally be different but made in the same way.

So? 'Balzac's passion for collecting things bordered on mono-mania'. We find this fetishism of objects in his novels, too, on hundreds and thousands of pages. Admittedly we are supposed to avoid such a thing. Lukács wags his finger at Tretyakov on this account. But this fetishism is what makes Balzac's characters individuals. It is ridiculous to see in them a simple exchange of the social passions and functions which constitute the individual. Does the production of consumer goods for a collective today construct individuals in the same way as 'collecting'? Naturally one can answer 'yes' here too.

(Adorno et al., 1988, 'Brecht against Lukács', p.78)

It becomes characteristic of the novel in English from the 1860s on to centre on the fascination exerted by desired but functionless objects. It is a commonplace for novels to be named after, and for their plots to revolve around, some supremely desired artefact. In Wilkie Collins's *The Moonstone* (1868) an elaborate sensation-plot of thefts and deceptions is generated by an Indian diamond plundered from a Hindu temple, bearing a curse and pursued around the world by its former Brahmin protectors. Anthony Trollope's *The Eustace Diamonds* (1873) also ponders, in a rather inert and literal-minded way, the status of objects and the legitimacy of ownership. The heroine pretends that the Eustace heirlooms of the title, given her by her husband, have been stolen and thus attempts to keep them from the acquisitive Eustace family. Henry James's *The Golden Bowl* (1904) circles, Balzac-like, the artefact of the title, human desires and destinies twining themselves around, and imaged in, the exquisite yet flawed objet-d'art. One feels James is elaborating hints from *Daniel Deronda*, that most Jamesian of Eliot's novels, where first Gwendolen's pawned turquoise necklace and later the ring Daniel has valued take on developing plot functions Eliot had not previously used objects to generate.

James is perhaps the author of the fetishised art-object par excellence. The milieu he brings for the first time into the purview of fiction is that specific to the last quarter of the nineteenth century, a world of culture-fetishising new wealth populated by connoisseurs, aesthetes, collectors and critics, the haunters of auction-houses, antique-shops, palaces and museums. Here is first registered in the novel the com-modification of the artwork Adorno analyses as a defining characteristic of capitalism in its world-monopoly phase, where artworks are shrivelled to the status of commodities and where commodities – through advertising or grandiose World Fairs and exhibitions where they are displayed like, or alongside, works of art – are swathed in an aesthetic allure. Here is an exhibition and museum culture in which Americans travel the European Old World trawling for, as another James novel title has it, 'spoils'. This is what Adam Verver does in *The Golden Bowl*. He is scouring Europe for objects to bring back to American City and install in his Palace of Art, a 'museum of museums' which 'was positively civilisation, condensed, concrete, consummate' (James, 1983, p.124). We find in James also exactly what Brecht observes in Balzac – an equation between possession and identity so that, in accumulating possessions, James's almost invariably wealthy characters foster a sense of identity inseparable from ownership. There is a provocative exchange in *The Portrait of a Lady* (1881) – yet another novel named after an aesthetic object – between Isabel Archer and Madame Merle on precisely this point. Wearied of her house, wealth and position Isabel asserts that these things do not define her and that nothing that belongs to her is any measure of her. 'I don't know if I succeed in expressing myself, but I know that nothing else expresses me'. Madame Merle disagrees. For her there is a precise equation of ownership, status and selfhood and she poses some pertinent questions.

> 'What shall we call our "self"? Where does it begin? Where does it end? It overflows into everything that belongs to us – and then it flows back again. I know a large part of myself is in the clothes I choose to wear. I've a great respect for *things*! One's self – for other people – is one's expression of one's self, and one's house, one's furniture, one's garments, the books one reads, the company one keeps – these things are all expressive.'
>
> (James, 1984, p.253)

The unresolved dialogue brilliantly encapsulates schisms within the fraught identities of James's own characters, torn between the notion of a romantic essentialism and an actual alienating refraction of identity through the signs of class and possession. Isabel and Madame Merle merely voice the opposed aspects of a single impossible position. It is precisely the annihilating perversity of identity under late capitalism that the subject's infatuation with itself and the fetishism of the object find their correlatives in each other. Human beings thus become the 'subjective-objective reality, a divided thing hinged together but not strictly individual' Lawrence analyses as the repulsive but all-too truthful characterisations of Galsworthy – he must have *The Man of Property* (1906) particularly in mind. The Forsytes have 'lost caste as human beings'. Entirely subject to the 'money-sway', they have violated their essential human 'naiveté' and consequently sunk to the level of the 'social being' in whom money 'goes right through the centre and is the controlling principle' (Lawrence, 1969, 'John Galsworthy', p.121; p.120).

Adorno analyses the museum culture and its construction of alienated identities with repugnance in *Prisms*. He discusses the opposed responses to museums of 'the two most knowledgeable men to have written about art in recent times', Valéry and Proust. Valéry loathes, Proust loves, museums but both reactions stem from a shared observation that museums are the mausoleums of their contents. Adorno cites Valéry's repulsion from the crammed, eclectic Louvre described in 'Le problème des musées' – one that recalls Dorothea's sense of the oppressive disorder of Rome and the 'titanic . . . struggling' of its artworks as well as Brecht's profound equation of collection and competition. 'Cold confusion, he says, reigns among the sculptures, a tumult of frozen creatures each of which demands the non-existence of the others, disorder strangely organised.' Of course Adorno is quick to find in the struggling chaos of the museum a metaphor for the anarchical production of desirous commodities in a fully developed bourgeois society. Perhaps more strikingly, Valéry himself makes the same equation by comparing the museum to 'the accumulation of excessive and therefore unuseable capital' (Adorno, 1983, 'Valéry Proust Museum', p.183; p.176; p.177).

The Proust argument is more complex: it is precisely the degree of alienation afforded by the museum which, by prising the artwork from any pre-existent context, makes it available for the individual's appropriation as an element within the transforming fabric of memory. The death-struggle amongst artworks Valéry perceives in the museum is for Proust a source of beauty, as objects submit themselves to the mingled ravages and affirmations of time.

> Valéry and Proust . . . agree even to the point of recognising something of the mortal enmity which exists among works and which accompanies the pleasure of competition. Far from recoiling before it, however, Proust affirms this enmity as though he were as German as Charlus affects to be. For him competition among works is the test of truth. Schools, he writes at one point in *Sodom and Gomorrah*, devour each other like micro-organisms and ensure through their struggle the survival of life.
>
> (Adorno, 1983, 'Valéry Proust Museum', p.179)

These meditations might strike the reader as somewhat untimely in their application to *Silas Marner*, and partly the intention is that their meaning will unfold in the ensuing discussion of *Romola* and *Daniel Deronda* which tease out further the issues around accumulation and the artwork evidenced in *Middlemarch*. *Silas Marner* – bucolic, fabular, homespun, warmly humanist – would seem to belong to another register altogether and to carry no whiff of the coming art-fetishising 'decadence' of a rabid commodity culture. *Silas Marner, Sodom and Gomorrah* and late, exquisite James make, I will admit, a provocative comparison even if Proust's characters are fond of reading and translating Eliot and Isabel Archer has been brought up on her. If *Daniel Deronda* is Eliot's most Jamesian novel, *Silas Marner* would appear to be her least. In fact *Silas* so precisely negates such a world as to be suspiciously disingenuous. To negate precisely a given form – as a sculptor's mould does, or a photographic negative – can be the means of its faithful reproduction. *Silas* is the anticipatory negative of a rabid, commodified, fetishistic, anti-humanist world. Thus Silas's revered broken pot is a humble ancestor of James's also cracked and fetishised golden bowl and the miserly Silas himself has been a (barely) living embodiment of the culture Valéry observes which, in its museums and elsewhere, requires 'the accumulation of excessive and therefore unuseable capital'. Readers will readily agree that *Silas* has mythic qualities, myths being those troublesome, indeterminate entities of *Middlemarch*. But why does one need a humanist myth unless everything it wishes to assert is under threat? If *Silas* is a myth it is so in the terms of Benjamin's dictum that while there is a beggar, there will be a myth. In other words myths are required to mask social tensions and oppressions for which they offer purely illusory resolutions.

The equation of the museum and the mausoleum analysed by Adorno, Valéry and Proust is continuous with the argument of Lukács that the nineteenth century is itself 'a charnel house of long-dead interiorities'. As Lukács describes it – and the Dickens of *Dombey and Son* had anticipated the analysis – the nineteenth century displaces nature by a charnel-house 'second nature' of human manufacture.

This second nature is not dumb, sensuous and yet senseless like the first: it is a complex of senses – meanings – which has become rigid and strange, and which no longer wakens interiority; it is a charnel-house of long-dead interiorities; this second nature could only be brought to life – if this were possible – by the metaphysical act of reawakening the souls which, in an early or ideal existence, created or preserved it; it can never be animated by another interiority.

(Lukács, 1878, p.64)

Here, in a somewhat mystified form, are all the Eliot cruces. Silas is in desperate need to be 'brought to life', to experience the wakening of his 'interiority', the 'metaphysical act of awakening'. *Silas Marner* is the Benjaminesque myth of that awakening. The novel offers an image of precisely what Lukács describes as what this period has made unattainable, the rescue from the 'charnel-house of dead interiorities' through the blessed 'act of reawakening' as one is 'animated by another interiority'. Eppie, the golden-haired child who tottering into Silas's cottage after the theft of his gold seems its miraculous human replacement, is that other, animating interiority. 'As the child's mind was growing into knowledge, his mind was growing into memory: as her life unfolded, his soul, long stupefied in a cold narrow prison, was unfolding too, and trembling gradually into full consciousness' (G. Eliot, 1973, p.185).

Eppie, in a phrase worth pondering in this context, is described as the antithesis of an object or, more contradictorily, as an object inspired with non-objective qualities: 'an object compacted of changes and hopes'.

> Unlike the gold which needed nothing, and must be worshipped in close-locked solitude – which was hidden away from the daylight, was deaf to the songs of birds, and started to no human tones – Eppie was a creature of endless claims and ever-growing desires, seeking and loving sunshine, and living sounds, and living movements . . . Eppie was an object compacted of changes and hopes that forced his thoughts onward, and carried them far away from their old eager pacing towards the same blank limit . . .
>
> (G. Eliot, 1973, p.184)

Two interdependent indices of growth mark Silas's progress in deserving, and achieving, his disenchantment from alienation; the slow shift in his vocabulary whereby he comes to call Eppie 'her' rather than 'it' and the commensurate erosion of his conception of her as his private property. This latter however is never fully extricated from the narrative's own fabular equation of the daughter with her father's treasure, a motif given emphatic stress also in the contemporaneous *Romola*. These are two novels giving utterly opposed readings of what it means for a daughter to be her father's wealth.

Eppie is an exemplary nineteenth-century heroine in having an essentially domestic function. Herself a human object miraculously disenchanted from her objectification, she revokes the alienation from the natural which has been Silas's burden and re-establishes him in his 'parental home'. 'Estrangement from nature (the first nature), the modern sentimental attitude to nature, is only a projection of man's experience of his self-made environment as a prison instead of as a parental home' (Lukács, 1978, p.64). The Lukácsian formulations derive from Hegel as, in some sense, does Marx's own analysis of alienation. For Hegel alienation is a facet of the wider contemporary need to feel at home within our own history, and art has the Eppiesque function of ushering us into this domestic/historical idyll.

The historical is only then ours . . . when we can regard the present in general as a consequence of those events in whose chain the characters or deeds represented constitute an essential link . . . For art does not exist for a small, closed circle of the privilegedly cultured few, but for the nation as a whole. What holds good for the work of art in general, however, also has its application for the outer side of the historical reality represented. It, too, must be made clear and accessible to us without extensive learning so that we, who belong to our own time and nation, may find ourselves at home therein, and not be obliged to halt before us, as before some alien and unintelligible world.

(Quoted Lukács, 1962, pp.57–8)

A novel both brave and defensive, *Silas Marner* first depicts, then denies the truth of nineteenth-century conditions before which Silas is 'obliged to halt . . . as before some alien and unintelligible world' – 'this life . . . from which . . . he had stood aloof as from a strange thing, wherewith he could have no communion'. Its very last line conjures the opposed possibility Hegel posits as the necessary contemporary message of art, the reassurance that we have a home in history. 'O father,' said Eppie, 'what a pretty home ours is! I think nobody could be happier than we are.'

II
'THE MUTILATED RELICS OF ANTIQUITY':
Romola

The great aim of archaeology is to restore the warmth and truth to life to dead objects.   Philipe Diole, *4000 Years Under the Sea*

Collections of antiquities of all sorts now become common. Ciriaco of Ancona (d.1457) travelled, not only through Italy, but through other countries of the old world, and brought back with him countless inscriptions and sketches. When asked why he took all this trouble, he replied, 'To wake the dead'.

Burkhardt, *The Civilization of the Renaissance in Italy*

97

To reconstruct a past world, doubtless with a view to the highest purposes of truth – what a work to be in any way present at, to assist in, though only as a lamp holder!

Eliot, *Middlemarch*

One can reconstruct antiquity, but one cannot bring it to life.

Flaubert, *Letters*

I have been all my life a dealer in antiquities and have imbibed the shadows of fallen columns at Balbec, and Tadmor, and Persepolis, until my very soul had become a ruin.

Poe, 'Manuscript Found in a Bottle'

In *The Historical Novel* a central illustration for Lukács' thesis that nineteenth-century bourgeois art deprives history of its dynamic by rendering it a static, objectified image is Flaubert's novel centring on and named after the priestess heroine of ancient Carthage, *Salammbô* (1862). Lukács finds the work a repository of all the anathematised features. It offers only a 'frozen, lunar landscape of archaeological precision', it is 'the ghostly illusion of life', 'a world of historically exact *costumes and decorations*, no more than a pictorial frame within which a purely modern story is unfolded' (original emphasis) (Lukács, 1962, p.224; p.225). As he points out, his objections had been anticipated in a famous contemporary critique by Saint-Beuve who had made a quintessentially Lukácsian observation to the effect that 'the dead environment of men, overwhelms the portrayal of men themselves' and that while Flaubert brilliantly describes all the material details of ancient life 'they do not add up to a whole' (Lukács, 1962, p.221).

> The political side, the character of the persons, the genius of the people, the aspects whereby the particular history of this seafaring and, in its own way, civilizing people is of concern to history in general and of interest to the great current of civilisation, are sacrificed here or subordinated to the exorbitant, descriptive side, to a dilettantism which, unable to apply itself to anything but rare ruins, is compelled to exaggerate them.
>
> (Lukács, 1962, p.222)

In fact, I only partly recognise *Salammbô* in Lukács's account of it. It is actually crowded with incident and characterised by an almost breathless activity accentuated by very short paragraphs of sometimes just one or two sentences. Indeed it is curiously hyper-active. Even the notorious descriptiveness of which Lukács and Saint-Beuve complain partakes of the prevailing restlessness, like the rapid eye movement required to scan a richly-wrought surface. In fact the novel is almost too active as if ever straining always towards more, and more striking, incident and display; hence the mathematical exuberance of the images of violence, sex and opulence for which it is chiefly known – not one crucified lion, but hundreds; not one virgin carried off, but one thousand five hundred; not huge wealth, but wealth 'inaccessible, inexhaustible, infinite' (Flaubert, 1977, p.129). Perhaps *Salammbô* is a novel already conscious and critical of the moribundity of historical representation Lukács laments and is hence a crowded, hectic over-compensation for it. In this sense at least it can be realigned with Lukács's critique. Certainly the facts of composition and Flaubert's own characteristically mordant self-commentary – the two hundred books he read in preparation, the famous dictum about the unimaginable sadness required to resuscitate Carthage and a confession that in the very midst of writing 'I understand nothing of it, neither I nor anyone else' – sketch the familiar Lukácsian dilemma of the ennui and distress of a historical project both monumental and meaningless. In his despair over composition Flaubert anticipates both the complaint of Lukács/Saint-Beuve about its details not 'adding up to a whole' and Adorno's formulation that 'The coming extinction of art is prefigured in the increasing impossibility of representing historical events'. 'I am now full of doubts about the whole, about the general plan; I think there are too many soldiers. That is History. I know quite well. But if a novel is as tedious as a scientific potboiler, then Good Night, there's an end to Art' (Lukács, 1962, pp.221–2)

Eliot's *Romola* however, which appeared the very next year, 1863, yields profitably to the readings of Lukács and Saint-Beuve and both illustrates and ventures a partial critique of the ubiquity of reified historical images they deplore. I will initially explore three strands of issues identifiable as within the spectrum of Lukácsian concerns; an insistence upon images of the abortion of play and representation that intimates a failure of self-confidence within the work's own creative ambition, oppressive motifs of reification, scriptedness and the unintelligble and, and this I will discuss most extensively, the motifs and issues surrounding Romola's own central dilemma, her responsibility towards her blind scholar father's antiquarian collection.

The purge of play

There is a quip about *Waiting for Godot* that it is a work in which nothing happens, twice. In *Romola* nothing happens really quite frequently. Eliot seems concerned to create a succession of images of the failure of event, of the abortion of representation that make the novel a series of strange negations of the shared premises of history and representation. Four examples: one chapter is named after 'The Unseen Madonna', an effigy of the Virgin which, entirely swathed and obscured, is displayed, if that is not precisely the wrong word, in an annual street procession, in a singular instance of a non-event, a teasing refusal of representation. Comparably uneventful is the eagerly anticipated 'Trial by Fire' of Savonarola, a public show for which the streets are thronged – the populace 'swarming . . . at every coign of vantage or disadvantage'. That ironic negation 'coign of disadvantage' is precisely apposite, there is nothing to be seen. To everyone's disappointment other than Savonarola's the spectacle is rained off. The 'Pyramid of Vanities' which Savonarola orchestrates is a holocaust of all the paraphernalia of play and display – wigs, make-up, mirrors, musical instruments, masks and costumes – and is topped by an effigy, 'the symbolic figure of the old debauched Carnival' (G. Eliot, 1984 (3), p.617; p.498). Savonarola attempts a purge of play. All these negations of event and representation are emphasised as chapter titles. While Eliot does offer a set-piece depiction of the thrilling occasion of Savonarola's preaching, and one can well imagine her relishing the aesthetic and intellectual challenge of such a recreation, it is balanced (cancelled?) by a notable companion passage describing Savonarola's empty pulpit after his arrest, the silent church and absent audience – an eerie evocation of the extinguishing of drama and event.

> Instead of upturned citizen-faces filling the vast area under the morning light, the youngest rising amphitheatre-wise towards the walls, and making a garland of hope around the memories of age – instead of the mighty voice thrilling all hearts with the sense of great things, visible and invisible, to be struggled for – there were the bare walls at evening made more sombre by the glimmer of tapers; there was the black and grey flock of monks and secular clergy with bent, unexpectant faces; there was the occasional tinkling of little bells in the pauses of a monotonous voice reading a sentence which had already been long hanging up in the churches; and at last there was the extinction of the tapers, and the slow, shuffling tread of monkish feet departing in the dim silence.
>
> (G. Eliot, 1984 (3), pp.539–40)

We might recall that it was partly the stale repetition of the uncomprehended 'good words' inscribed in the church which in *Silas Marner* Eliot tried to make an object of just reverence and a component of the healthily socialising discourse which revives the protagonist. Here their monotonous authority intones the death of drama. The monks' 'bent, unexpectant faces' recall Silas at his most withdrawn, who had no conception of 'the unexpected' (G. Eliot, 1973, p.90).

The importance for nineteenth-century discourse of images of the abortion of play and performance such as these central to *Romola* can hardly be exaggerated and deserves a study of its own. Eliot makes an intriguing complement here to the writer in other respects her antithesis, Dickens. The first set-piece of his novelistic career is, resonantly, the harrowing death of a clown fallen on hard times at the beginning of *The Pickwick Papers* (1836–7) and the death of play and performance is again prefigured as Little Nell and her grandfather come across Mr Punch 'all loose and limp and shapeless' (Dickens, 1980, p.180) straddling a gravestone in *The Old Curiosity Shop* (1840–1). The motifs recall Bakhtin's conclusion that 'Parody has grown sickly, its place in modern literature is insignificant' (Bakhtin, 1981, p.75) and suitably preface a novelistic career which can be read as a prolonged post-mortem for play. With striking congruence Latimer in 'The Lifted Veil', a singularly miserable protagonist, has been assimilated into the same pattern. 'I had been the model of a dying minstrel in a fancy picture' (G. Eliot, 1985, p.20).

The nineteenth century indeed proves Hard Times for play, as Dickens's novel of 1854 writes large its impotence under industrial capitalism. Sleary's circus peddles a tame and self-depreciating 'amuthement' to the Coketown proletariat as imagination slides into a circumscribed comedy, as Fact colonises Fancy in Mr M'Choakumchild's pedagogic system and as work subsumes play. The novel's own uncharacteristically subdued, dispirited 'realist' treatment seems itself to enact and reproduce the subduing of art which is the ostensible object of its protest. The Dickensian issues survive in Lawrence. The creepy Loerke's artistic chef-d'oeuvre in *Women in Love* (1921) is a circus painted on a factory wall. Industrial capitalism commissions a façade of play to mask its exigencies, a transaction which the bourgeois English novel has both lamented and facilitated, sometimes simultaneously. Thus Eliot and Dickens would prove equivalently problematic instances for Bakhtin's argument that the modern novel is privileged to have retained at its heart the fool's cap and bells, a subversive residue of play and performance surviving from the parodic-travestying genres of classical and medieval literature and festival. Dickens's novelistic career, beginning with a dying clown, can be read rather as the extirpation of Bakhtin's dissentient tradition. 'We do not have the cap and bells of the jester but the bunch of keys of capitalist reason' say Adorno and Horkheimer (1989, p.142) and bring to mind both Dickens's debilitated clowns and, in *Bleak House* (1853), Esther Summerson taking a fetishistic pleasure in her jingling chatelaine. In *Romola* the fool's cap and bells would have ended up on the Bonfire of the Vanities. 'In vain Dolfo Spini and his companions had struggled to get up the dear old masques and practical jokes, well spiced with indecency. Such things were not to be in the city where Christ had been declared king' (G. Eliot, 1984 (3), p.497). Protest rather than lament seems a rarity. Poe enjoys a malicious dream of play revenged of its contemporary subservience in the story 'Hop-Frog'. A much abused court jester, a crippled dwarf more laughed *at* than *with*, orchestrates as his last jest his own purging bonfire – a practical joke which concludes with the king and his councillors hanged, tarred and immolated.

Complementing *Romola's* images of aborted performance are images and intimations of a world where nature and humanity are repulsively reified. Romola's brother Dino stalks her to tell her of the eerie vision he has had of her alienated amidst moribund antiquarian script and human flesh rendered as statuary. This vision frankly seems to have no real function in the plot and seems rather to spring from the psyche of the work itself as a self-descriptive intuition. 'And at last you came to a stony place where there was no water, and no trees or herbage: but instead of water, I saw written parchment unrolling itself everywhere and instead of trees and herbage; I saw men of bronze and marble springing up and crowding round you' (G. Eliot, 1984 (3), p.215). Dino's vision here explodes Mr Deane's assurance in *The Mill on the Floss* (their names suggest a curious alignment?) that 'the world isn't made of pen, ink and paper'. Mr Deane is a successful capitalist entrepreneur, and his comment comes in the context of priming Tom Tulliver for a comparable career – 'and if you're to get on in the world, young man, you must know what the world's made of' (G. Eliot, 1983, p.309). As such he suggests a necessary affinity between the projects of capitalism and realism in their shared need to affirm that, whatever 'the world's made of' it is not script. The tricky project of the realist literary artist is precisely to align script and world while preserving their assumed ontological distinction. Intimations that the world is turning to script as this of Dino's must penetrate such a project like shock waves.

The novel is also tainted with the corrosive suspicion that – in the very era of realist prose – the world is proving illegible. Tito's father is, like Romola's, a humanist scholar. He has been captured and held for a ransom which Tito refused to pay but has escaped after a shipwreck and now seeks to challenge the son who disowned him and claims him to be dead. Appearing in Florence a raving and destitute figure, he is challenged by city notables to prove his claim to be the famous scholar by reading from a manuscript.

> The book was open before him, and he bent his head a little towards it, while everybody watched him eagerly. He turned no leaf. His eyes wandered over the pages that lay before him, and then fixed on them a straining gaze. This lasted for two or three minutes in dead silence. Then he lifted his hands to each side of his head, and said, in a low tone of despair, 'Lost, Lost'.
>
> (G. Eliot, 1984 (3), pp.424–5)

One recalls Lukács's formulation about the bourgeois world as 'a complex of . . . meanings – which has become rigid and strange, and which no longer wakens interiority' (Lukács, 1978, p.64). One might recall also a rash of nineteeth-century images of the illegible: illegible man, illegible world, illegible history.

> *He is the man of the crowd.* It will be in vain to follow; for I shall learn no more of him, nor of his deeds. The worst heart of the world is a grosser book than the 'Hortulus Animae,' and perhaps it is but one of the great mercies of God that *es lässt sich nicht lesen.*
>
> (Poe, 1986, 'The Man of the Crowd', p.188)

> A solemn consideration, when I enter a great city by night, that every one of those darkly clustered houses encloses its own secret . . . No more can I turn the leaves of this dear book that I loved, and vainly hope in time to read it all . . . It was appointed that the book should shut with a spring, for ever and for ever, when I had read but a page.
>
> (Dickens, 1990, p.44)

> History . . . that complex Manuscript, covered over with formless inextricably-entangled unknown characters.
>
> (Carlyle, 1987, p.91)

Romola has her own intuition of the veracity of Dino's vision in the form of a frightening encounter with some masquers representing Time and Death.

> And as he spoke there came slowly into view . . . a huge and ghastly image of Winged Time with his scythe and hour-glass, surrounded by his winged children, the Hours . . . a troop of the

sheeted dead gliding above blackness . . . A cold horror seized on Romola, for at the first moment it seemed as if her brother's vision, which could never be effaced from her mind, was being half fulfilled.

(G. Eliot, 1984 (3), p.262)

Brides of quietness

Romola has the ponderous, descriptive manner Lukács would recognise. Its mode of representation is always only a step away from the mannered stasis he calls 'still-life' (one is reminded that the French term is the Lukácsian 'nature morte') – and sometimes actually realises it in an artful descriptive hiatus: 'the inner room, in which were some benches, a table, with one book in manuscript and one printed in capitals lying open upon it, a lute, a few oil-sketches, and a model or two of hands and ancient masks' (G. Eliot, 1984 (3), p.78). Similar antiquarian bric-a-brac, and the meticulous descriptive style that picks it over, form the initial setting of its heroine. She is introduced as a compositional component of an antiquarian still-life, a feature of her father's collection.

a long, spacious room, surrounded with shelves, on which books and antiquities were arranged in scrupulous order. Here and there, on separate stands in front of the shelves, were placed a beautiful feminine torso; a headless statue, with an uplifted muscular arm wielding a bladeless sword; rounded, dimpled, infantine limbs severed from the trunk, inviting the lips to kiss the cold marble; some well-preserved Roman busts; and two or three vases from Magna Grecia. A large table in the centre was covered with antique bronze lamps and small vessels in dark pottery. The colour of these objects was chiefly pale or sombre: the vellum bindings, with their deep-ridged backs, gave little relief to the marble livid with long burial; the once splendid patch of carpet at the farther end of the room had long been worn to dimness; the dark bronzes wanted sunlight upon them to bring out their tinge of green, and the sun was not yet high enough to sends gleams of brightness through the narrow windows that looked on the Via de' Bardi.

The only spot of bright colour in the room was made by the hair of a tall maiden of seventeen or eighteen, who was standing before a carved *leggio* or reading-desk . . .

(G. Eliot, 1984 (3), p.93)

Romola, like *Silas Marner*, centres on the equation of a daughter with her father's treasure. The two works are entwined, at least this was the history of their composition. Eliot wrote *Silas* as a break from the enervating rigours of researching and writing *Romola*, a kind of holiday. One can see how a novel dramatising the protagonist's disenchantment from objectification and finding his Hegelian home in history can serve as relief from a project that envisages for its heroine no such release and no such home. I want to pause here with Romola amidst her father's collection, as I did over the comparable depiction of Dorothea's alienation amidst Roman art and culture, to consider the theoretical implications of this emphatic Eliot motif: the eerie and problematic status of antiquities and the antique. One way of putting the issues here is to ask whether Dino's vision of his sister alienated amidst a world turning to script and statuary were not here already fulfilled. 'The marble fragments of the past', 'the unchanging, mutilated marble' (G. Eliot, 1984 (3), p.92; p.98) (the adjectives in this last phrase are curiously contradictory) as here evoked bespeak human intimacies, sexual politics, historical relics and violences and oppressive reverence towards the antique conflated in a strange inextricability and rendered as a still collection of stony fragments. The passively 'beautiful' and ungesturing 'feminine torso' is ominously juxtaposed to the victorious gesture of male power, paradoxically emasculated and bladeless as if itself the loser in some obscure contention. The child's sculpted limbs, actually a popular Victorian ornament when modelled from life – Victoria had all her children modelled in this way – complete the grisly, mutilated family redolent of some ancient domestic carnage. The dismembered fragments both signify immemorial sexual violences and anticipate Freud's Oedipal model of the family, the mother/father/child triangle of tragic contention. Here are another set of Benjaminesque relics which as memorials of violence can only be contemplated with disquiet.

An absolutely authentic nineteenth-century response is registered in the narrator's poignant displacement of a sensual/sexual longing on to the inanimate cultural artefacts – 'inviting the lips to kiss the cold marble'. As Hardy does through the figure of Somerset in *A Laodicean* who invites the heroine to join him in a sensuous stroking of architectural details in her castle's shady vault, Eliot here registers a vain attempt to draw historical objects back into human relation, to render the historically inanimate, humanly intimate. One is reminded also of those drawings by Ruskin lovingly detailing all the sensuous intricacies of architectural or unworked stone and giving them the look of living flesh or hair. He subjects the stones to the intimacies of minute seeing as if projecting on to their unthreatening inanimacy the sexual/sensual longing for which he never found an appropriate human object. Dorothea will be a compound of comparable needs who 'longed for objects who could be dear to her, and to whom she could be dear' and yearned to feed 'her affection with those childlike caresses which are the bent of every sweet woman, who has begun by showering kisses on the hard pate of her bald doll, creating a happy soul within that woodenness from the wealth of her own love. That was Dorothea's bent'. But the stone will not be seduced, nor the woodenness animated. There is no living soul in things. 'Their susceptibilities will clash against objects that remain innocently quiet' (G. Eliot, 1981, p.516; p.230; p.223). Eliot's brilliant reworking of the statue scene from *The Winter's Tale* in *Daniel Deronda* into a form that can state nineteenth-century concerns will extend the problematic representation of the desire to touch stone and find it flesh.

The poignancy of historical dislocation evoked in these attempts to touch the ancient object is something Lawrence knew and meditated in *Etruscan Places* (1932). The figures depicted in Etruscan tomb art 'really have the sense of touch' lost to later art, and life. 'There is plenty of pawing and laying hold, but no real touch. In pictures especially, the people may be in contact, embracing or laying hands on one another. But there is no soft flow of touch. The touch does not come from the middle of the human being. It is merely a contact of surfaces, and a juxtaposition of objects' (Lawrence, 1985, p.88). Such a 'juxtaposition of objects' recalls Lukács's conception of the debilitating descriptiveness of capitalist representation with its characteristically lingering, static depiction of reality as an object or scattered array of disparate objects, a 'still-life'. Eliot's own term from *Romola* after another meticulous description of an interior, Piero's studio, is 'heterogeneous still-life' (G. Eliot, 1984 (3), p.245). 'Juxtaposition of objects', 'heterogeneous still-life': these phrases emphatically invert another of Lukács's formulations who, borrowing from Hegel, laments the loss of an ideal 'totality of objects' as represented in Classical epic art. Lukács argues that in the Classical epic, and the cultures that produced them, objects are held in a vital tension of significance with individuals and with social forms. The essence of the epic world, Lukács citing Hegel asserts, is,

the 'totality of objects which' is created 'for the sake of connecting the particular action with its substantial basis'. Hegel stresses sharply and rightly that this does not mean an autonomous object-world. If the epic poet makes the object-world autonomous, then it loses all poetic values. In poetry things are important, interesting and attractive only as objects of human activity, as transmitters of relations between human beings and human destinies. But in epic they are there neither as decorative background nor as technical instruments for directing the action, of no real interest in themselves. An epic work which presents only the inner life of man with no living interaction with the objects forming his social and historical environment must dissolve into an artistic vacuum without contours or substance.

(Lukács, 1962, p.102)

Things ain't what they used to be. Lukács's idealising strategy of positing a lost historical totality is, to say the least, open to objection. The ancients who are supposed to embody this totality themselves had recourse to the same model in the concept of the Golden Age. However the Greek epic does furnish one striking paradigmatic instance of the epic object as Lukács describes it. This is the burgeoning human and narrative significance of Achilles's shield in Book 18 of *The Iliad*. It is embossed with multiple scenes and narratives which, as the poem elaborates them, become themselves subsidiary events within the meta-narrative of *The Iliad*. The poem teases an object out into events and narratives as if not recognising a perhaps quintessentially modern distinction between object and action. The shield – object, event, narrative? – is that which can only appear under modern conditions as a paradox, an 'object of human activity', 'an object compacted of changes and hopes'.

Lawrence values the recovered Etruscan artefacts – urns, amphorae, tomb statuary – as evidences of the non-acquisitive, non-imperialist culture the Romans obliterated, and for still bearing the aura of Lukács's epic objects. He finds the promise of a personal restoration in contemplation of and identification with 'those "brides of quietness" which have been only too much ravished'.

Life was not only a process of rediscovering backwards. It is that, also: and it is that intensely. Italy has given me back I know not what of myself, but a very, very great deal. She has found for me so much that was lost: like a restored Osiris. But this morning in the omnibus I realise that, apart from the great rediscovery backwards, which one *must* make before one can be whole at all, there is a move forwards . . . But one must have perfected oneself in the great past first.

(Lawrence, 1985, p.88; *Sea and Sardinia* p.123)

107

Lawrence's invocation of the Osirian mysteries is exactly apposite. The Egyptian king was murdered and dismembered but his wife Isis, who was also his sister, sought for, re-assembled and actually re-animated his remains. Deleuze and Guattari, who in fact do extensive honour to Lawrence, would refute his imagery and ambition here of pursuing the ancient past's promise of psychic wholeness, of recovering oneself 'like a restored Osiris'.

> We live today in the age of partial objects, bricks that have been shattered to bits, and leftovers. We no longer believe in the myth of the existence of fragments that, like pieces of an antique statue, are merely waiting for the last one to be turned up, so that they may be glued back together to create a unity that is precisely the same as the original unity. We no longer believe in a primordial totality that once existed, in a final totality that awaits us at some future date. We no longer believe in the dull gray outlines of a dreary, colorless dialectic of evolution, aimed at forming a harmonious whole out of heterogeneous bits by rounding off their rough edges.
>
> (Deleuze and Guattari, 1984, p.42)

So Deleuze and Guattari are like Lukács in recognising that modern conditions render reality a scattering of 'heterogeneous bits', but unlike him in denying that these once formed a 'primordial totality' ('primitive tissue'?) requiring reconstruction. One of their favourite metaphors is that things always were mutilated, even in their origination. 'This is the place to say it, if there ever was one: *the mutilation is prior, pre-established*' (Deleuze and Guattari, 1988, p.447). Sylvia Plath's great statement of the burdens of female creativity, 'The Colossus', realises a Deleuzeoguattarian vision of modernity as the speaker vainly struggles to piece together the shattered and scattered 'old anarchy' of the ancient male monument of the title. 'I shall never get you put together entirely / Pieced, glued, and properly jointed'. Mary Shelley, George Eliot, Sylvia Plath: women writers seem locked in problematic identification with the reconstructive labours of Isis driven to rebuild a possibly monstrous and certainly moribund husband/father. Casaubon's work relied precisely on the Lukácsian assumption of a lost totality, a recoverable colossus, as he seeks to 'reconstruct' the Ur-myth now scattered amongst 'mythical fragments' – 'he had undertaken to show . . . that all the mythical systems or erratic mythical fragments in the world were corruptions of a tradition originally revealed'. In the project's tortuous resistance to completion Eliot sketches the modern condition Deleuze

108

and Guattari envisage. As her husband's amanuensis Dorothea feels the despair of Plath's speaker in assembling ancient fragments that refuse to reform a totality – or never did form one. 'And now she pictured to herself the days, and months and years which she must spend in sorting . . . fragments of a tradition which was itself a mosaic wrought from crushed ruins' (G. Eliot, 1981, p.46; p.519).

Freud's consulting rooms in Vienna and then London – now preserved as the Freud Museum – were more disordered versions of Bardo's study, filled with the ancient tomb statuary – Assyrian, Babylonian, Cycladic, Egyptian, Etruscan, Greek, Minoan–Mycenaean, Roman – of which he was an avid and expert collector. One cannot help conjecturing that, reposing on the bier-like couch amidst the tomb-furnishings, Freud's predominantly female analysands must have felt like Romola – as a fractured tomb-relic, or the corpse itself, amongst the Freud/father's collection. The psychoanalytic project itself formalises Lawrence's archaeological ambition of 'rediscovering backwards' and Freud's discourse is, especially in relation to his female subjects, a tissue of archaeological/antiquarian metaphors. 'Our insight into [the pre-Oedipus] phase in the little girl's development comes to us as a surprise, compatible . . . with . . . the discovery of the Minoan–Mycenaean civilization behind that of Greece' (Freud, 1931, p.195). In the context of his analysis – or rather his 'Fragment' of one – of 'Dora', an adolescent victim of a sexual assault and subsequent hysteric, he concludes 'I had no choice but to follow the example of those discoverers whose good fortune is to bring to the light of day after long burial the priceless though mutilated relics of antiquity. I have restored what is missing' (Freud, 1987, p.41). The Freudian metaphors assimilate the female subject to the antique, her psyche a trove of 'the mutilated relics of antiquity' just as her sexual organs are in Freud's notorious conception another site of 'mutilation'. Freud once showed H.D. around his antiquarian collection and she records an anecdote which wryly evokes this Freudian equation of the antique object, fracture, impotence and the female.

> '*This* is my favorite,' he said. He held the object toward me. I took it in my hand. It was a little bronze statue, helmeted, clothed to the foot in carved robe with the upper incised chiton or peplum. One hand was extended as if holding a staff or rod. 'She is perfect,' he said, '*only she has lost her spear*'. I did not say anything.
>
> (H.D., *Tribute to Freud*, 1985, pp.68–9)

109

Evidently Freud equates his fractured stauettes and his female analysands. They are equally '"brides of quietness" which have been only
too much ravished'.

PATRIARCHY AND PARALYSIS

Let us return to *Romola*. The novel branches from this initial complex
image of Romola's relation to her father's collection into a tortuously
self-contradictory representation of sexual/historical loyalties. Within
the novel conflicting claims are strenuously debated but with a recessive,
self-cancelling ambivalence. The dilemma posed by Bardo's collections
evidences one such crux. On the one hand they embody the moral
imperative of preserving antiquarian artefacts and their attendant
scholarship, rightly reverenced and authoritative, the repository of a
healthily liberal Classicism opposing the philistine orthodoxies of
clericism. On the other, that same script is figured as moribund,
unmeaning and sinisterly ousting nature and those same artefacts as the
mutilated relics of immemorial violences. As Bardo's daughter (he has
disowned his monk son) these artefacts and issues become Romola's
responsibility and dilemma, and as such become charged with sexual
politics. The daughter's relation to her father mirrors and enacts her
relation to history. For Romola, father, desire, law, history and the
historical monument/artefact conflate as a composite authority in a
paradigmatic instance of a female experience under patriarchy also
registered by Sylvia Plath in 'The Colossus' – 'O father, all by yourself |
You are pithy and historical as the Roman Forum'.

Romola herself is, in one sense, little more than the point of torsion
where conflicting claims and stresses warp and twist: to the historian
father and his museum of scholarship; to a disloyal brother turned monk
whom the father has disowned; to a husband duplicitous sexually,
politically and as the betrayer of her father's will and dissipator of his
collection; to her mentor Savonarola who imperiously reminds the
fleeing heroine of her duties to husband, city, church, history and duty
itself. The proliferation of authorities renders patriarchy omnipresent
and multiform as, indeed, Romola finds herself subject to an embarrassment of father figures. Savonarola habitually addresses her as 'daughter'
and, as well as her own father, her godfather Bernardo and Tito's father
Baldassarre all claim a paternal role – 'I am your father', 'Ah! you would
have been my daughter' (G. Eliot, 1984 (3), p.535; p.530). 'Baddo' is a
term for Daddy used in the novel and Bardo, Bernardo and Baldassarre

are all, phonetically at least, near-indistinguishable variants on a many-headed patriarchy. She even lives on the Via Bardi.

Romola experiences a tortuous daughterliness. She poses for a painting of Antigone – but Antigone as the dutiful daughter of a great blinded father of *Oedipus at Colonus*, not the tragic rebel of *Antigone* whose 'defiant hardness' is an object of judicious admiration in 'The *Antigone* and its Moral'. Eliot's fascination with Sophocles' heroine would seem to derive from the latter's duplex, yet somehow not duplicitous, relation to patriarchy. She is simultaneously rebellious and loyal, defiant and deferent, the bane of Creon but the prop and eyes of Oedipus – a near-impossible simultaneity of which Romola is a much more stressed and contradictory embodiment. The novel's proliferation of patriarchy is further highlighted by the conspicuous absence of matriarchy. No adult character appears to have a mother and mothering is imaged either as nauseatingly callow – winsome Tessa toying with her babies like dolls – or impossibly spiritualised and wish-fulfilling – 'Madonna' Romola ministering to the obligingly leprous islanders.

The issues of patriarchal loyalties are played out again in the figure of Tito who, faced with a comparable set of choices to Romola, makes all the rebellious gestures she resists. He breaks up and sells off Bardo's collections, pretends that his own scholar father is dead when he is in fact held captive for want of the ransom Tito withholds and, when he does present himself, disowns him and declares him mad. One is tempted to read Tito as the out-and-out villain through whom Eliot can enjoy the relief of imagining every excess of iconoclasm and filial/historical disloyalty denied the heroine without appearing to condone or indulge. At the same time, the novel is spiked with vivid and vehement moments of protest against the claims to loyalty of the oppressive triumvirate of script, history and patriarchy – a dream in which manuscripts displace nature, a distraught scholar lamenting 'Lost! Lost!' over an incomprehensible script, the 'cold horror' inspired by the masque of Time and his hours, Romola cutting at a stroke her web of loyalties and attempting to flee Florence only to be turned back by Savonarola and returned, as the next chapter title has it, to 'her Place'.

But Eliot chooses to enact this dense and ambiguous play of loyalties and disloyalties within an obsessively loyal historicist project. The novel may speak of forms of historical rebellion and protest, but the meta-language which contains these itself bespeaks a loyal historicism. G.H.Lewes commented that *Romola* was a historical novel more extensively researched than most histories. The evidence of the journals and letters is that Romola's tormented consciousness of restraint, and her deflected rebellion, were prefigured in the author's own sense of entrapment within the tortuously emergent novel. 'Got into a state of so much wretchedness in attempting to concentrate my thoughts on the construction of my story that I became desperate, and suddenly burst my bonds, saying, I will not think of writing!' 'Shall I ever be able to carry out my ideas? Flashes of hope are succeeded by long intervals of dim mistrust', 'Dreadfully depressed about myself and my work', 'Utterly despondent about my book'. Lewes describes Eliot's 'immoveable . . . conviction that she *can't* write the romance because she has not knowledge enough. Now as a matter of fact I know that she has immensely more knowledge of the particular period than any writer who has touched it; but her distressing diffidence paralyses her' (MS Journal, 30 July, 10 Nov., 11 Dec., 28 Oct. 1861. Quoted Haight, 1985, p.351).

The notion of paralysis here is precisely apposite as Eliot herself experiences the form of debility to which her own characters are peculiarly prone. In *The Historical Novel* Lukács quotes a remark of Balzac distinguishing between 'the characters of a novel' and 'historical characters' – 'The former must be roused to life, the latter have already lived' (Lukács, 1962, p.43). It would be difficult to think of a novelist of whom it is more true that her characters have to be 'roused to life' than Eliot. An occupational hazard of being an Eliot character is to experience the need of being 'roused to life' with peculiar urgency. 'The Lifted Veil' turns on an experiment in re-animation as Latimer and Meunier resurrect the corpse of Mrs Archer. Silas is subject to catatonic seizures and has to be recalled from a comparable ethical and emotional catatonia. Mr Transome in *Felix Holt* has 'the unevenness of gait and feebleness of gesture which tell of a past paralytic seizure'. Maggie's father has suffered a paralysis after a fall from his horse just as Romola's is subject to 'sudden fits of numbness' and, metaphorically, Romola herself is 'benumbed to everything but inward throbbings'. Dorothea finds her life 'wretchedly benumbing' and Lydgate tells her he is 'afraid of creeping paralysis'. Gwendolen, subject to attacks of paralysing panic, has such a seizure just at the moment when, acting Hermione, the statue should 'bequeath to death' its 'numbness' (G. Eliot, 1982 (1), p.88; 1984 (3), p.393, p.825; 1981, p.516). *Romola*, the monumental historical project attempting to rouse to life an entire age, results for the author in the reduction to debility her work seems everywhere to fear. Eliot embodies a formidable erudition still craving an impossible completeness of knowledge, a completeness which is itself a form of paralysis. As Nietzsche puts it 'A historical phenomenon, known clearly and completely and resolved into a phenomenon of knowledge, is, for him who has perceived it, dead' (Nietzsche, 1983, p.62).

The dreary, ageing experience of researching and writing *Romola* must have fed into the characterisation of Casaubon, who admits to living 'too much with the dead' and whose mind is 'something like the ghost of an ancient, wandering about the world and trying mentally to construct it as it used to be, in spite of ruin and confusing changes'. His vocabulary reworks her own complaint with regard to *Romola* of 'trying to write, trying to construct, and unable' (1981, p.40; MS Journal, 6 Oct. 1861. Quoted Haight, 1985, p.351). Both Casaubon and Eliot fall victim to the historicist delusion against which Benjamin warns. 'To articulate the past historically does not mean to recognise it "the way it really was" (Ranke)' (Benjamin, 1973, p.257). Eliot had a guilty sensitivity to her own 'Casaubon-tints'. She told Harriet Beecher Stowe 'I fear that the Casaubon-tints are not quite foreign to my own mental complexion' (1954, vol. 5, p.322). Myers cites an anecdote. 'Asked by a young friend "But from whom, then, did you draw Casaubon?" George Eliot, with a humorous solemnity, which was quite in earnest, nevertheless, pointed to her own heart' (Myers, 1881, p.60).

The death-tints of that Casaubon complexion – he looked like 'a death's-head fleshed over for the occasion' – are the symptoms of a sufferer from Benjamin's historical *acedia*. This is the sadness attendant upon the bourgeois historian's doomed and delusory 'process of empathy' and pursuit of an absolute reconstruction. Like Lukács, Benjamin cites the Flaubert of *Salammbô* as his example.

> To historians who wish to relive an era, Fustel de Coulanges recommends that they blot out everything they know about the later course of history. There is no better way of characterising the method with which historical materialism has broken. It is a process of empathy whose origin is the indolence of the heart, *acedia*, which despairs of grasping and holding the genuine historical image as it flares up briefly. Among medieval theologians it was regarded as the root cause of sadness. Flaubert, who was familiar with it, wrote: '*Peu de gens devineront combien il a fallu être triste pour ressusciter Carthage*'. The nature of this sadness stands out more clearly if one asks with whom the adherents of historicism actually empathise. The answer is inevitable: with the victor.
>
> (Benjamin, 1973, p.258)

It is a curiously self-destructive literary/historical project which, claiming validity from the density of its historical knowledge, dramatises, in an echo of Adorno's 'blind spots' of bourgeois historical insight, the blindness of a terminally anxious historical scholar and the dissipation of his researches and collections. Here again is the curiously self-collapsing structure of *Middlemarch*. Both works appear to establish an ambitious reconstructive historical project but that very project then finds ironic, belittling reflection within the work itself in the doomed – uncompleted or dissipated – projects of the scholars/collectors/historians on which they centre. These are novels that are unpicking themselves. In *Romola*, the work which is Eliot's most obviously historicist project, where her own role is most evidently that of a historian, she is beginning what she is to find the painfully self-implicating process of distancing herself from the figure and function of the historian. The representation of Casaubon in *Middlemarch*, with whom Eliot admitted a guilty affinity, takes the process a stage further, more consciously focusing within one witheringly judged character the sterile historicism which had in the earlier novel been Eliot's own project.

Antigone, Athena, Prometheus, Penelope

What is the core of the problem? Why was writing *Romola* such an ordeal, and why is its project as a densely researched slab of historical reconstruction so persistently sabotaged by oppressive motifs of reification, scriptedness and the abortion of play and representation? Why is its central image of history that of a father's collection of mutilated artefacts which a daughter feels duty-bound to preserve while struggling to avoid assimilation within it? My thinking on these issues has benefited from a short story 'Prometheus' by Alasdair Gray from *Unlikely Stories, Mostly* (1984). As references back to my own work will indicate, I regard Gray as a valuable commentary not merely on these Eliot issues but on all the key concerns of this work.

The story is the first person narration of M. Pollard, a reclusive French intellectual as old as the twentieth century, of contentious fame, adopted by structuralists and compared variously to Chomsky, Kierkegaard and Lévi-Strauss. He begins, as Eliot does *Daniel Deronda*, by meditating what she calls 'the make believe of a beginning'. He is paraphrasing one of his own works, *Sacred Sociology* (1934), which ponders first causes and how various cultures construct the myths of their originating authorities, with particular stress on the implicit politics of these aetiologies. For instance Roman Catholics and Milton conceived of Creation as magisterial and Heaven as 'a mansion where God lives in luxury among angelic flunkies', a notion 'very reassuring to people with power and those weaklings and parasites who admire them'. He prefers the Jewish Genesis as he pictures it, feeling empathy with a lonely, existentially traumatised God who, sounding like Beckett as Adorno describes him, cries 'Let there be light' not as a serene fiat but rather as 'a desperate prayer to our unknown powers' and 'a scream rejecting everything we know by committing us to an unimaginable opposite'. This is a version Pollard does not find incompatible with the scientific one of 'the splitting of that grand primordial atom', and one from which he traces his own descent (Gray, 1984, pp.199–20).

Pollard moves near to the time of the narration and his encounter in a café with a female poet, Lucie, on what we later surmise to be the eve of the Paris uprisings of 1968, who asks his opinion on her work. She says she regards him as an almost total reactionary but admits that her twin early influences in learning to love freedom and language were de Beauvoir and his own seminal *A Child's Plainchant Dictionary of Abstractions*. Attracted to her, he studies the poems and finds her a formidable feminist talent, 'vivisecting her mauled sexual organs to display the damage and making the surgery icily comic by indicating . . . "It's even more fun when I slice him up"' (p.208). She is a sort of Dora grown angry, radical and articulate over her sexual 'mutilation'. Her work indicates her desire for 'a world-wide anarchic commonwealth' releasing human souls from the imprisonment of camps, hospitals, asylums, marriages. Impressed he writes an exhaustive commentary which she regards as an almost complete misrepresentation but notwithstanding useful. He is perturbed by her characterisation of him as reactionary. Surely his works were dedicated to the liberating analysis that

> For centuries men have been misled by words like God, fate, nature, necessity, world, time, civilisation and history: words which hide from us our cause and condition. The bourgeois say that because of these things our state can change very little . . . But these words are nothing but names for *men*. *We* are our God, fate, nature, necessity, world, time, civilisation and history.
>
> (Gray, 1984, p.211)

Lucie dismisses this with a proverb she likes – 'The good wine of truth cannot be poured out of filthy old bottles'. He had been taken in by the sexual status quo and merely reaffirmed the old lie of the maleness of all originating authority. Pollard humbly acknowledges that this is his weakness and that the radicalism of his work has been lost through bourgeois appropriation 'as they appropriate all splendid things'. 'My art is solving injustice through historical metaphor and even there I may be defeated.'

The story comes to its crux. Pollard describes the long-cherished, unfinished project to which his life's work has tended. Will Lucie help him complete it? The glory of Greece and the great, originating, tragic and egalitarian statement of Western culture was the second play, Aeschylus's *Prometheus Bound*. Its explosively liberating sequel *Prometheus Unbound* was written, but suppressed and is now lost. Pollard intends to repair this immemorial damage to the egalitarian tendency of the world by completing Aeschylus's work and writing *Prometheus Unbound*. He does not here seem to be aware that he is thus part of a Romantic tradition of such re-writers; Shelley wrote his own *Prometheus Unbound* and Mary Shelley *Frankenstein: A Modern Prometheus*. He sketches the background. The gods and the titans are at war for control of the world and titan Prometheus, seeing the future lies with the gods, aids their leader Zeus with the armoury craft of the Cyclops and fighting power of mortal men. Once established in power Zeus turns tyrant and condemns mankind to death. Prometheus defies him by arming them with the divine prerogatives of hope and fire, inspiring them to be forever resistant to government. He is punished by crucifixion to a rock where, immortal, he writhes to this day having predicted that eventually he will be released and tyranny cast down. Lucie agrees that this story of a 'new administration crushing a clumsy old one with the help of the skilled workers, common people and a radical intellectual, and then taking control with the old threats of prison and bloody punishment' is, though savage, not remote. Pollard's completion begins with Zeus's bogus claim to be the creator impotently contested by mother-earth. The way Pollard describes her mode of declamation, an intriguing instance of a male imagining of *écriture féminine*, reminds me of Eliot's contemporary and admirer Emily Dickinson who in poems such as 'I cannot live with You' dispenses with punctuation and teases out a patriarchal imperative into liberating conditionals. 'She is twisting a huge statement into a question and does not divide what she knows into separate sentences and tenses' (p.221).

But Pollard cannot imagine beyond this point. He now requires a heroine as the instrument of liberation and Lucie's genuine *écriture féminine* to create her. She considers, and rejects, the collaboration. She has decided to abandon poetry and its cowardly immersion in language, preferring to make her life – and some unnamed political action – the book in which her beliefs can be read. She also rejects the rationale of the whole project in a letter in terms that unfold the story into the uneasy dialogue of a feminist deconstruction with a romantic reconstructive liberalism.

> You see civilisation as an unfinished story the Athenians started and which a few well-chosen words will help to a satisfactory finish! You are wrong. The best state in the world was that primitive matriarchy which the Athenians were foremost in dismantling . . . The rational Greek foundation of things has been unbuilt, unlearned. And you did not notice! My poor dwarf, you are the last nineteenth-century romantic liberal. That is why a corrupt government wishes to make you a national institution.
>
> (pp.229–30)

Pollard reads the letter with despair, and a reaction reminiscent of Tito's father before the dead letters of the unmeaning manuscript. 'I sat holding it, feeling paralysed, staring at the words until they seemed dark stains on a white surface like THIS one, like THIS one.' The story ends with Pollard in this (Eliotesque?) paralysis. Students urge his support for the évènements – he quotes Marx to support De Gaulle and Lenin to condemn the students. In a last cry of loneliness he reverses the conceit of the opening, identifying himself not now with God, but rather with the still bound Prometheus whose picture is the story's final illustration, as it had been its first.

I would like to entwine this story of Gray's with the argument of Martin Bernal in *Black Athena*. He shows that modern historiography and classical studies emergent as a discipline in the eighteenth century and established in the nineteenth as the very cornerstone of the humanities had, whether in history, archeology, philology or textual exegesis, one central, urgent project. This was to refute and discredit the view held by the ancient Greeks themselves – Aeschylus, Herodotos and Plato are cited – that their culture derived from Egyptian and hence black settlement. This was a long and bitterly fought intellectual and political campaign, but staggeringly successful in that by the second half of the nineteenth century it was little short of heretical to agree with the Greeks and posit anything other than an ethnically pure, autochthonous Aryan Ancient Greece. I cannot do justice here to the immense erudition and rich implications of Bernal's work but can perhaps point some intriguing areas of affinity with our own argument. There are some fascinating affinities with Gray. For example just as a key text for Pollard is Aeschylus's supposed second play *Prometheus Bound*, Bernal uses his first, *The Suppliants*. He sees the play as a partly cryptic depiction of what Aeschylus believed to be a historical truth, Greece's origination in Egyptian settlement. He even sees the title as punning on the affinity between the Greek words for 'suppliants' and 'Egyptians'. The intellectual connotations are fascinating – the very source-statement of our autochthonous culture is, self-deconstructively, a demonstration of a prior hybridisation. To quote myself paraphrasing Foucault – 'the apparently authoritative source refers elliptically to something still further back and so on ad infinitum . . .'.

The reader of George Eliot will also be intrigued to learn from Bernal that the French scholar and revolutionary Charles Dupuis wrote a massive work *Origin of all Cults* (1795) which 'argued that all mythologies and religions could be traced to one source' (p.182). Strikingly, in relation to Casaubon's comparable project, Bernal regards this as a genuinely radical revisionist masterwork because the origin it posited was Egyptian rather than Greek. Here is one of the points where the complex and perhaps confused ideological positioning of Bernal's own work surfaces as a problem. On the one hand *Black Athena* is radical in overturning a long-lived, oppressive and ethnically exclusive myth of origination for purely 'Western' – in fact Semitic and Afroasiatic – culture. On the other it merely replaces the top jobs in the historical hierarchy with new candidates selected on equal opportunities principles without disturbing the wearisome arborescent structure of it all and the persistent reactionary model which venerates whatever was there first, grants automatic authority and authenticity to whatever can claim to be pre-established. This surely exhausted model has a new lease of life in *Black Athena* and Bernal's argument needs to engage with positions such as those offered by Foucault and Deleuze and Guattari to liberate its own genuine radical potential. Perhaps my own argument is a sketch of what such an engagement would look like.

I hope readers will see for themselves ways in which both Gray's rehearsal of the issues around history, gender and representation and Bernal's account of how the nineteenth century makes such politically urgent issues out of notions of historical origins and the reconstruction of ancient cultural models resonate with Eliot's dilemma in *Romola*. Why should the woman artist wish to reconstruct a world in which she has never been welcome? The appeal of the Italian Renaissance for a nineteenth-century woman artist must be a curiously ambivalent one. Where there does she find her counterparts? This supposed very acme of cultural achievement and glorious first flowering of all that is best in subsequent Western culture is one in which women appeared to have played no part whatever – except, of course, as objects of representation. This was not in fact entirely the case – see for instance Germaine Greer's championing of the obscured career of painter Artemisia Gentileschi in *The Obstacle Race* (1979). It is true, however, that nineteenth-century representations of the Renaissance, such as Burckhardt's *The Civilisation of the Renaissance in Italy* (1860) with its seminal identification of the period's 'discovery of Man', effectively suppressed recognition of such determining female presence. It is amazing how this historiography never tires of uncovering, wherever it looks, the moment of self-discovery of the male Western humanist subject. The Renaissance, as the nineteenth century understood it, was a double helping of such discovery, both the birth of humanism and the re-discovery of an ancient precurser for that humanism. One wonders whether a history of womens' experience would need to acknowledge the Renaissance as an event at all except as a particularly vigorous stage of the immemorial patriarchal reconstructive project.

As for the discursive context within which Eliot must write, we need only recall our instance of *Salammbô* to illustrate how grossly sexist was the prevailing literary/historical language, rewriting all time so as to place male violence at its core. It centres on the rape by the barbarian leader Matho first of the sacred veil of which Salammbô is the keeper and then, and inevitably, of Salammbô herself. The novel is heterosexual male appetite run riot. The rape scene is one of ludicrous macho prurience with Salammbô agog at the sight of Matho's 'bronze belt set with leather thongs which hung down to his knees, more solid than marble'. A seer Salammbô consults in her distress voices an unequivocally phallocentric creed – 'all that he saw of earthly things forced him to acknowledge the male exterminating principle as supreme' (Flaubert, 1977, p.168) – and one looks in vain for the novel that contains him to offer any higher belief. As a historical reconstruction it seems rather a determined attempt to establish that same principle as the very meaning of history.

A novel which appeals, as *Romola* does, to a sexual justice in the mid nineteenth century is evidently constrained from the word go by the oppressive presuppositions of its age. In *Romola* Eliot works within a triumvirate of superadded constraints: the sexual conservatism of the historical period the novel addresses and the very same sexual ideology as it is reproduced in the nineteenth century through the genre of historical fiction and within the academic historicism she so painstakingly imitates, even out-historicising historicism. Unlike Gray's

Lucie, Eliot does not make the separatist gesture of refusing to amelio-
rate the great patriarchal projects. Indeed she seems to load herself with
a set of titanic tasks of renovation, reconstruction – of antiquity, of the
Renaissance, of the writing of history, of the historical novel. She accepts
the onerous and perhaps self-destructive duty of revising, feminising,
humanising them.

I have so insistently stressed Romola's position because it is evidently
Eliot's own: gingerly turning over the mutilated relics of her patriarchal
inheritance, torn between reverence and revulsion before the detritus to
which she can feel herself being assimilated. I presented Gray's story as
the tense and aborted dialogue between a feminist deconstruction and a
reconstructive romantic liberalism. I would suggest that George Eliot
embodies both figures. They are the oppositely charged poles between
which the current of her art springs. A feminist deconstruction?
Dorothea surveying Rome and its accretions of cruel culture – ancient,
Renaissance, contemporary – with such despair will be at least tweaking
the thread that could unravel that great fabric. And yet Eliot identifies
Casaubon as the figure drawn from her own breast. His work, to which
Dorothea attempts to contribute, will be the great patriarchal reconstructive project – Lydgate, Lawrence, Lukács, Flaubert, Freud and
Pollard are all working on their versions – seen in all its grisly sterility.
Bernal quotes Barthold Niebuhr, author of *History of Rome* (1810–11),
quickly recognised as the foundation of modern classical studies and a
key text in Bernal's depiction of the emergence of a pernicious ethnic
principle in historiography. Niebuhr's serene justification of his enterprise as an ideal reconstruction exactly articulates the normative
assumptions of nineteenth-century historicism with which we have seen
George Eliot has so very problematic a relation.

> I am an historian, for I can make a complete picture from separate
> fragments and once I know where the parts are missing and how
> to fill them up, no one believes how much of what seems lost can
> be restored.
>
> (Bernal, 1987, p.302)

Eliot's project is more complex and onerous. Eliot weaving the web of
her works is like Penelope at hers. She staves off subjection by subvert-
ing the day work of synthesis through the night work of deconstruction.
The danger she fears is that, like the weaving of the Lady of Shalott, all
will unweave to an anarchy that shatters representation, 'Out flew the
web and floated wide | The mirror crack'd from side to side' (ll.114–15).

III
'NO STATUES IN THE UNCONSCIOUS':
Daniel Deronda

The penultimate chapter of *Daniel Deronda* carries an epigraph from *The Prelude*. The epigraph is thus in fact the penultimate literary reference (the final chapter ends with *Samson Agonistes*) of a densely allusive novelistic career and one crucially concerned with the problematic nature of inheritances – financial, literary, cultural, historical, ideological. Since the reference itself is an arresting but ambiguous definition of identities and inheritances and their interdependence one is tempted to seek something definitive within it, a summation.

> The human nature unto which I felt
> That I belonged, and reverenced with love,
> Was not a punctual presence, but a spirit
> Diffused through time and space, with aid derived
> Of evidence from monuments, erect,
> Prostrate, or leaning towards their common rest
> In earth, the widely scattered wreck sublime
> Of vanished nations . . .
> (Wordsworth, *The Prelude*, 1850 version, Book 8, ll.608–15)

The citation is ambiguous, problematic and perhaps, in Eliot's hands, wishful. We have seen how *Middlemarch* pointedly negates 'Tintern Abbey' and the latter's promise of psychic restoration in identification with ruins. Romola feels more ambivalent than Wordsworth here about being defined amidst monuments. What precisely Wordsworth identifies with is itself ambiguous. The assertion of a human identity characterised rather by 'diffusal' than 'presence' seems an anticipatory negation of the enclosed 'individualistic' identities of the nineteenth-century bourgeoisie (Eliot uses the 1850 text, but this only minimally alters this quotation from that of 1804–5). It even anticipates post-modern conceptions of identity, or perhaps this passage might alert us to such conceptions' prior presence within Romanticism. It is in the context of praise of *Frankenstein* (1818) for instance that David Musselwhite offers a quintessentially post-modern definition – 'The self is not an original identity, but the produced effect, mobile rather than static, nomadic rather than fixed, of fabulous plays of differences' (1987, pp.49–50). But Wordsworth predicates this diffused spirit on the emphatically 'static' and 'fixed' Ozymandian 'monuments'. Or perhaps not; these are strangely declining to the 'common rest' which suggests their obliteration. They are 'erect' at the end of one line, 'prostrate' at the start of the next, so one is not sure whether it is their survival as monuments, or their declining to dust which is the characteristic with which the poet identifies. He seems both to affirm and deny an identification with monuments which is itself ambiguous – is it with survival or demise? Shelley conveys a forceful sense of the politics of monuments, a subject about which Wordsworth seems curiously innocent. The 'shattered visage' of Ozymandias still bears the 'sneer of cold command' and the pedestal bears the ironically superseded inscription 'Look on my works ye mighty and despair'. Such politics is much less directly articulated in Wordsworth. The dissolution of the monasteries is not an object of enquiry in 'Tintern Abbey'.

It is easy to understand how the author of *Silas Marner* would be attracted to a definition of 'human nature' that refutes the 'punctual presence', the 'lone thing' as Silas calls himself. Silas is such a presence who wriggles out of his own insistent punctuation. Before the advent of Eppie he is a figure in whom 'thought was arrested' which seems a good definition of the function of punctuation. In this 'ant-like' figure identity is, to use an Eliot phrase from another context, 'pinched to its pilulous smallness'. It is a sign of the nineteenth-century times that this 'punctual presence' can be exactly stated. One could not think of a more crisply exact, indeed punctual, phrase. Its negation, however, and the obscure object of Wordsworth's desire is, like 'the history of the lights and shadows', something not quite articulable. 'With aid derived | Of evidence from' stumbles as a phrase as if the master cannot quite get to his meaning. For all the impalpability there remains something haunting and provocative in the image of the sublimely diffused, historical self. Here is a radically alternative and seemingly liberated identity; a function of, but not quite identified with, historical monuments and inscriptions, objects themselves riven with historicity, change and decline. Here is a massive, ruinous historical meaning scattered far beyond the enclosures of monadic selfhood.

Perhaps the most remarkable features of Eliot's oeuvre are the leaps – ethical, thematic, methodological – she makes between novels. Each work starts again, as it were, from a degree zero of literature, thoroughly revising and reappraising the ethical and aesthetic assumptions of its predecessors. It is surely characteristic of her that having written *Middlemarch* – that prodigious and paradigmatic realist text – her next novel is in so many ways even more ambitious and ambiguous, the 'singularly dark and glittering' (Beer, 1986, p.228) *Daniel Deronda* in which all Eliot readers recognise a new voice. I have tried to suggest precise parallels between Eliot and Matthew Arnold, but one never senses in Eliot what Hardy so justly sensed in Arnold when he paid him the double-edged compliment of being 'a finished writer' (T. Hardy, 1982 (1), p.437). George Eliot seems always to be beginning again, not least of all in this final novel which itself begins with a famous meditation on the nature of beginnings. What we sense new in the tone of *Daniel Deronda* is difficult to articulate precisely except we might call it menace, a sense of violence coiled at the heart of things. Everywhere the novel registers the nuanced workings of power and particularly their diffusal through sexual relations. The especial brilliance of the Gwendolen plot is its evocation of the tissue of covert coercions, of violences cloaked, transmuted and internalised to which the heroine, with only partial awareness, is subject. These erode with grim relentlessness a vain and naive woman's illusion of her own pre-eminence. Gwendolen is painfully disabused of her sense of feminine command within a society – or that section of society which calls itself Society – that allows women only an illusory, metaphoric power. Exactly registered is a sense of the violence latent within the drill of sexual decencies and deferences by which men regulate human relations, issues focused in Grandcourt's stately sadism and in an insistent patterning of antithetical motifs of stasis and action. 'The correct Englishman, drawing himself up from his bow into rigidity, assenting severely, and seeming to be in a state of internal drill, suggests a suppressed vivacity, and may be suspected of letting go with some violence when he is released from parade . . . ' (G. Eliot, 1984 (2), p.145).

Of course thematic concerns persist through Eliot's fiction, but their forms of presentation are mercurial, all their shapes and figures revised. I have focused in this and the previous chapter on the repetition and revision of certain key scenes or settings in which Eliot protagonists are variously linked or juxtaposed to cultural artefacts that oppress or negate them: Dorothea alienated amidst Rome's culture, Romola surrounded by her father's antiquarian collection, Silas with the cold comfort of his hoard of coins. In this section I want to examine just one key scene in *Daniel Deronda* which reworks and extends this nexus of concerns and is also charged with the pain and urgency which is this novel's particular stress: Gwendolen's fractured playing of Hermione in the tableau-vivant she stages of the statue-scene from *The Winter's Tale*. I hope to draw a thread of connection between this scene in which in effect Eliot doubles Shakespeare's device and shows a monument turn into a woman turn into a monument and Wordsworth's ambiguous vision of the possibility of a historical self, strangely both predicated on, and yet freed from the fixity of, monuments. Clearly the psychology of containment and stasis of which Gwendolen's story is an elaboration has here a complex articulation.

The tableau of Hermione was doubly striking from its dissimilarity with what had gone before: it was answering perfectly, and a murmur of applause had been gradually suppressed while Leontes gave his permission that Paulina should exercise her utmost art and make the statue move.

Hermione, her arm resting on a pillar, was elevated by about six inches, which she counted on as a means of showing her pretty foot and instep, when at the given signal she should advance and descend.

'Music, awake her, strike!' said Paulina (Mrs Davilow, who by special entreaty had consented to take part in a white burnous and hood).

Herr Klesmer, who had been good-natured enough to seat himself at the piano, struck a thunderous chord – but in the same instant, and before Hermione put forth her foot, the moveable panel, which was on a line with the piano, flew open on the right opposite the stage and disclosed the picture of the dead face and the fleeting figure, brought out in pale definiteness by the position of the wax-lights. Everyone was startled, but all eyes in the act of turning towards the opened panel were recalled by a piercing cry from Gwendolen, who stood without change of attitude, but with a change of expression that was terrifying in its terror. She looked like a statue into which a soul of Fear had entered: her pallid lips were parted; her eyes, usually narrowed under their long lashes, were dilated and fixed. Her mother, less surprised than alarmed, rushed towards her, and Rex too could not help going to her side. But the touch of her mother's arm had the effect of an electric charge; Gwendolen fell on her knees and put her hands before her face. She was still trembling, but mute, and it seemed that she had self-consciousness enough to aim at controlling her signs of terror, for she presently allowed herself to be raised from her kneeling posture and led away, while the company were relieving their minds by explanation.

(G. Eliot, 1984 (2), pp.91–2)

For me this scene, in which the woman identified with a statue (Gwendolen is frequently so identified) is arrested at the very moment of being roused to life, is the high-point of Eliot's art. I cannot think of a comparable scene in fiction in which an author has achieved the forceful articulation of so many of her long-considered themes. All the essential issues discussed in relation to *Middlemarch*, *Silas Marner* and *Romola* are here: the woman quelled and stilled, the possibilities and impossibilities of action, the need to be roused to life, a fraught and ambivalent relation to antiquity and one's own assimilation within it, anxiety over an art threatening to freeze into Arnoldian reification (Gillian Beer has observed how the novel's surge of emotions keeps 'freezing into tableaux' (Beer, 1986, p.214)), the abortion of play and representation. As an elaborate Shakespearean reference the scene is a radical, indeed iconoclastic, revision. Eliot shatters the scene's wonted meaning, scoring through with panic a moment famed as ineffable, serene. In a recent assessment Wilbur Sanders finds something rapturous in Shakespeare's enactment of stone becoming flesh, a gesture pregnant with humanist promise. The issue that we have seen to be so problematic for Eliot – how to be roused to life – is worked into a sublime affirmation.

> You might almost say that this is the single most important discovery of *The Winter's Tale* – the discovery of warmth. The word echoes throughout the last scene. And perhaps its most healing aspect is its simplicity as sensation. In that absolving simplicity, its adversary, numbness can be finally bequeathed to death where it belongs. Stone becomes flesh. Dear life redeems it. Breath parts the lips that seemed eternally stilled, for 'The very life seems warm upon her lip'. If Leontes, after that embrace, has very little to say, it is because he has only one thing to say, only two words left in his vocabulary: 'warm life'. And the wonder of that subsumes everything else.
>
> (Sanders, 1987, p.118)

Evidently for Sanders Shakespeare's statue-scene is the high-point of a positively sacramental Renaissance humanism which is itself still 'warm' and contact with which is rejuvenation – warmth in a winter's tale. For me Eliot's statue-scene is the high-point of the nineteenth century's very different art where humanism is cut through with contradiction, arrested at the very moment of its apparent assertion. Eliot seems regularly to risk the coherence of her own work in set-piece scenes that test to breaking-point some of the innermost presuppositions of the realist mode. Romola amidst her father's collection exposes as oppressive and problematic the profound association Brecht identifies between realist representation and acquisition/accumulation. Dorothea's experience of Rome as unsurveyably conflictual and chaotic is the occasion for questioning the premise of an objective seeing and the conception of cultural coherence and continuity that underwrites it. When Silas breaks his beloved pot and keeps the useless fragments as a memorial, Eliot suggests an act of mourning for a lost intimacy between humanity and the object, for the now severed relation of subjectivity and the world of things. The recovery or synthesis of such relation is another key realist premise (or promise). Now here in Gwendolen's strangely arrested statue-scene realism's humanist premises, its claim to be animated by lived experience, are challenged.

One might note that, in this extract at least, it is the scene as experienced by Leontes that Sanders depicts, not the woman's experience of being the stone that becomes flesh which was Eliot's emphasis and which Sanders for all his empathy and psychological reconstruction leaves unimagined. *The Winter's Tale* seems to speak with a particular urgency to the nineteenth century and this scene specifically carries an extraordinary charge, the moment of transformation for a woman it depicts a focus of strange pressures and contradictions. This is how it is described by Helena Faucitt, an acclaimed Victorian actress whom Eliot admired and visited. There is evidence that *The Spanish Gypsy* (1868) began as a play in which Eliot intended Faucitt to star. Hermione was a favourite role but the statue-scene was for the actress a strange meeting-point of strains and pressures that was gruelling to perform.

The arm and hand were gently lifted from the pedestal; then, rhythmically following the music, the figure descended the steps that led up to the dias, and advancing slowly, paused at a short distance from Leontes. Oh, can I ever forget Mr Macready at this point! At first he stood speechless, as if turned to stone; his face with an awe-struck look upon it. Could this, the very counterpart of his queen, be a wondrous piece of mechanism? Could art so mock life? He had seen her laid out as dead, the funeral obsequies performed over her, with her dear son beside her. Thus absorbed in wonder, he remained until Paulina said, 'Nay, present your hand'. Tremblingly he advanced, and touched gently the hand held out to him. Then what a cry came with, 'O, she's warm!' It is impossible to describe Mr Macready here. He was Leontes' very self. His passionate joy at finding Hermione really alive seemed beyond control. Now he was prostrate at her feet, then enfolding her in his arms. I had a slight veil or covering over my head and neck, supposed to make the statue look older. This fell off in an instant. The hair, which came unbound, and fell on my shoulders, was reverently kissed and caressed. The whole change was so sudden, so overwhelming, that I suppose I cried out hysterically, for he whispered to me, 'Don't be frightened, my child! don't be frightened! Control yourself!'. All this went on during a tumult of applause that sounded like a storm of hail. Oh, how glad I was to be released, when, as soon as a lull came. Paulina advancing with Perdita, said, 'Turn, good lady, our Perdita is found'. A broken, trembling voice, I am sure, was mine, as I said, 'You gods, look down', etc.

(Faucitt, 1887, p.390)

Here is the very inversion of Sanders's hushed humanist sublime. Sanders had compared the reunion of Leontes and Hermione to that of Coriolanus and Virgilia and their kiss with which 'all the structures of military domination crumble into insignificance' (Sanders, 1987, p.118). Here a strangely frantic Macready is quick to assert domination at the moment which might seem to dissolve it. He runs the gamut of stereotypical nineteenth-century male responses to woman, in quick-fire declension – reverence, affection, despoiling and command. He turns the wife into the daughter requiring first protection – 'Don't be frightened, my child!' – and then firmly quelled at the very moment of her supposed self-assertion – 'Control yourself!' commands a Leontes, himself 'beyond control'. This statue-scene is like Eliot's in provoking panic and being one where the woman's moment of action is forcefully checked. Faucitt's experience is evidently threaded with panic that turns apparent adoration into an act of violence. A Macready 'beyond control' despoils her dress and hair, so disorientating her that she only 'supposes' that she cried out – with that degrading woman-word upon which Freud founds a science – 'hysterically'. Even the applause is cruel Lear-weather.

Macready is over-acting, in a precise use of the term. He evidently cannot bear that the woman at her moment of assertion can be the centre of attention and ensures that her single gesture is swamped with his excess of male action/acting. For Faucitt the tension between her need to act – Shakespeare's scene is essentially the beautifully concentrated staging of a woman *acting* – and Macready's need to turn her back into an object of contemplation, controlled and stilled by her own will and his male imperative, amounts to a terrifying moment of panic and debility. She sounds here like Gwendolen suffering one of her attacks of existential anxiety 'in the midst of which she was helplessly incapable of asserting herself' (G. Eliot, 1984 (2), p.95). Gwendolen is a sufferer from the psychic malaise described by Baudelaire as 'oases of panic in a desert of ennui' ('La Mort').

'There is no action possible without a little acting' comments Eliot's Sir Hugo. Equally there is no acting possible without a little action, but in Eliot's scene even the most minimal action – the tableau is to be momentarily animated by Gwendolen's single gesture of descending from her pedestal – is instantly extinguished by the spell of reification. The tableau had been fittingly described, in a tautology to ponder, as a mere 'imitation of acting' (G. Eliot, 1984 (2), p.90). As a chill evocation of performance Gorgonised the passage re-states as crisis Dickens's comic stroke when in *Great Expectations* (1860–61) Pip describes Mr Wopsle's performance as Hamlet in Arnoldian terms as 'massive and concrete' (Dickens, 1986, p.277). Reification is evidently so much more than a theoretical construct, a passage such as this registers the fear of it with vivid anguish.

The denial of action, and particularly the artistic representaion of such, is a source of disquiet for Arnold and in one sense Eliot had dramatised his anxieties when he asks

> What then are the situations, from the representation of which, though accurate, no poetical enjoyment can be derived? They are those in which the suffering finds no vent in action; in which a continuing state of mental distress is prolonged, unrelieved by incident, hope, or resistance; in which there is everything to be endured, nothing to be done.
>
> (Arnold, 1987, pp.655–6)

Eliot even more than Arnold is the great nineteenth-century artist of the crisis where there is nothing to be done:

> For a long while she had been oppressed by the indefiniteness which hung in her mind, like a thick summer haze, over all her desire to make her life greatly effective. What could she do, what ought she to do?
>
> (G. Eliot, 1981, p.50)

> 'But what can I do?' she went on, more quickly. 'I must get up in the morning and do what every one else does. It is all like a dance set beforehand'.
>
> (G. Eliot, 1984 (2), p.507)

> 'I must do as other men do, and think what will please the world and bring in money . . . that is the sort of shell I must creep into and try to keep my soul alive in'.
>
> (G. Eliot, 1981, p.825)

> 'I can do so little – have I done it well?' is the perpetually recurring thought . . .
>
> (G. Eliot, 1973, pp.214–5)

Daniel Deronda is patterned as a great, unresolved dialectic between 'event' and 'deadlock'. In the Daniel and Mordecai relation and their vision of a galvanised Jewish world-consciousness, the issues are writ large as the shadowy possibility of a world-historical change. Mordecai conceives the whole Jewish mission as the necessary realisation of choice and action. 'Shall man, whose soul is set in the royalty of discernment and resolve, deny his rank and say, I am an onlooker, ask no choice or purpose of me? That is the blasphemy of this time. The divine principle of our race is action, choice, resolved memory.' In Gwendolen's financial and psychological oppressions, her soured ambitions and tyrannical marriage, the same dialectic is enacted in close focus; private, localised, lost to history. The craving for event is the same, whether that event be marriage or a messiah. Daniel asks 'But how and whence was the needed event to come?' Gwendolen, considering Grandcourt's proposal, contemplates in her own terms the difference between 'event' and 'deadlock'. 'The young activity within her made a warm current through her terror and stirred towards something that would be an event – towards an opportunity in which she could look and speak with the former effectiveness. The interest of the morrow was no longer at a deadlock' (G. Eliot, 1984 (2), p.598; p.413; p.337).

I am trying to formulate something which, I will admit, is not absolutely within my grasp – with the perhaps partial justification that neither was it really within Wordsworth's or Eliot's and found in them only ambiguous or fractured articulation. Since it is only a projection, a possibility, it is perhaps not fully articulable until the society comes about that could realise it. In Eliot's statue-scene the Arnoldian statue-world and its refusal of action is, if not toppled, then at least momentarily shaken. For an instant Eliot articulates the panic of containment within such a world and dreams the possibility of release from it. Like Wordworth imagining a diffused, dispersed, richly historical self, she imagines identity freed of reification, though she does not seem able to do it without panic and an almost immediate retreat. Gwendolen is quickly again 'like a statue' within a novel which itself habitually 'freezes into tableaux'.

In *Anti-Oedipus: Capitalism and Schizophrenia* Deleuze and Guattari synthesise into a single anti-capitalist critique elements and motifs dispersed through my own work. They see the oppressions of nineteenth-century Hellenism with its fetishism of archetypes and the tragic, mythic figures as complicit with an industrial capitalism fetishistic of objects and rendering its human subjects as such objects. *Black Athena* with its insight into the politics of such Hellenism provides another strand we can entwine with their critique. Freud they judge an elaborator rather than a critic of these 'Hellenistic' emphases. Deleuze and Guattari's particular anathema is, as their title suggests, what I have discussed as the archaeologial strand in Freud: his love of mythic figures, tragedy, statuary, his poring over the unconscious as over 'the mutilated relics of antiquity', all castigated by Deleuze and Guattari in terms of their metonym, the Oedipus complex. Freud has merely helped us internalise the mythic bric-a-brac beloved of nineteenth-century ideology, images of which crammed his own consulting room, so that we even believe it to occupy an unconscious from which it can never be extirpated. We are thus perfected as bourgeois subjects: securely located within the tragic neurosis of an infinitely recessive subjectivity whose field of play is solely childhood/familial crisis with no larger conception of society or history. Oedipus and the ego must be dethroned (perhaps by Prometheus – or Antigone?).

In the nineteenth century, the argument goes, the fetishised mythic figures were never anything other than disguised images of the nineteenth century's real fetish, capital. 'Capitalism is constructed on the ruins of the territorial and the despotic, the mythic and the tragic representations, but it re-established them in its own service and in another form, as images of capital' (1984, p.303). Deleuze and Guattari cite approvingly what they see as Nietzsche's conversion whereby he came to reject the tragic representations venerated in *The Birth of Tragedy* (1872) and Engels whom they cite as commenting incredulously on nineteenth-century Hellenists 'you'd think they really believed in all this – in myth, in tragedy' (1984, p.303; p.338). Instead of the oppressions of psychoanalysis they propose the liberation of their own 'schizoanalysis' which aims to fragment the conception of personal identity. This conception they see as in collusion with those other pernicious constructions – temporal sequence, historical process and even the very inter-relation of belief, action and event. All these are disintegrated by their critique as is any global account of reason, history, progress. The first job is to reject the old models.

> The schizoanalyst is not an interpreter, even less a theater director; he is a mechanic, a micromechanic. There are no excavations to be undertaken, no archaeology, no statues in the unconscious: there are only stones to be sucked, à la Beckett, and other machinic elements belonging to deterritorialized constellations.
>
> (Deleuze and Guattari, 1984, p.338)

The ideas of Adorno and Deleuze and Guattari enter into configuration. *Prisms* and *Anti-Oedipus* both dream the possibility of a dispersed, historical identity, encompassing cultural artefacts but not identified with them, a transcendence equally of monadic selfhood and the capitalist chaos of cultural goods. Deleuze and Guattari castigate Freud for keeping sexuality within the tight frame of Narcissus and Oedipus, the ego and the family, and for refusing to believe that the libido 'invests' the social field. Their argument sounds like a gloss on our extract from *The Prelude*.

> We have seen on the contrary that what the libido invested, through its loves and sexuality, was the social field itself in its economic, political, historical, racial, and cultural determinations: in delirium the libido is continually re-creating History, continents, kingdoms, races and cultures. Not that it is advisable to put historical representations in the place of the familial representations of the Freudian unconscious, or even the archetypes of a collective unconscious. It is merely a question of ascertaining that our choices in matters of love are at the crossroads of 'vibrations', which is to say that they express connections, disjunctions, and conjunctions of flows that cross through a society, entering and leaving it, linking it up with other societies, ancient or contemporary, remote or vanished, dead or yet to be born. Africas and Orients, always following the underground thread of the libido. Not geohistorical figures or statues, although our apprenticeship is more readily accomplished with these figures, with books, histories, and reproductions, than with our mommy.
>
> (Deleuze and Guattari, 1984, p.352)

Adorno finds comparable possibilities in Proust, an artist in whom the influences of both Eliot and Hardy are generously acknowledged – characters translate Eliot and Marcel has a particular fondness for *The Well-Beloved*. Eliot particularly would surely recognise her own ambition for art in Adorno's formulation that in Proust we sense how an art disenchanted from its wonted alienation 'returns . . . to life'.

> The procedure which today relegates every work of art to the museum, even Picasso's most recent sculpture, is irreversible. It is not solely reprehensible, however, for it presages a situation in which art, having completed its estrangement from human ends, returns, in Novalis' words, to life. One senses something of this in Proust's novel, where physiognomies of paintings and people

131

glide into one another almost without a break and memory traces of experience fuse with those of musical passages. In one of the most explicit passages in the work, the description of falling asleep on the first page of *Du côté de chez Swann*, the narrator says, 'It seemed to me that I was the thing the book was about: a church, a quartet, the rivalry between Francis the First and Charles the Fifth'. This is the reconciliation of that split which Valéry so irreconcilably laments. The chaos of cultural goods fades into the bliss of the child whose body feels itself at one with the nimbus of distance.

(Adorno, 1983, p.185)

Eliot is not Proust and she would balk at the tremendous shattering of tradition which is one aspect of the modernism of which he is an exemplar – though in another respect Proust is the twentieth century's great recuperator of nineteenth-century realism in extravagantly over-elaborated, even self-parodic, forms. Only fleetingly and in ways that threaten the whole stability of her realist project does Eliot sketch this possibility of the rejection of the 'chaos of cultural goods', of a diffused identity liberated rather than burdened by its rich historicity, a field of monuments, conflicts and artefacts, and at one with – Hardyesque phrase – 'the nimbus of distance'.

STASIS, SIGNS AND SPECULATION

Nostromo and history

THE NAME OF NOWHERE

Joseph Conrad admired Henry James to idolatry and enshrined his enthusiasm in 'Henry James: An Appreciation' (1921). There is one point, however, on which Conrad feels he must dissent from the master. He is unhappy with James's equation of the novelist and the historian. James had written:

> It is impossible to imagine what a novelist takes himself to be unless he regard himself as a historian and his narrative as a history. It is only as a historian that he has the smallest *locus standi*. As a narrator of fictitious events he is nowhere; to insert into his attempts a backbone of logic, he must relate events that are assumed to be real. This assumption permeates, animates all the work of the most solid storytellers . . .
>
> (James, 1987, 'Anthony Trollope', p.178)

Conrad readers will understand his discomfort. What James regards as prerequisites for novel-writing – firm ground under one's feet, a secure grasp of the real, a sense of personal solidity – always eluded Conrad. These things were what his fiction sought, not the pre-established conditions of its creation. James's term for what fiction must contain, 'backbone', would have had a chill reverberation for the author of 'Heart of Darkness' with that work's astonishingly sustained permutation of the imagery of bones, teeth, skeletons, ribs, skulls, raw ivory and its products, billiard-balls and piano-keys. Marlow, like James, admires backbone, which is exactly what one would expect from an Edwardian narrator. The term seems to crystallise the normative values of the age. He is impressed by the dapper Company Accountant who is eternally in starched collars and cuffs even when surrounded by dead and dying Congolese: 'in the great demoralisation of the land he kept up his appearances. That's backbone' (Conrad, 1981, p.26). Two paragraphs earlier had ended with the head of a skeletal Congolese falling wearily upon his 'breastbone', another victim of the ivory exploiters' 'back-breaking' trade. That also is backbone.

Conrad's response to James makes some striking claims for the relations between fiction, history and truth.

> In one of his critical studies, published some fifteen years ago, Mr Henry James claims for the novelist the standing of the historian as the only adequate one, as for himself and before his audience. I think that the claim cannot be contested, and that the position is unassailable. Fiction is history, human history, or it is nothing. But it is also more than that; it stands on firmer ground, being based on the reality of forms and the observation of social phenomena, whereas history is based on documents, and the reading of print and handwriting – on second-hand impression. Thus fiction is nearer truth. But let that pass. A historian may be an artist too, and a novelist is a historian, the preserver, the keeper, the expounder, of human experience.
>
> (Conrad, 1986 (2), pp.65–6)

Conrad makes striking distinctions. History's relation to truth is oblique and thoroughly mediated, truth having to be inferred from implicitly unreliable interventions of documentation, deciphering and hearsay. Fiction's relation to truth, however, is immediate – unmediated. Fiction is founded on the real and material and partakes rather of the directness of seeing – 'observation' – than the obliqueness of writing. These distinctions seem to reverse the most basic and familiar of received assumptions: that while fiction is opaquely literary, existing only as 'documents' and conveying authorial 'second-hand impression', history claims a more direct relation to truth.

In the preceding paragraph Conrad had made a very direct statement that history is, in essence, conflict. He has evoked the death-throes of civilisation when a single artist, reduced to a voice speaking out in the growing gloom of the dark night of the world's destruction, will speak a final, hopeful utterance. This figure sounds very like Marlow as he is introduced in 'Heart of Darkness', heard rather than seen amidst the 'brooding gloom' of sunset over the Thames. This utterance 'Will sleep on the battlefield among its own dead, in the manner of an army having won a barren victory. It will not know when it is beaten'. He then justifies his 'warlike images' which 'come by themselves under the pen; since from the duality of man's nature and the competition of individuals, the life-history of the earth must in the last instance be a history of really very relentless warfare' (Conrad, 1986 (2), p.65).

For a moment Conrad voices a classic Marxist position of history as 'relentless warfare'. He echoes Engels who had argued that 'Competition is the completest expression of the battle of all against all which rules in modern civil society' (Engels, 1987, p.111). He also echoes a Marxist position that in a conflictual culture, individual psychology is itself correspondingly riven with contradiction. However, Conrad seems to balk at the central innovation of Marxist analysis that it is social being that precedes and determines consciousness rather than the other way round; for Conrad here a seemingly immutable 'duality of Man's nature' precipitates historical conflict, rather than historical conflict precipitating a historically specific division within consciousness. He reaches a Marxist conclusion through non-Marxist premises.

That a specifically Marxist position on history concerned Conrad is evident from the fact that such an analysis is the object of satire when Michaelis in *The Secret Agent* holds forth on history, his argument drawing heavily on Marx's great historiographic meditation, *The Eighteenth Brumaire of Louis Bonaparte* (1851). 'History is made by men, but they do not make it in their heads. The ideas that are born in their consciousness play an insignificant part in the march of events. History is dominated and determined by the tool and the production – by the force of economic conditions' (Conrad, 1980, p.42).

It is clear that Michaelis, the over-fed pet of a trendy lady aristocrat, is the target of some really rather cheap and irrelevant authorial satire which Conrad seems to keep in store for characters who voice socialist positions.

> He had come out of a highly hygienic prison round like a tub, with an enormous stomach and distended cheeks of a pale, semi-transparent complexion, as though for fifteen years the servants of an outraged society had made a point of stuffing him with fattening foods . . . and ever since he had not managed to get his weight down by an ounce.
>
> (Conrad, 1980 (1), p.42)

But in *Nostromo* the narrator articulates a perspective on history's cause and effect which is very close to Michaelis's materialist position. 'Material changes swept along in the train of material interests. And other changes more subtle, outwardly unmarked, affected the minds and hearts of the workers' (Conrad, 1986 (1), p.417). The causal sequence here is clear; material interests effect material changes which themselves bring about mental and emotional changes in individuals. This was in essence Michaelis's argument, that economic conditions drive all before them, consciousness, a wonted explanation for historical change in the 'humano-anecdotical' school, included.

Two passages concerned with imagining history will focus and expand these issues. Both from the opening of 'Heart of Darkness', they are opposed versions of Britain's colonial history. The novella's initial narrator eulogises Tudor colonial adventurers.

> The tidal current runs to and fro in its unceasing service, crowded with memories of men and ships it had borne to the rest of home or to the battles of the sea. It had known and served all the men of whom the nation is proud, from Sir Francis Drake to Sir John Franklin, knights all, titled and untitled – the great knights-errant of the sea. It had borne all the ships whose names are like jewels flashing in the night of time, from the *Golden Hind* returning with her round flanks full of treasure, to be visited by the Queen's Highness and thus pass out of the gigantic tale, to the *Erebus* and *Terror*, bound on other conquests – and that never returned. It had known the ships and the men. They had sailed from Deptford, from Greenwich, from Erith – the adventurers and the settlers; kings' ships and the ships of men on 'Change; captains, admirals, the dark 'interlopers' of the Eastern trade, and the commissioned 'generals' of the East India fleets. Hunters for gold or pursuers of fame, they all had gone out on that stream, bearing the sword, and often the torch, messengers of the might within the land, bearers of a spark from the sacred fire. What greatness had not floated on the ebb of that river into the mystery of an unknown earth! . . . The dreams of men, the seed of commonwealths, the germs of empires.
>
> (Conrad, 1981, p.7)

There are a number of ironies here it is hardly necessary to point out: the germs of empires that could be the sort that are spread rather than sown, ships named *Erebus* and *Terror* as if as metonyms for their enterprise, torches that could illuminate or ignite, the 'gigantic tale' of colonial history which might well be a big lie. More interestingly perhaps colonial history is pictured in terms of the medium through which its traffic was conducted – not London and colonial settlements, but the Thames and the ocean, the space between centres of dominion, the traffic between centre and outposts. What constitutes the *activity* of colonial ventures is thoroughly obscured. The succession of nouns designating colonial agents – 'Hunters', 'pursuers', 'bearers', 'messengers' – slides from a sense of an *activity* of colonialism to a mere sense of *mediation*. Agents are 'messengers of the might within the land'. In fact the term 'agent' – rather as in the title and novel of *The Secret Agent* – is rendered problematic.

'The mystery of an unknown earth!' 'Mystery' and the 'unknown' are, for colonialism, both the inherent qualities of the uncolonised territories and peoples and also strategies which inhere in the activities of the colonial venture itself. Colonial activity is by definition conducted at a far remove from those inhabitants of the colonising power whose acquiescence, or positive enthusiasm, is – in a nominal democracy – required to endorse it. Its site of activity is the far-flung 'outpost of progress'. Geographically and morally it takes place at 'the end of the tether'. As Marlow says of his Congo experience, 'It was the the farthest point of navigation and the culminating point of my experience'. Speaking to Antonia, Decoud in *Nostromo* – the work Conrad describes as 'my remote novel' – describes history in terms which rework precisely these emphases.

> 'No, but just imagine our forefathers in morions and corselets drawn up outside this gate, and a band of adventurers just landed from their ships in the harbour there. Thieves, of course. Speculators, too. Their expeditions, each one, were the speculations of grave and reverend persons in England. That is history, as that absurd sailor Mitchell is always saying'.
>
> (Conrad, 1986 (1), p.168)

History is the distance – geographical and moral – between the intentions of 'grave and reverend persons' who promote colonial expeditions, and the activities of the armed 'thieves' and 'adventurers' themselves in far off territories, never fully observed. The term 'speculation' links their activities linguistically where there is little link in terms of knowledge. The 'speculations' (financial adventuring) of colonial agents are the 'speculation' (conjecture) of those who send them in hope of profit. In a sense 'speculation' is being misused here with the cavalier aplomb typical of the coloniser's appropriation of language – it has been completely stripped of its root meaning of 'observation'. History is here precisely that which is *not* observed. Colonial agents are all 'secret agents'. 'The speculations of grave and reverend persons in England' could refer to the whole gamut of pro-colonial discourses ungrounded in observation – legal, journalistic, parliamentary, religious and fictional. History is doubly 'speculation' – an entrepreneurial venture and an unverifiable conjecture.

If history is a kind of tenuous mediation between mutually unknowing activities, then so, in a sense, is language, which can thus be utilised as a natural ally of history under this obfuscating guise. Here language is made to play a crucial role, bearing the responsibility for articulating colonialism's meaning which few, other of course than colonised populations and colonising forces, see or experience. Language under such circumstances enjoys a large degree of autonomy, not having visual or experiential evidence to compete with since it addresses something which does not actually pass under one's observation. The nub of colonial activity is always 'hidden out of sight somewhere' as Marlow says of the natives suffering the onslaught of the French man o'war firing blindly into the obscuring bush in an incident paradigmatic of the unseeing, unconscious, mediated death-dealing of colonial conquest. Language and colonialism are both forms of mediation. Conrad makes a central observation about the referenceless discourse of colonialism in the figure of Kurtz, who speaks and writes with thrilling 'eloquence' and yet commits 'unspeakable acts'. Speech is cut free from reference to action. Thus the narrator here, as colonialism's apologist, glories in colonial history as a play of 'names', splendidly detached from reference, flashing out from a void 'like jewels flashing in the night of time'. Names can be put to some things, not to others – colonial history, like its heroes, remains both 'titled and untitled'. The colonies themselves – and their native inhabitants – seem to be the unlocated, unnameable nowhere. Ships simply 'return' – where from? – their 'round flanks' now mysteriously 'full of treasure', the highpoint of their career being purely ceremonial, 'visited by the Queen's Highness'. The discourse of colonialism is structured on the model indicated by the manager when he has a round table constructed to pre-empt squabbling over precedence amongst his agents, 'Where he sat was the first place – the rest was nowhere'. It is as just such an unlocated, unnameable, nowhere that uncolonised territories are represented on the maps that fascinate Marlow as a boy – challengingly mysterious 'blank spaces on the earth' as yet unviolated by naming. The Congo is 'the biggest, the most blank', although 'it had got filled since my boyhood with rivers and lakes and names'. Colonialism is the inscribing of previously blank spaces with exported 'names'. This is almost ludicrously evident in maps of the Congo of the 1880s, where the ironically entitled 'Free State' is littered with variants on the names of its Western 'discoverer' and owner labelling its geographical features – Stanleyville, Stanley Falls, Stanley Pool, Lake Leopold II, Leopoldville.

All this is evidenced in the opening narrator's eulogy of the 'knights-errant' of Tudor colonialism with its unmistakable reference to contemporary colonialism, conducted by those Kipling praised as 'The New Knighthood'. But in 'Heart of Darkness' this historical vision is not allowed to stand alone and is immediately countered by Marlow who imagines Britain's colonial history under quite different lights. He imagines ancient Britain, the victim rather than the victor of colonialism, and seen from the perspective of the conquerors. He gives an image of history that is a precise inversion of the initial narrator's. He imagines the feelings of a Roman invader sensing 'the utter savagery' of ancient Britain close around him.

The discourse of colonialism is a paradigm of ideologically bound language in the metaphysical tradition as Derrida has described it in carving reality into binary oppositions, one term dominant, the other secondary. The initial narrator's eulogy has such a morally loaded dualistic structure – 'the rest of home . . . the battles of the sea', 'the adventurers and the settlers', 'bearing the sword, and often the torch', 'hunters for gold or pursuers of fame', 'the titled and the untitled', as well as dividing the world in accordance with the manager's managing model whereby where power sits is 'the first place' and everywhere else 'nowhere'. The metaphysical, binary mode of thought has been identified, particularly within feminism, as essentially predicated on conflict and, to use Conrad's term, 'a really very relentless warfare'. Hélène Cixous, appropriating Derrida's arguments for feminism, indicates how the death-dealing binary oppositions upon which patriarchal discourse is founded – the Ur-opposition of which, from the feminist perspective, is man/woman – require urgent deconstruction. She locates death at work in this kind of thought and discourse. For one of the terms to acquire meaning, she claims, it must destroy the other. The 'couple' cannot be left intact: it becomes a general battlefield where the struggle for supremacy is forever re-enacted (Moi, 1985, pp.104–5). In *Under Western Eyes* Razumov compiles his own list of such oppositions, seen precisely as antagonists, and headed by History.

> History not Theory.
> Patriotism not Internationalism.
> Evolution not Revolution.
> Direction not Destruction.
> Unity not Disruption.
>
> (Conrad, 1979, p.62)

Marlow's account of Roman Britain is structured so as to undermine this mode of thought and discourse. The passage is based on reversals – centrally Britain as colony rather than imperial centre. Britain here is the 'unknown' 'nowhere' – 'mysterious', 'the very end of the world', 'lost in a wilderness'. History for the initial narrator was the unfolding of 'a gigantic tale' which, ironic connotations aside, suggests the secure progress of sequential time. Marlow collapses historical time into a moment; Britain was apparently a colony only yesterday, time is both an eternity and an instant – 'nineteen hundred years ago – the other day', 'we live in a flicker – may it last as long as the old earth keeps rolling!'

The most fundamental of these oppositions upon which colonial discourse is structured, conqueror/conquered, is undermined by the very juxtaposition of the opposed versions of British history. In his final soliloquy, Othello kills himself as the climax to a story of how

> . . . a malignant and a turban'd Turk
> Beat a Venetian, and traduc'd the state,
> I took by the throat the circumcised dog,
> And smote him thus.

> (V.ii.354–7)

Thus he dies, 'Perplexed in the extreme' in one sense through embodying the dual figure of conquered and conqueror, both avenger of Venetian honour and Turkish victim of that revenge. Othello, Moorish agent of Venetian power defending its Cypriot colony from Turkish invasion, dies unable to sustain the overlaid contradictions of being both agent and victim of imperial power. Conrad's use of the opposed versions of British history as the opening to 'Heart of Darkness' seems to be sketching a similar schizophrenic psychology in British history and identity, where the figures of oppressor and victim have become confounded. So Marlow's opening to his Congo narrative is a radical gesture of historical deconstruction; reversing the figures, inverting the hierarchies and unravelling the oppositions that structure the colonial discourse of which the initial narrator's Tudor eulogy is a model. The passage forcefully indicates that the power to name and categorise other people's reality always falls to the conquerors. This narrative beginning is a powerful paradigm of how Conrad habitually depicts history – a 'gigantic tale' that can be inverted and all its figures reversed.

So, in short, Conrad's historical concerns focus three overlapping issues. First, fiction must clearly distinguish itself from historical discourse. Received history is a tissue of mediations – 'based on documents, on the reading of print and handwriting – on second hand impression' which always needs to be approached with Marlow's caution, 'If we can believe what we read'. This sets it in opposition to fiction, which, being 'based on the reality of forms and the observation of social phenomena' is 'nearer truth'. Second, history is a site of conflict – material, ideological and linguistic – where the struggle for signifying supremacy is continually re-enacted. Discourses struggle to assert their rival claims to authenticity rendering history 'a gigantic tale' all of whose figures and meanings can be reversed in alternative tellings. Third, Conrad is much exercised by a contradiction inherent in the term *history* previously identified as problematic by Eliot and Hardy – is it an action, an artefact or a discourse? The 'materiality' of history seems insistently evidenced by Conrad's use of 'material' as an adjective for the 'interests' and 'changes' which constitute history. Yet within a particular historical context where an unsecured language roams free of reality – autonomous names 'flashing in the night of time' – actions and facts threaten to dissolve into discourse. Troubling is the thought that we can say of history what Marlow says of Kurtz, the novel's prime 'agent' of colonialism, 'I made the strange discovery that I had never imagined him as doing, you know, but as discoursing'.

BIG LIES/PLAIN TALES

A comparison of 'Heart of Darkness' with a Kipling short story 'Thrown Away' (1888), will illustrate how different are these authors' negotiations with the dominant discourse. Kipling's story is like a 'Heart of Darkness' drained of Marlow's agonised self-scrutiny and re-stated to endorse rather then problematise the colonialist position. 'Thrown Away' describes how a naive young English officer fresh from Sandhurst named only as 'The Boy' is posted to a British station in India. 'Sensitive to the marrow', he was ill suited to 'a slack country where all men work with imperfect instruments' and where he 'had no one to fall back on in time of trouble except himself' and, fatally, 'took all things seriously' (Kipling, 1987, p.41). He quarrels with his fellow officers who tease rather than pet him as his parents had done, drinks, gambles and has heavy losses. Upbraided by his colonel and slighted by a woman's remark he charges off the station, 'to shoot big game'.

A major and another officer who turns out to be the narrator of the story set out for the rest house he had made for, and find him dead on the bed: 'He had shot his head nearly to pieces with his revolver'. He has left letters to be sent to his parents and girlfriend full of the 'disgrace which he was unable to bear', 'indelible shame' and 'criminal folly'. The major and narrator feel 'It was utterly impossible to let the letters go Home. They would have broken his father's heart and killed his mother after killing her belief in her son'. This would have been a '"Nice sort of thing to spring on an English family!"'. Instead the major and narrator begin a 'grimly comic scene'. The major asks his subordinate 'Can you lie?' and he smartly replies 'You know best . . . It's my profession'. They then agree upon 'the concoction of a big, written lie' – 'it was no time for little lies, you understand' – that the Boy, an exemplary officer and much loved, had died of cholera. They dispose of the remains – 'I am not going to write about this. It was too horrible' – and send their 'lie'. The story ends with the mother replying with 'the sweetest possible things about our great kindness, and the obligation she would be under to us as long as she lived. All things considered, she was under an obligation; but not exactly as she meant' (Kipling, 1987, pp.43–6).

There are intriguing details of affinity between the tales. The Boy charges off the station with 'a revolver and a writing case' rather as Conrad's papier-mâché Mephistopheles carries bullets in one pocket and a book in the other, both instances evoking an affinity between the violence and the discourse of colonialism. Kipling's narrator's construction of a 'big lie' recalls the 'gigantic tale' of Western colonial venturing evoked by Conrad's initial narrator. The Boy, like the Intended, is never named, but, like her, the existence of a name is evoked but not spoken – 'calling for the Boy by name', 'the last word he pronounced was – your name'. Both authors acknowledge an area of 'horror' in their narrative, which can be gestured towards but not shown. Both use the sensitivities of women back home to stand for the distanced, conventional views of the colonial venture which narrators lie to protect.

There are also, obviously, broad structural and thematic affinities. Both stories focus colonial concerns on the crises of doubt and disillusion that can drive a sensitive colonial agent to 'the end of the tether' in an alien 'outpost of progress'. The Boy conflates issues which Conrad needs a range of characters to dramatise; he is like Marlow in his initial boyish enthusiasm for his venture and the subsequent disabling sensitivity he brings to it, like Kurtz in carrying the promise of a European education and high hopes of a fine colonial career, like the Intended in having no name and living with unsustainably high moral standards. He perhaps most closely resembles a modern version of Marlow's 'decent young citizen in a toga – perhaps too much dice you know' encountering 'powerless disgust' in his colonial posting. But whereas Marlow's imagining of this figure at the beginning of his narrative, and his subsequent encounter with the doctor who is something of an 'alienist' or psychologist interested in 'the mental changes in individuals', prepares for a narrative similarly psychologically concerned, Kipling avoids depicting the Boy's evidently disturbed psychology and so avoids the question of the mental pressures of the coloniser's role. The story begins with a repetitive preamble where the narrator complains of parents who bring their children up under the soft 'sheltered life system'. The story needs to contort itself into duplicitous positions to occlude problems. The Boy has to be seen as the exceptional product of a peculiarly ill-advised upbringing while the spareness of his characterisation, scrupulous avoidance of interiorisation and his being dubbed merely 'the Boy' all tend to suggest that his story – 'the tale is as old as the hills' – is typical rather than exceptional. The story is duplicitous also in beginning as if an omniscient narration in which the strictures on bad parenting carry the authoritative weight of a supra-individual perspective, then turn out to be the words of one of the Boy's fellow officers, who, being merely another character, claims areas of ignorance which the story can then conveniently ignore – 'Of course, we could not tell how his excesses struck him personally' (Kipling, 1987, p.42).

In Conrad's story, Marlow's puncturing his narrative with outbursts of anxiety over lies acts as a paradigm of Conrad's own fraught narrating position. In Kipling, a similar image of his own storytelling function is offered when the major asks the gruffly practical officer/narrator if he can lie and he smartly replies 'It's my profession'. This is essentially as much hesitation as Kipling's story evinces on the matter. Perhaps Kipling, the popular storyteller of colonialism, would make a similar reply. In a conflation of duplicitous ironies, this story, in which 'big lies' are sent abroad appeared in the volume *Plain Tales from the Hills*.

FOUL SKIES/HEAVY WEATHER

Nostromo is not merely a self-conscious, but actually a self-critical text. It acknowledges a possibly debilitating paradox at the heart of its own project in that it attempts to analyse the historical development of capitalism and its correlative colonialism, while being itself a strand within the discourse of capitalism/colonialism and hence disposed to endorse its values. Characteristic of the novel is a sense of oppressive deadlock of which its epigraph – 'So foul a sky clears not without a storm' – is exactly expressive. This deadlock can be seen to derive from its combination of a frank analysis of its own implication within conservative positions, and a fearful reticence about imagining political alternatives. Typical of Conrad is a thoroughly fraught and unstable representation of his characters' ideas – and sometimes his own – when they appear to have a Marxist cast. In Conrad, an irrational loathing directed at Marxist characters is indicative of something plausible in their perspective which he is afraid to acknowledge – 'There are some things I *must* leave alone'. The novel is uncertain as to what it fears most; the 'foul sky' of current political formations, or the 'storm' that would remove them.

In the 'Author's Note' to *An Outcast of the Islands*, written in 1919 and hence the decade after *Nostromo*, there are a couple of instances where Conrad describes his experience of artistic impasse and eventual activity in terms which echo the characterisation of Charles Gould and suggest an affinity of concerns and mental states.

> [Mr Gould's] face was calm with that immobility of expression which betrays the intensity of inner struggle.
>
> (Conrad, 1986 (1), p.321)

> I was a victim of contrary stresses which produced a state of immobility.
>
> (Conrad, 1984, 'Author's Note', p.7)

> Charles Gould . . . was the visible sign of the stability that could be achieved on the shifting ground of revolutions.
>
> (Conrad, 1986 (1), p.16)

> And thus a dead point in the revolution of my affairs was insidiously got over.
>
> (Conrad, 1984, 'Author's Note', p.17)

I would suggest that Conrad is particularly prone to setting off verbal echoes between his self-characterisation in non-fictional writings and his fictional characterisations. These are admittedly slight connections, but in line with Freud's conception of jokes and slips-of-the-tongue can be seen as articulations from within the unconscious of the text of affinities and relationships not acknowledged on its surface. Famously, there is the term 'standing jump' he used for his renunciation of all his family and class affiliations in leaving Poland for a career at sea echoing Lord Jim's 'jump' which proves so crucial and ambiguous an act of desertion or betrayal (Reilly, 1991, pp.17–18). In *The Nigger of the 'Narcissus'* (1897) there is a single moment of insight into the mind of the despised and feared Jimmy Wait in a description of his delirious dream of a ship discharging grain: 'and the wind whirled the dry husks in spirals along the quay of the dock with no water in it. He whirled along with the husks – very tired and light' (Conrad, 1983, p.97). The memorable husks image is reworked in the 'Author's Note' to *The Secret Agent*, describing Conrad's mental exhaustion on completing *Nostromo* which 'made me feel (the task once done) as if I were left behind, aimless amongst mere husks of sensations' (Conrad, 1980 (1), 'Author's Note', p.8).

While these examples from *Lord Jim* and *The Nigger of the 'Narcissus'* show Conrad empathising at a perhaps unacknowledged level with disgraced and despised figures who seem challengingly disruptive or unconventional to those around them, in *Nostromo* the telling verbal affinities are not with anyone equivalently positioned within that novel but rather with the great Gould, 'King of Sulaco', agent of Western material interests and hence the novel's pivot of historical and economic power. That Conrad's affinity here is particularly with the embodiment of capitalism suggests the degree to which Conrad and the novel are enmeshed within conservative positions and capitalist/colonialist assumptions and the degree to which, if it is a critique of such positions, the novel simultaneously acknowledges – in a possibly debilitating paradox – that such a critique is articulated from *inside* such positions rather than from *outside*. Indeed, an aspect of *Nostromo*'s honesty and profundity is its insistence upon capitalism's ability to consume and digest all opposition, even that offered by *Nostromo* itself. In the novel the outside-ness of outsiders – variously manifested as their rebelliousness, detachment or heroic independence – proves illusory as even figures as variously detached and independent as Viola, Decoud and Nostromo find themselves enmeshed within a capitalism so arrogantly monumental as to suffer the existence of no 'outside' and no 'outsiders'.

A play on words crystallises this issue. Antonia and Decoud have a crucial dialogue about the possibility of being 'disinterested'.

> 'Men must be used as they are. I suppose nobody is really disinterested, unless, perhaps, you, Don Martin.'
> 'God forbid! It's the last thing I should like you to believe of me.'
>
> (Conrad, 1986 (1), p.439)

Antonia and Decoud are partly speaking at cross-purposes. Antonia means by 'disinterest' Decoud's apparent ironic detachment from the political commitments she holds so dear, while he is trying to bend her words into a personal and romantic meaning and so protests at the idea that he is emotionally 'disinterested' in her. But in a novel so obviously and centrally concerned with the immanence of 'material interests' the 'idle boulvardier's' admission that not even he is 'disinterested' is a telling indication of how spurious is the pose of detachment. The term is used again by Mrs Gould of Nostromo, 'I prefer to think him disinterested, and therefore trustworthy' (Conrad, 1986 (1), p.204), but the novel subsequently unpicks both Decoud's and Nostromo's belief in their own disinterest. No one in capitalist culture is 'disinterested' in 'material interests'. Part of the brilliance – and characteristic excruciating sense of heaviness, tension and deadlock – of *Nostromo* stems from its attempt to analyse 'material interests' in the light of a full recognition that there is no critical perspective or narrating position which can escape them. Capitalism in its world monopoly phase comes to erode a favoured dichotomy of eighteenth- and nineteenth-century discourse between detachment and participation. Conrad undertakes a scathing analysis of material interest where there can be no pretence of 'disinterest'. To cite Adorno,

> The detached observer is as much entangled as the active participant; the only advantage of the former is insight into his entanglement, and the infinitesimal freedom that lies in knowledge as such. His own distance from business at large is a luxury which only that business confers.
>
> (Adorno, 1974, p.26)

Thus the novel can be seen to be highly self-conscious about its own enclosure within the conditions capitalism demands. The novel's eponymous hero comes to feel he has 'silver welded into his veins' and silver is the novel's own alpha and omega – its first words, in the title of the first part, are 'The Silver of the Mine', its last sentence describes a cloud formation as 'like a mass of solid silver'. Gold and silver underpin capitalism, not merely in a vaguely metaphorical sense, but quite specifically in that they are the 'security' held in reserve by countries and their banks which guarantees the value of the bonds and paper money which are in immanent circulation. One aspect of the sense of debilitating stalemate the novel creates, paradoxically in contrast to its apparent welter of political drama, is the difficulty Conrad has in acknowledging any 'Other' to this capitalist hegemony. The representation of Communistic ideas exposes Conrad's deepest insecurites and draws from him quite unstable and contradictory formulations.

One aspect of Conrad's evidently very fraught attitude towards Communistic ideas is the absurd, spluttering invective he directs at the characters who voice them. He reserves for them a physical loathing never otherwise apparent in his characterisation, the virulency of which

anticipates the grossest of twentieth-century anti-semitic or racial propagandist abuse where physical repulsion poses as moral criticism.
Donkin in *The Nigger of the 'Narcissus'* who insists that 'I can look after
my rights' and is prepared to 'kick up a bloomin row' to defend them is a
landlubbing shirker and physically disgusting.

> a man with shifty eyes and a yellow hatchet face . . . a squeaky
> voice . . . He looked as if he had been cuffed, kicked, rolled in the
> mud; he looked as if he had been scratched, spat upon, pelted
> with unmentionable filth . . . his neck was long and thin; his
> eyelids were red; rare hairs hung about his jaws; his shoulders were
> peaked and drooped like the broken wings of a bird; all his left
> side was caked in mud . . . He stood repulsive and smiling.
>
> (Conrad, 1983, p.20)

The prose here itself scratches, pelts and spits at a character it loathes.
The Nigger of the 'Narcissus' is in this respect continuous with the deeply
anti-egalitarian import of the sea-stories which were favourite boyhood
reading of Conrad's. In Captain Marryatt's *Mr Midshipman Easy*, an
especial favourite, the eponymous hero is educated out of the pernicious egalitarianism he has picked up from Paine's *The Rights of Man*
and transformed from spineless liberal landlubber to exemplary officer
by the rigours, and rigorous hierarchies, of naval life. We have seen how
the narrator of *The Secret Agent* never tires of pointing out that
Michaelis, leading light of the moribund Marxist/Anarchist cell 'The
Future of the Proletariat', is grotesquely overweight. In *Nostromo* it
comes as no surprise that a character described as 'an indigent, sickly,
somewhat hunchbacked little photographer, with a white face' turns out
also to have 'a magnanimous soul dyed crimson by a bloodthirsty hate of
all capitalists, oppressors of the two hemispheres' (Conrad, 1986 (1),
p.436).

This is all fear masquerading as loathing, and perhaps an unacknowledged sense of recognition. Conrad loathes his Communistic
characters with an irrational virulency that cannot help but make the
reader feel that he somewhere senses a veracity that refuses to be
dismissed by uneasy sneering. One moment in *Nostromo* comes close to
bringing this recognition to consciousness – significantly, given the
novel's acknowledgement of capitalism's monopoly on discourse, it is
conveyed via a wordless moment of connection. Alone at Nostromo's
death-bed is the Communist, at whom the 'Man of the People' directs 'a
glance of enigmatic and profound enquiry' (Conrad, 1986 (1), p.462).

There is an insistent duplicity in the presentation of Marxist ideas by this 'homo-*duplex*' – Conrad coined this famous self-definition in a letter contemporaneous with, and discussing, the composition of *Nostromo*. For example, one can place statements made by the Marxist slob Michaelis ranting to his fellow supine activists side by side with some of the most pithy and insightful political assessments voiced in *Nostromo* with all appearance of an intellectual continuity. Michaelis and *Nostromo* share classic Marxist/materialist analyses. Capitalism spells conflict:

'The possessors of property had not only to face the awakened proletariat, but they had also to fight among themselves. Yes. Struggle, warfare, was the condition of private ownership. It was fatal . . .'.

(Conrad, 1980 (1), p.42)

'No!' interrupted the doctor. 'There is no peace and no rest in the development of material interests. They have their law, and their justice. But it is founded on expediency, and is inhuman; it is without rectitude, without the continuity and the force that can be found only in a moral principle. Mrs Gould, the time approaches when all that the Gould Concession stands for shall weigh as heavy upon the people as the barbarism, cruelty, and misrule of a few years back.'

'How can you say that, Dr Monygham?' she cried out, as if hurt in the most sensitive part of her soul. (Conrad, 1986 (1), p.423)

History and consciousness are the product of economic relations and not vice versa:

'History is made by men, but they do not make it in their heads. The ideas that are born in their consciousness play an insignificant part in the march of events. History is dominated and determined by the tool and the production – by the force of economic conditions.'

(Conrad, 1980 (1), p.42)

Material changes swept along in the train of material interests. And other changes more subtle, outwardly unmarked, affected the minds and hearts of the workers.

(Conrad, 1986 (1), pp.417–18)

Nostromo, the novel of 'material interests', both depicts and, in its own deadlocked and embattled narrative, actually enacts Conrad's insight in

'Autocracy and War': 'Democracy, which has elected to pin its faith to the supremacy of material interests, will have to fight their battles to the bitter end' (Conrad, 1970, p.85).

DESCRIPTIVE DEADLOCK

In the 'Author's Note' to *An Outcast of the Islands* Conrad described his drained and debilitated state on completing *Almayer's Folly*. For Conrad the completion of a novel was invariably accompanied by a physical and mental collapse – and none more than *Nostromo*, 'Months of nervous strain have ended in complete nervous breakdown . . . the M.S. . . . lays on a table at the foot of the bed and he lives mixed up in the scenes and holds converse with the characters' (Conrad, 1983–90, vol. 4, p.87). Thus Conrad's statement here can serve as one instance of a characteristic deadlock.

> *Almayer's Folly* had been finished and done with. The mood itself was gone. But it had left the memory of an experience that both in thought and emotion was unconnected with the sea, and I suppose that part of my moral being which is rooted in consistency was badly shaken. I was a victim of contrary stresses which produced a state of immobility. I gave myself up to indolence. Since it was impossible for me to face both ways I had elected to face nothing. The discovery of new values in life is a very chaotic experience; there is a tremendous amount of jostling and confusion and a momentary feeling of darkness. I let my spirit float supine over the chaos.
>
> (Conrad, 1984, 'Author's Note', p.7)

Conrad relishes the exactitude of technical expression, so perhaps we can detect a metaphor drawn from the science of materials in the formulation 'I was a victim of contrary stresses which produced a state of immobility'. Marlow in the Congo is fascinated by his discovery of Towson's manual on the breaking-strains of ships' cables. Conrad's own works are about testing breaking-strains – physical, ethical and emotional – and his metaphor here suggests an instance from Towson of the cable stretched taut by opposed forces. This is Conrad at 'the end of the tether'. The submerged metaphor surfaces in *Nostromo* to evoke unforgettably Decoud's devastating alienation alone on the *Isabel*. 'In the daytime he could look at the silence like a still cord stretched to breaking-point, with his life, his vain life, suspended from it like a weight' (Conrad, 1986 (1), p.414).

'Stillness' and 'immobility' that indicate, not repose, but the near-tearing tautness of contrary forces – this is the characteristic tension of *Nostromo*. The novel, like its author here, is debilitated by an 'immobility' affecting characters, setting and narrative alike. At its heart is the contradiction that a work so obviously concerned with the movement of historical change is everywhere mesmerised by immobility. The word is repeatedly evoked, far more frequently than the key-term always cited in criticism, 'material interests'. The regularity of its reappearances both evokes an immanent inertia and actually clogs the novel's apparent narrative and historical movement with a congealing repetitiveness.

[Mr Gould's] face was calm with that immobility of expression which betrays the intensity of mental struggle.

(Conrad, 1986 (1), p.321)

The Garibaldino – big erect, with his snow-white hair and beard – had a monumental repose in his immobility, leaning upon a rifle.

(Conrad, 1986 (1), p.455)

Behind him the immobility of Mrs Gould added to the grace of her seated figure the charm of art, of an attitude caught and interpreted forever . . . Mrs Gould's face became set and rigid . . . her still and sad immobility . . .   (Conrad, 1986 (1), p.430–1)

And the old man, bent forward, his head in his hand, sat through the day in immobility and solitude.   (Conrad, 1986 (1), p.390)

his eyes met again the shape of the murdered man suspended in his awful immobility, which seemed the uncomplaining immobility of attention . . .   (Conrad, 1986 (1), p.365)

Father Corbelan had remained quite motionless for a long time with that something vengeful in his immobility which seemed to characterise all his attitudes.   (Conrad, 1986 (1), p.185)

a great land of plain and mountain and people, suffering and mute, waiting for the future in a pathetic immobility of patience.

(Conrad, 1986 (1), p.102)

A big green parrot . . . screamed out ferociously '*Viva Costaguana!*' . . . and suddenly took refuge in immobility and silence.

(Conrad, 1986 (1), p.88)

Only in one instance is immobility equated with repose – otherwise it is the grim parody of repose of the 'awful' immobility of the hanged Hirsch; it is 'sad', 'vengeful', 'pathetic', a betrayal of 'inner struggle'.

The Shadow-Line (1917) develops a triple analogy between the dilemma of a captain whose ship languishes in a slough so absolute that the sails hang like granite, the ordeal of the contemporary generation of youth to whom the novel is dedicated bogged in the slough of the First World War and Conrad's own sense of creative impasse. Conrad would complain of being, like the ship in the novel, 'complétèment embourbé' – completely stuck. In *Nostromo* also, immobility is a central metaphor implicating the novel's *action*, the *historical context* which it addresses, and the writer's own sense of *artistic deadlock*. The form of description characteristic of the novel is endless variation on an apparent 'universal repose of all visible things'.

> All at once, in the midst of the laugh, he became motionless and silent as if turned to stone.
>
> (Conrad, 1986 (1), p.373)

> [Dr Monygham] sitting . . . so motionless that the spiders, his companions, attached their webs to his matted hair . . .
>
> (Conrad, 1986 (1), p.318)

> The solid wooden wheels of an ox-cart, halted with its shaft in the dust, showed the strokes of the axe . . .
>
> (Conrad, 1986 (1), p.103)

> the equestrian statue of the King dazzlingly white in the sunshine, towering enormous and motionless above the surges of the crowd with its eternal gesture of saluting . . .
>
> (Conrad, 1986 (1), p.327)

> For a long time even [Nostromo's] eyelids did not flutter upon the glazed emptiness of his stare.
>
> (Conrad, 1986 (1), p.410)

> Perfectly motionless in that pose, expressing physical anxiety and unrest, [Nostromo's mother] turned her eyes alone towards Nostromo.
>
> (Conrad, 1986 (1), p.224)

> The Capataz frowned: and in the immense stillness of sea, islands, and coast, of cloud forms on the sky and trails of light upon the water, the knitting of that brow had the emphasis of a powerful gesture. Nothing else budged for a long time; then the Capataz shook his head and again surrendered himself to the universal repose of all visible things.
>
> (Conrad, 1986 (1), p.410)

The novel's crucially developed descriptive motifs are such emphases writ large; the ever-lowering monumentality of Mount Higuerota, the absolute, black, solid stillness of the aptly-named Golfo Placido, the statuesque bearing of Nostromo on horseback, the mesmerised spectators of Hirsch's statically suspended corpse, Decoud's equivalent metaphorical suspension alone on the Isabel.

Talking about novels within the traditions of nineteenth-century realism, Lukács argues in 'Narrate or Describe?' that the subversive potential of works apparently critical of capitalism is usually smothered at birth by a conservatism latent within their style. This style is characteristically a debilitating, reifying, descriptiveness. The presence of this monumental and moribund descriptiveness indicates how these works are in fact absolutely subservient to an ideology congenial to capitalism which denies the possibility of change and hence monumentalises and eternalises capitalism itself. His instances of static, debilitating description, as opposed to the dynamic and engaging *narration* of process Scott, Balzac or Tolstoy achieve, are Flaubert and Zola. In these authors, 'the characters are merely spectators, more or less interested in the events. As a result, the events themselves become only a tableau for the reader, or, at best, a series of tableaux. We are merely observers' (Lukács, 1970, p.130). A Marxist and a Nietzschean analysis are strikingly congruent. What Nietzsche said of the nineteenth century's experience of history – that we are no longer participants, but merely strolling spectators visiting an exhibition – is here Lukács's vision of nineteenth-century fictional characters' relation to their world and, by extension, the readers' relation to theirs – 'merely observers' of 'a series of tableaux'. Lukács also decisively echoes an assertion of Conrad's from *A Personal Record* (1912) where he describes reality as 'the sublime spectacle', even positing 'the conception of a purely spectacular universe' (Conrad, 1988, pp.92–3). Peculiarly apposite to Decoud is the notion of a character who, a 'mere spectator', is 'more or less interested in the events'. We can recall the ironically detached 'idle boulevardier's' tangled relation to 'disinterest'.

In fact there are striking instances of congruity between Conrad's writing practice in *Nostromo* and Lukács's analysis of capitalist fiction's descriptive deadlock and delivery of the reified image of a reified world. This is essentially the argument of Kiernan Ryan in 'Revelation and Repression in Conrad's *Nostromo*'. He suggests that the immobility immanent in characters, setting and narrative structure alike qualify it as an even better model than Lukács's own instances of the densely descriptive and essentially moribund capitalist text which, while appearing to activate the subversive potential within historical change, in fact smothers history and denies even the existence of such change. One of the points on which I depart from Ryan's analysis is that I would argue that – unlike Zola and Flaubert as Lukács characterises them – Conrad foregrounds and renders self-conscious and hence problematic his leanings towards Lukácsian 'description'.

For Lukács 'Description contemporises everything. Narration recounts the past . . . the contemporaneity of the observer making a description is the antithesis of the contemporaneity of the drama. Static situations are described, states or attitudes of mind of human beings or conditions of things – still lives' (Lukács, 1970, p.130). I am reminded of the opening page of *Nostromo* where the reader is at first invited to expect a 'narration' that 'recounts the past': 'In the time of Spanish rule, and for many years afterwards, the town of Sulaco . . . had never been commercially anything more important than a coasting port . . .'. But by the next paragraph the style has gelled into 'description' which 'contemporises everything' introducing its extended present-tense set-piece of Costaguanan geography and topography. 'On one side of this broad curve in the straight seaboard of the Republic of Costaguana, the last spur of the coast range forms an insignificant cape . . . On the other side, what seems to be an isolated patch of blue mist floats lightly on the glare of the horizon.' In fact the description lingers over an evocation of the 'prevailing calms of its vast gulf' that suggests that Costaguanan geography has ensured the preservation of Lukácsian 'static situations . . . still lives'. 'Sulaco had found an inviolable sanctuary from the temptations of a trading world in the solemn hush of the deep Golfo Placido as if within an enormous semi-circular and unroofed temple open to the ocean, with its walls of lofty mountains hung with the mourning draperies of cloud' (Conrad, 1986 (1), all p.39). The image captures two crucial aspects of the 'descriptive version of the world'; the denial of capitalist history – 'sanctuary from the temptations of a trading world' – and the *staged*, but not *dramatised*, aspect of reality – Sulaco here sounds like an abandoned amphitheatre.

Description for Lukács renders the world an array of discrete, reified elements with no vital connection, and the style of the descriptive novel is an equivalently bitty and scattered form of seeing such a world. In *Lord Jim* there is a descriptive passage which evokes with a startling exactness Luckács's formulation that 'The false contemporaneity of description transforms the novel into a kaleidoscopic chaos'.

There was, as I walked along, the clear sunshine, a brilliance too passionate to be consoling, the streets full of jumbled bits of colour like a damaged kaleidoscope: yellow, green, blue, dazzlingly white, the brown nudity of an undraped shoulder, a bullock-cart with a red canopy, a company of native industry in a drab body with dark heads marching in dusty laced boots, a native policeman in a sombre uniform . . .

(Conrad, 1980 (2), p.122)

Conrad exactly reproduces Lukács's 'kaleidoscopic chaos' and actually self-consciously characterises not merely Marlow's vision here but his own descriptive technique as 'like a damaged kaleidoscope'. The world fractures into a neurotic scattering of momentarily arresting details, vision jerking from one detail to the next with no stepping back to see the larger composition – a lurid, unblending pointillism. Sentence structure and speaker's vision are alike slackly additive, paratactic rather than structured and syntactic. Marlow's walk anticipates the urban wanderings of later modernist protagonists – Prufrock, Mrs Dalloway, Septimus Smith and Bloom – whose perceptions are all slackly successive fragments of observation but most precisely, the vision of Decoud who, on the *Isabel*, 'beheld the universe as a succession of incomprehensible images' (Conrad, 1986 (1), pp.413–4).

A description of goods on display in Anzani's shop in *Nostromo* is like a realisation in miniature of another of Lukács's formulations about the descriptive style:

The result is a series of static pictures, of still lives connected only through the relations of objects arrayed one beside the other according to their own inner logic, never following one from the other, certainly never one out of the other. The so-called action is only a thread on which the still lives are disposed in a superficial, ineffective fortuitous sequence of isolated, static pictures.

(Lukács, 1970, p.144)

It was next to Anzani's great emporium of boots, silks, ironware, muslins, wooden toys, tiny silver arms, legs, heads, hearts (for ex-voto offerings), rosaries, champagne, women's hats, patent medicines, even a few dusty books in paper covers and mostly in the French language.

(Conrad, 1986 (1), p.157)

The list captures in miniature the novel's 'series of static pictures . . . objects arranged one beside the other'. In fact it is almost a checklist of the novel's contents, as well as an enactment in miniature of its static array of discrete, reified elements. Limbs and hearts rendered in silver –

154

as in further memorable instances of the novel's reification imagery Nostromo has silver welded into his veins and Mrs Gould's heart turns to silver brick – and all scattered, dismembered, dispersed, as Nostromo feels he has been dispersed, 'Nostromo here and Nostromo there – where is Nostromo?' (Conrad, 1986, p.351). There are the 'boots' and 'ironware' of revolutionary and counter-revolutionary forces; 'rosaries' and 'offerings' which evoke the pervasive fetishism and 'purely spiritual value' of objects which trouble characters and narrator alike and of which the perverse mutability of the San Tomé silver is emblematic, and even, in the dusty French books, something of a homage to the French fiction to which Conrad's own style is indebted. Flaubert is both Lukács's great instance of the debilitating descriptiveness of capitalist art, and Conrad's acknowledged literary master.

With great acumen Conrad has used a display of shop goods to exemplify the contents and form of his own novel. A display of goods is the fundamental structuring principle of capitalist expression, even its art. Captain Mitchell's tedious official account of Sulacan 'historical events' narrates how Sulaco became 'the Treasure-House of the world'. Henry James – with whom Conrad disagreed over the relations between fiction and history – dubbed *Middlemarch* 'a treasure-house of details' (James, 1987 (*Galaxy*, March 1873), p.75), a perverse irony given how repulsed Dorothea is by Rome's accumulation of cultural trophies. Under capitalism everything from states to art-works is readily translated into displays of possessions. *Nostromo* – a succession of highly-wrought set-pieces, brilliantly detailed – is, in perhaps a debilitating sense, another 'treasure-house of details'.

As Kiernan Ryan describes it, the novel itself is Anzani's display of essentially unrelated objects writ large, each reified element held in the gel of a dense descriptiveness.

> The descriptive strategy of *Nostromo* is most immediately evident in its meandering mode of advance through set-piece tableaux rendered with a lingering profusion of detailed circumstances. One thinks of the opening frieze of life at the Casa Viola; of the O.S.N. convité on the *Juno*; of the Goulds frozen silent in their house; the troops' embarkation under Barrios; the Goulds' party, with Decoud and Antonia on the balcony; Decoud alone at night in the Casa Viola: the hypnotic Placido Gulf scene: Nostromo and Monygham spellbound before the grotesque suspended corpse of Hirsch; Decoud lost out of time in the infinite solitude of the island. The novel delivers no sense of developing action emerging through the vital interplay of the characters with each other and

their world. Quite the reverse. The narration does not flow, it coils and eddies through a configuration of still centres, congealed *settings for* action which, if recounted at all, is not fully narrated from the 'inside' as well – through the evolving subjectivity of active participants – but statically depicted as a ready-made phenomenon, a finished product.

(Ryan, 1982, p.167)

The last two phrases evoke Marx's concept of the fetishised object of production which I shall argue finds echoes everywhere in the novel as well as Anzani's arrangement of goods on display. Conrad's comments on his own writing add useful evidence of the justice of Ryan's analysis, and his own acknowledgement of his descriptive impasse. Ryan quotes a letter to Garnett: 'It is evident that my fate is to be descriptive and descriptive only. There are things I *must* leave alone' (Conrad, 1983–90, vol. 4, p.89). One could cite also the admission in the 'Author's Note' to *An Outcast of the Islands* and relating to that novel: 'The mere scenery got a great hold of me as I went on, perhaps (I may just as well confess that) the story itself was never very near my heart' (Conrad, 1984, 'Author's Note', p.8).

'Mere scenery' overwhelming 'story itself' is exactly the disaster of capitalist prose Lukács diagnoses in 'Narrate or Describe?'. One instance in the novel seems to bring all these concerns with Lukácsian description to a head – the pivotal moment when we learn, as Charles Gould announces it to his wife, that his father has died. The death precipitates Charles's exploitation of the Gould Concession which, abandoned under Gould senior who urged his son not to take it up, becomes the transforming force in Sulacan history.

> She was the first person to whom he opened his lips after receiving the news of his father's death.
>
> 'It has killed him!' he said.
>
> He had walked straight out of town with the news, straight out before him in the noonday sun on the white road, and his feet had brought him face to face with her in the hall of the ruined *palazzo*, a room magnificent and naked, with here and there a long strip of damask, black with damp and age, hanging down on a bare panel of the wall. It was furnished with exactly one gilt armchair, with a broken back, and an octagon columnar stand bearing a heavy marble vase ornamented with sculptured masks and garlands of flowers, and cracked from top to bottom. Charles Gould was dusty with the white dust of the road lying on his boots, on his

shoulders, on his white cap with two peaks. Water dripped from under it all over his face, and he grasped a thick oaken cudgel in his bare right hand.

She went very pale under the roses of her big straw hat, gloved, swinging a clear sunshade, caught just as she was going out to meet him at the bottom of the hill, where three poplars stand near the wall of a vineyard.

'It has killed him!' he repeated.

(Conrad, 1986 (1), pp.82-3)

This is, like the opening description of Sulaco, suggestive of an amphi-theatre awaiting a performance, 'semi-circular and unroofed . . . with its walls of lofty mountains hung with . . . mourning draperies' (Conrad, 1986 (1), p.39). Both descriptions illustrate exactly Ryan's observation about Conrad offering '*settings for* action' which then fails to mater-ialise. What a splendid set designer Conrad would have made on the evidence of this austerely ruined palazzo with its sculptural furnishings, fractured and monumental. The stage is set for an absent epic action, a tragedy – a Sophocles or a Racine – which fails to turn up or which swept off long ago. Only an Oedipus or a Phèdre would fail to be swamped and intimidated by such a setting, as their understudies the Goulds so evidently are. Or perhaps the formulation '*settings for* action' is inap-propriate. Instead of the setting being the backdrop for action, it almost seems as if the action is mere pretext for the setting. Descriptive 'background' and dramatised 'foreground' have changed places, a great chunk of static 'scene-setting' interrupting the very articulation of Gould's crucial announcement of rupture and change.

Here we can understand Conrad's concern over the centrality of 'mere scenery' and his being 'descriptive and descriptive only'. We wait for something to happen only to have the same words of Gould's repeated as if action is congealing to become as monumental as its setting. Speeches have to be repeated, setting is precise and final – '*exactly one* gilt armchair'. As if moving over a canvas the eye is guided by compositional structures – a strip of black, a block of gilt, the central sculptural form of the urn. Here Conrad is achieving his ambition 'To make you *see*', efficiently aping 'the plasticity of sculpture . . . the colour of painting'. Conrad called *Nostromo* 'my largest canvas' (Conrad, 1980 (1), 'Author's Note', p.8). The Classical vase, Keats's image of imme-morial stillness and evocative also of Arnold's monumentally objective Classical art, is compositionally central and a metonym for the monu-mentality of the whole. Ornament (masks and flowers) encrusts the vase, as the Goulds (mask-like and be-flowered respectively) merely ornament their setting. Ornamentation – the term Marlow used for Kurtz's human decor of severed heads – is both repeated motif and fundamental stylistic principle in Conrad's prose. And Charles Gould – so often depicted as reified as when his 'steady poise' on horseback echoes the equestrian statue of Charles IV he passes – completes the statuesque arrangement and as such enacts another of Lukács's formulations, 'When men are portrayed through the descriptive style, they become mere still lives' (Lukács, 1970, p.143). He is even, like the books in Anzani's shop, dust-covered.

The mesmerising reification will not be shaken off. 'She was too startled to say anything; he was contemplating with a penetrating and motionless stare the cracked marble urn as though he had resolved to fix its shape forever in his memory . . . while he stood by her, again perfectly motionless in the contemplation of the marble urn' (Conrad, 1986 (1), p.83). The Goulds *are* Arnold's reified spectators of reification – fixing statuary with 'riveted gaze'. But as so often in Conrad, the immanent stillness and reification is evidence not of repose but of barely contained tensions, as with Conrad describing himself as 'a victim of contrary stresses which produced a state of immobility'. 'Contrary stresses' here have broken the back of the regal gilt seat and cracked the immemorial urn. The great images of authority and stasis are fractured.

This is a good point at which to part company with Ryan's Lukácsian comparison. If one's Marxist critical model was provided by Brecht/ Benjamin rather than Lukács one would be more sympathetic to the possibility of critical energies within a consciously stilled representation. Benjamin explains Brecht's dramatic method in precisely these terms.

> The task of epic theatre . . . is not so much the development of actions as the representation of conditions . . . This discovery (alienation) of conditions takes place through the interruption of happenings. The most primitive example would be a family scene. Suddenly a stranger enters. The mother was just about to seize a bronze bust and hurl it at her daughter; the father was in the act of opening the window in order to call a policeman. At that moment a stranger appears in the doorway. This means that the stranger is confronted with the situation as a startling picture: troubled faces, an open window, the furniture in disarray. But there are eyes to which even more ordinary scenes of middle-class life look almost equally startling.
>
> (Benjamin, 1973, 'What is Epic Theatre?', pp.152–3)

Benjamin's metonym of the bronze bust within the composition standing for the reification of the whole is very reminscent of the method of
Nostromo, a masterpiece of 'the interruption of happenings'. To return
to Conradian breaking-strain imagery, where Ryan sees monumental
reification everywhere in *Nostromo*, it appears rather that Conrad
scrutinises, like Gould opposite the cracked urn, an utterly unstable
tension – 'contrary stresses' – between reification and dissolution,
atrophy and evanescence. The fractured monument – the Amarilla club,
Mitchell's tedious tourist monologue observes, contains a bust of a
bishop with its nose broken – is a splendid image for an apparently solid
surface straining against dissolution, an erection that hints at collapse.

A PLAY OF SIGNS

Conrad's preoccupation with the term 'material interests' is telling. He
returns to it repeatedly as if continually turning it at different angles,
examining it in different contexts, to get as many opportunities as
possible to discern whatever evanescent 'glimpse of truth' it contains –
to use his own phrase about what his novels might ideally offer (Conrad,
1983, 'Preface', p.13). *Nostromo* might be regarded as simply Conrad's
supporting medium for voluminous puzzling over the nagging enigma
of this phrase. And it is an enigma, because wealth and value within
capitalism are, as Marx explained in relation to the commodity, a bizarre
and unprecedented category, neither fish nor flesh, entity nor abstraction. 'A commodity appears, at first sight, a very trivial thing, and easily
understandable. Its analysis shows that it is, in reality, a very queer thing,
abounding in metaphysical subtleties and theological niceties' (Marx,
1977, p.225). The root of this ontological oddity is that commodities are
products characterised by 'division . . . into a useful thing and a value'
with no comprehensible, stable or discernible relation between these
two characteristics. The comprehensible social character of the labour
that created the commodity is appropriated by the commodity itself in
the form of its market value so that workers' relation to their own labour
ceases to be a comprehensible social one and becomes instead a quality
of relations between objects.

> This is the reason why the products of labour become com-
> modities, social things whose qualities are at the same time
> perceptible and imperceptible by the senses.
>
> (Marx, 1977, p.436)

the existence of the things *qua* commodities, and the value relation between the products of labour which stamps them as commodities, have absolutely no connection with their physical properties and with the material relations arising therefrom. There it is a definite social relation between men, that assumes, in their eyes, the fantastic form of a relation between things.

(Marx, 1977, p.436)

Marx offers an eloquent illustration – a table may be made out of that humble material, wood,

But, so soon as it steps forth as a commodity, it is changed into something transcendent. It not only stands with its feet on the ground, but, in relation to all other commodities, it stands on its head, and evolves out of its wooden brain grotesque ideas, far more wonderful than 'table-turning' ever was.

(Marx, 1977, p.435)

The commodity is at once banally material and an utter abstraction. It appears to abstract itself of its own volition, out of its own 'brain', and its consequent transcendence – like the spiritualistic sham of 'table-turning' – is of a peculiarly fake and nonsensical nineteenth-century kind.

Is not Conrad in the term 'material interests' approaching a similar analysis – the oxymoronic conjunction of the 'perceptible and imperceptible', the actual and the transcendent? 'Material' is material, but 'interests' – investments, commitments, concerns, excitements – are abstractions. Indeed it seems absolutely typical of Conrad to meditate upon categories of experience – whether history, money, power or meaning itself – which he sees as presenting the same perplexing ontological duality. All are poised between fact and discourse, materiality and immateriality. He stresses that history is 'speculation' which as a term conflates the contradictions of 'material interests' – it means both investments and conjecture. Gould argues that his stash of dynamite is both a 'weapon' and an 'argument'. Marlow thinks of Kurtz as less 'doing' than 'discoursing'.

Undoubtedly a crucial concern in the representation of the Gould Concession's central historical meaning is an analysis very much akin to Marx's on how the mine's wealth and influence transmutes – now materially solid, now an idea. Marx famously declared that under capitalism 'All that is solid melts into air' (Marx, 1977, p.225). Conrad seems equivalently concerned with the dissolving of fact into 'idealism', 'abstraction', 'spiritual value' and a corresponding contrary movement

160

whereby ideas beome monuments – his central instance being, like Marx's, money. Uneasy shiftings in Mrs Gould's view of the mine, and her husband in relation to it, focus these issues. Economic facts, and even geographic ones, become abstractions.

> 'Charley an idealist!' she said, as if to herself, wonderingly. 'What on earth do you mean?'
>
> 'Yes', conceded Decoud, 'it's a wonderful thing to say with the sight of the San Tomé mine, the greatest fact in the whole of South America, perhaps, before our very eyes. But look even at that, he has idealized this fact to a point – ' He paused. 'Mrs Gould, are you aware to what point he has idealized the existence, the worth, the meaning of the San Tomé mine? Are you aware of it?'
>
> (Conrad, 1986 (1), p.199)

Those who live by such abstractions become themselves abstractions.

> Mrs Gould watched his abstraction with dread . . . Charles Gould's fits of abstraction depicted the energetic concentration of a will haunted by a fixed idea. A man haunted by a fixed idea is insane.
>
> (Conrad, 1986 (1), p.322)

All reality has its solidity dissolved into a purely spiritual value.

> 'Upon my word, doctor, things seem to be worth nothing by what they are in themselves. I begin to believe that the only solid thing about them is the spiritual value which everyone discovers in his own form of activity.'
>
> (Conrad, 1986 (1), p.275)

Ideas, and those controlled by them, reify into monuments.

> The fate of the San Tomé mine was lying heavy upon her heart. It was a long time now since she had begun to fear it. It had been an idea. She had watched it with misgivings turning into a fetish, and now the fetish had grown into a monstrous and crushing weight. It was as if the inspiration of their early years had left her heart to turn into a wall of silver-bricks . . .
>
> (Conrad, 1986 (1), pp.204–5)

In this last quotation particularly, Marx and Conrad speak with one voice – or at least one vocabulary. The foregoing comments from Marx come from the section of *Das Kapital* (1867), 'The Fetishism of Commodities'. Both writers reach for the term *fetish* to evoke the nature of capitalist wealth and value – commanding submission, incomprehensibly powerful, but above all, perversely both monumental and essentially idealised, abstract.

Everywhere in *Nostromo* Conrad seems to be concerned to imagine this perplexing impossiblity of the material/immaterial entity. He uses descriptive phrases – particularly relating to the peculiar density of darkness over the Gulf – to evoke the perverse inter-penetration of presence and absence.

> He could bear no longer that expressionless and motionless stare, which seemed to have a sort of *impenetrable emptiness* like the black depth of an abyss.
>
> (Conrad, 1986 (1), p.300)

> this almost *solid stillness* of the gulf.
>
> (Conrad, 1986 (1), p.242)

> this mysteriousness of the great waters spread out strangely smooth, as if their restlessness had been crushed in the *weight of that dense night*.
>
> (Conrad, 1986 (1), pp.230–1) (all my emphases)

The tormenting, tantalising materiality/immateriality, absence/presence of all things! In relation to it Conrad evokes in reader and characters alike a frustration comparable to that of Sortillo desperately and vainly dredging the Gulf for the silver he feels sure has been ditched there, 'stamping his foot and crying out, "And yet it is there! I see it! I feel it!"' (Conrad, 1986, p.403).

Nostromo, Decoud and Mrs Gould all have experiences of being tormented by the impalpability of the seemingly solid. For them money, and even human action and history, dissolve at the touch.

> [Nostromo] yearned to clasp, embrace, absorb, subjugate in unquestioned possession this treasure, whose tyranny had weighed upon his mind, his actions, his very sleep.
>
> (Conrad, 1986 (1), p.436–7)

> [Mrs Gould] had laid her unmercenary hands, with an eagerness that made them tremble, upon the first silver ingot turned out still warm from the mould; and by her imaginative estimate of its power she endowed that lump of metal with a justificative conception, as though it was not a mere fact, but something far-reaching

and impalpable, like the true expression of an emotion or the emergence of a principle. (Conrad, 1986 (1), p.117)

The Capataz, extending his hand, put out the candle suddenly. It was to Decoud as if his companion had destroyed, by a single touch, the world of affairs, of loves, of revolution, where his complacent superiority analysed fearlessly all motives and all passions, including his own.

(Conrad, 1986 (1), p.241)

The conjunction of these quotations throws into relief what I feel is the central and brilliant insight of *Nostromo*, nowhere exactly stated but everywhere implied in the novel's repeated configuration of two dominant elements. Under capitalism, two apparently distinct categories of experience – the value of commodities and the fact of history – are actually perversely inter-related and share a common fate in dissolution and abstraction. In these quotations characters are frustrated in their attempts to find the values that govern their world – whether financial, romantic or political – palpable. Not only does a newly moulded silver ingot prove 'impalpable . . . an emotion . . . a principle' but the very 'world of affairs, of loves, of revolution' (Conrad decisively conflates personal and political history) dissolves at the touch. *Nostromo* is centrally about money and history and, more precisely, it is about their shared status as newly abstract – a bizarre state of affairs to which Conrad alerts us when he has Decoud call history 'speculation'. 'Speculation' is money made abstract and Decoud's usage applies the term also to history rendered abstract, conjectural, hypothetical. This de-materialising is what he here actually experiences as the extinguishing in an instant of 'the world of affairs, of loves, of revolution'.

Such de-materialising can appear to be conferred via the fiat of capitalists. Their acts of naming are decisive. Gould discloses that he has a stash of dynamite so that he can protect the San Tomé mine from seizure by threatening to destroy it if it is claimed by the Monterists.

'The Gould Concession has struck such deep roots in this country, in this province, in that gorge of the mountains, that nothing but dynamite shall be allowed to dislodge it from there. It's my choice. It's my last card to play.'

The engineer-in-chief whistled low. 'A pretty game,' he said, with a shade of discretion. 'And have you told Holroyd of that extraordinary trump card you hold in your hand?'

'Card only when it is played; when it falls at the end of the game. Till then you may call it a – a –'

163

'Weapon,' suggested the railway man.

'No. You may call it rather an argument,' corrected Charles Gould, gently. 'And that's how I've presented it to Mr Holroyd.'
(Conrad, 1986 (1), p.192)

A card? A weapon? An argument? The explosive material of historical power – literally here dynamite – can strangely mutate and even shed its materiality. Dynamite, a material substance whose function is to de-materialise itself and the matter around it with shattering violence, is an apposite metaphor for this dangerously de-materialising principle. The railway man cuts through the deft evasions of Gould's formulation – dynamite is patently a weapon. Gould, however, insists on transmuting that weapon into 'a card' or 'an argument' – a sign or a discourse. Here Conrad brilliantly highlights how, under capitalism, the duality inherent in the term history – is it action or discourse? – is peculiarly knotty and confounded. Gould, here the representative and agent of Western material interest, deftly transmutes a weapon into an argument, as his capitalist/colonialist culture collapses the distinction between violence and discourse. In the sign-saturated, densely scripted capitalist/colonialist world weapons become words, and words, weapons. Decoud notes how when the Monterists seize the print offices Don José's magnum opus on the history of Costaguana and the moveable type used to print it become literal (literary?) ammunition, 'fired out as wads for trabucos loaded with handfuls of type' (Conrad, 1986, p.213). In 'Heart of Darkness' the papier-mâché Mephistopheles carries a book in one pocket, bullets in the other. In Gould's own study there are two cabinets, one of books, one of firearms.

Gould's metaphor of the card-game is a rich one. A playing card is like a banknote, a share certificate or even a word according to Derrida's conception of linguistic 'différance'. These are all signs which on their own carry no intrinsic meaning or value, point to no objective signified. A thoroughly labile and relative value, however, is activated when the sign circulates in the play of other signs which make up its sign-system – the card-game, monetary system, stock-market or discourse. As Gould so perceptively remarks, the card/sign only has value – only *is* a sign – 'when it is played'. It is a meaningless blank when not circulating within the sign-system, literally insignificant. The clinching moment of its activity when played to win the game is also its 'fall', its death and that of the system – except of course only in a card-game is the play of meaning ever decided and terminated. Economic and linguistic systems always outlast the defeats or victories enacted within them.

The analogy Gould's metaphor suggests between capitalist violence/ economics and the card-game is provocative. The game is a play of signs – an argument between signs – that signify wealth without actually embodying it. The meaning of signs is thoroughly dependent upon their participation in the play of competition. The play of signs, the discourse, in a game played for money, serves purely to facilitate the circulation of capital. The game enacts the absolute subjection of the sign. Signs are hoarded, guarded, played, won or relinquished all as part of the individual's strategy within the play of competition – and fall dead and silent when not facilitating that competition. In a game of cards there is no distinction between the competitive activity and the discourse, the play of signs, which embodies it. Activity and discourse are one and the same and signs only speak when called to serve the game's purpose.

The 'considerable personage' talking to Charles Gould sums up the trammelling of discourse, volition and identity by capitalism and the absolute subjection of the sign it enacts:

> 'We shall be giving the word for everything: industry, trade, law, journalism, art, politics, and religion, from Cape Horn clear over to Smith's Sound, and beyond, too, if anything worth taking hold of turns up at the North Pole. And then we shall have the leisure to take in hand the outlying islands and continents of the earth. We shall run the world's business whether the world likes it or not. The world can't help it – and neither can we, I guess.'
>
> (Conrad, 1986 (1), p.94–5)

Capitalism 'gives the word' for everything – including 'art' and therefore the novel within which these words are articulated. Like colonialism which inscribes the supposedly 'blank places of the earth' with exported names, capitalism speaks itself into a total linguistic dominion. Though capitalism likes to see itself as a market-place, a site for exchange, there is no linguistic exchange, no conversation envisaged here. Capitalism is an interminable monologue – rather like Mitchell's tedious narration of 'historical events' – that brooks no interruption. Notice that the imposition of discourse precedes actual conquest – 'giving the word' prepares the way for 'taking in hand' and 'running the world's business' – and that capitalism's word-givers find themselves as drained of volition as those they name – 'The world can't help it – and neither can we'. Capitalism can do what the individuals within it cannot – 'take' their world 'in hand'.

THE DEATH OF WRITING

I have suggested that late Victorian and Edwardian capitalism is a peculiarly sign-dense culture where the ideological import of reading and writing is supreme. Perhaps this position ought to be modified since in fact the dense literariness of this culture is another aspect of its apparent monumentality which, on closer inspection, appears fissured. Deleuze and Guattari in *Anti-Oedipus: Capitalism and Schizophrenia* suggest that the type of communication proper to capitalism in this period and after is not grounded in the sign/signified model at all, but is rather a matter of technically processed information flows in which messages convey, not meanings, but instructions.

> the capitalist use of language is different in nature: it is realised or becomes concrete within the field of immanence peculiar to capitalism itself, with the appearance of technical means of expression that correspond to the generalised decoding of flows . . . Language no longer signifies something that must be believed, it indicates rather what is going to be done, something that the shrewd or the competent are able to decode, to half understand.
> (Deleuze and Guattari, 1984, p.250)

I am not proposing an exact equation between this linguistic theory and Conrad's depiction of the discourse of capitalism, or his own prose as a strand within that discourse. However there are suggestive affinities with his writing practice. Deleuze and Guattari stress that capitalism demands, not reading skills, but decoding ones. In 'Heart of Darkness' Marlow is intrigued by what he takes to be code – actually annotations in Russian – he finds in the margins of a copy of the seafarer's manual *Towson's Enquiry*. The pleasure Marlow takes in the refreshing lucidity of Towson's exact and technical usages – a delight in technical expression Conrad shared – is offset by the puzzling opacity of the accompanying code. Kurtz writes a work of characteristic eloquence in his report for 'The Society for the Suppression of Savage Customs'. As such it might be seen as a classic instance of the language which 'signifies something that must be believed', as, indeed, Marlow's whole discourse struggles with the burden of constructing something that can be believed – 'would you believe it?' (Conrad, 1981, p.12) – but concludes with a lie. Kurtz's report rather reverses this movement, ending with the plain-spokenness of the scrawled postscript 'Exterminate all the brutes'. In effect his meretricious and pietistic ramble finally provides its own decoding. Thus his text finally admits that, as Deleuze and Guattari put it, it is not appealing to belief but conveying an order, telling 'what is going to be done'.

In *Under Western Eyes* (1911) the teacher of languages who narrates seeks the 'key-word' which 'could stand at the back of all the words covering the pages, a word which, if not truth itself, may perchance hold truth enough to help the moral discovery which should be the object of every tale' (Conrad, 1979, p.62). The word he hits upon is 'cynicism'. The discourse of capitalism/colonialism is characterised by cynicism, it 'no longer signifies something which must be believed'. All the Plain Tales from the Hills of this culture which contain 'big lies' do not ask to be believed, they can even, like 'Thrown Away', foreground their own activity of constructing deception.

Kurtz's report finally decodes itself, as Marlow eventually learns that the 'coded' annotations were in Russian. Both texts are experienced as a 'delayed decoding'. This phrase has famously been used to characterise the strategy of Conrad's own texts by Cedric Watts, instances from 'Heart of Darkness' being his illustration. With Deleuze and Guattari's argument in mind, we can begin to take the full measure of the idea that Conrad's prose enacts 'delayed decoding'. More than an idiosyncrasy of a modernistically experimenting literary style, Conrad's foregrounding of 'delayed decoding' can be seen as articulating a crucial shift within the discourse of his culture, from the reading of expressive signs to the partial decoding of information and instructions.

Deleuze and Guattari refer to what 'the shrewd or the competent are able to decode, to half understand'. I have suggested something of the relevance of the nature of decoding to Conrad. 'Half understanding' can be seen also as something with which Conrad's texts are crucially concerned. In *Joseph Conrad: Language and Fictional Self-Consciousness* (1979), in order, rather like the teacher of languages, to find a key-term suggestive of the form of consciousness which Conrad's texts address, Jeremy Hawthorn chooses 'half-ignorance'. He quotes the stanzas of Keats's *Isabella* detailing the exploitation of foreign workers which Isabella's brothers conduct at a comfortable distance, 'Half-ignorant, they turn'd an easy wheel | That set sharp racks at work, to pinch and peel' (XV.119–20). Hawthorn stresses

> Keats's portrayal of the indirect way in which this pain is inflicted; *half-ignorant* is just right, and it applies perfectly to what we see going on in 'Heart of Darkness' . . . The mechanical metaphor used by Keats – the 'easy wheel' – is also very precise. It is the industrial revolution, with its revolutionising of production and communication, that allows human beings to inflict pain on their

167

fellows in half-ignorance. Oppression is not new, but oppression by those hardly aware that they are oppressors is peculiarly modern.

(Hawthorn, 1979, p.25)

I would wish to extend Hawthorn's analysis of 'half-ignorance' here. Conrad seems to be articulating how, under capitalism, the 'revolutionising of . . . communication' creates a *discourse* predicated on, and productive of, in Hawthorn's Keatsian term, 'half-ignorance', in Deleuze and Guattari's, 'half-understanding'.

It might be objected here that Deleuze and Guattari are talking of a phase of capitalism later than Conrad's in which the audio-visual and information technologies – television, film, video, telecommunications, computers, satellites – on which their argument is predicated are developed far beyond what an Edwardian imagination could conceive. However, *Nostromo* does show itself perceptive in the importance it places on technology's new, non-verbal, non-scripted forms of communication. The Monterist revolution pivots on their success in seizing and silencing the wireless office at Esmerelda, from which the news had been broken of the crucial defection of a garrison from the Ribierist to the Monterist cause. Victory falls to those with the power to silence or activate informational 'flows'. There is also one moment when the text seems to acknowledge that, amidst its characters' – and its own – voluminous literary activity, is stealthily establishing itself a form of communication more efficient, more free of human contact, and more deadly in achieving capitalism's ends: 'the sparse row of telegraph poles strode obliquely clear of the town, bearing a single, almost invisible wire far into the great *campo* – like a slender, vibrating feeler of that progress waiting outside for a moment of peace to enter and twine itself about the weary heart of the land' (Conrad, 1986 (1), p.162).

There is a specific sense in which Conrad can be regarded as the last great literary artist. By this I mean that as a writer he is working at the last moment when it is possible to feel that the literary medium in which the novelist works is also the medium in which the controlling discourse of the culture he addresses is conducted, and Conrad actually takes this fact as his subject. We could regard Conrad's texts as the last articulations of an essentially nineteenth-century sign-dense, literary culture. Carlyle, in the 1830s, fulminates against a suffocation in signs. 'Alas, move whithersoever you may, are not the tatters and rags of superannuated worn-out Symbols (in this Ragfair of a world) dropping off everywhere, to hoodwink, to halter, to tether you; nay, if you shake them not aside, threatening to accumulate, and perhaps produce suffocation!'

(Carlyle, 1987, p.171). As we have seen in *Nostromo* the suffocating feeler waiting to 'twine itself about the weary heart of the land' is now the medium of Deleuze and Guattari's encoded 'pulses and flows' rather than Carlyle's 'Symbols'.

For Deleuze and Guattari,

> Writing has never been capitalism's thing. Capitalism is profoundly illiterate. The death of writing is like the death of God or the death of the father: the thing was settled a long time ago, although the news of the event is slow to reach us, and there survives in us the memory of extinct signs with which we still write.
>
> (Deleuze and Guattari, 1984, p.240)

We could reformulate this by saying that capitalism's voluminous writing activity serves more often to disguise than articulate its essentially secret, unarticulated actions – 'The inner truth is hidden – luckily, luckily' (Conrad, 1981, p.47). Kurtz writes and speaks with thrilling 'eloquence', yet commits acts which are 'unspeakable'. Gould, also, can turn not speaking to his advantage.

> But Charles Gould, openly preoccupied now, gave not a sign, made no sound. The impenetrability of the embodied Gould Concession had its surface shades. To be dumb is merely a fatal affliction; but the King of Sulaco had words enough to give him all the mysterious weight of a taciturn force. His silences, backed by the power of speech, had as many shades of significance as uttered words in the way of assent, of doubt, of negation – even of simple comment. Some seemed to say plainly, 'Think it over'; others meant clearly 'Go ahead', a simple, low 'I see', with an affirmative nod, at the end of a patient listening half-hour was the equivalent of a verbal contract . . .
>
> (Conrad, 1986 (1), p.190)

We have seen elsewhere in *Nostromo* how Conrad emphasises that capitalism 'gives the word for everything' and thus secures a combined linguistic and political dominion. Here he seems to back-track, or perhaps rather anticipate a further phase in the development of capitalism which has nothing to do with words and signs. Perhaps it is hardly more than a hint, but Gould's 'taciturn force' here, where his audience (not auditors) have to decode silences rather than read words and signs and where communication is a matter of disseminating instructions and concluding contracts rather than expressing belief, appears convincingly Deleuzeoguattarian. Culture seems in movement from a sign-dense discursiveness to a taciturnity stripped of signs to which we might apply Carlyle's term 'the signless inane'. The Goulds' parrot, trained to squawk 'Viva Costaguana' would seem another instance of a communication which can be decoded to provide a congenial political message but which is not the expression of a meaning or an intention.

For reasons about which we might wish to speculate in this context, Conrad refused Roger Casement's invitation to contribute to his notorious report of 1904 detailing Belgian atrocities in the Congo. If 'Heart of Darkness' is one of the last texts of the sign-dense culture, Casement's text can be seen as a seminal work of the emergent, technological, unscripted communication. I have called it a text, but in fact it was as a photographic record that this work produced its enormous impact, becoming one of the great public topics of the year and, as such, duly recorded in *Ulysses* as the subject of an indignant pub conversation (Joyce, 1985, p.274). The scandal it caused helped turn the tide of popular support for colonialism – a far more palpable impact than that of 'Heart of Darkness'. It was the first great work of photo-journalism with memorably repulsive images, such as a Congolese gingerly holding up from one finger a severed hand. Belgian agents were accused of wasting ammunition on shooting game and so had to bring in a human hand for every bullet with which they had been issued. Such images had an impact we, in our audio-visual, news-saturated culture, can only dimly conceive. In comparison, Conrad's Congo accountant who tabulates horrors as figures kept in 'apple-pie' order seems a timid representation of this regime's combination of meticulous bureaucracy with appalling violence. In response to the report Mark Twain wrote a prose piece 'King Leopold's Soliloquy' (1905) in which the Belgian monarch bemoans the invention of the easily portable camera which has cut straight through the duplicity and obfuscations of colonialist discourse.

The kodak has been a sore calamity to us. The most powerful enemy that has confronted us, indeed. In the early years we had no trouble in getting the press to 'expose' the tales of the mutilations as slanders, lies, inventions of busy-body American missionaries and exasperated foreigners . . . Yes, all things went harmoniously and pleasantly in those good days, and I was looked up to as the benefactor of a down-trodden and friendless people. Then all of a sudden came the crash!

(Twain, 1963, p.122)

Casement – he has a splendidly apposite name – used new photographic technology to *show* colonialism. Photographic 'exposure' outstrips linguistic, words are devastatingly discredited. Perhaps Conrad refused Casement because he intuited in his project the beginning of the end of the literary culture which he had struggled to render lucid enough 'before all, to make you *see*' (Conrad, 1983, 'Preface', p.13). The communist in *Nostromo* whom Conrad describes with disgust but on whom Nostromo bestows his last look of 'profound and enigmatic enquiry' is, for no reason apparent in the text, a photographer.

Conrad's work thus exemplifies how, in his period, the critical writer's position – already constrained within a culture which enacts the absolute subservience of the sign – is further marginalised by a revolution in the way capitalism communicates. The sign/signified structure of the old culture is deconstructed by the innovation of signless flows signifying nothing. So the writer has to negotiate both with, to use Conrad's term, a pervasive 'cynicism' about capitalism's self-serving deployment of signs, and an emerging redundancy of signs themselves. The writer who addresses history as his subject finds that – in line with the abstracting impulse at work within capitalism in which, for example, dynamite can be thought of as an 'argument' – history itself has dissolved into 'speculation'.

BIBLIOGRAPHY

Adorno, Theodor (1974) *Minima Moralia: Reflections from a Damaged Life*, trans. E.F.N. Jephcott, London: Verso.

—— (1983) *Prisms*, trans. Samuel and Shierry Weber, Cambridge, Mass.: The MIT Press.

—— (1990) *Negative Dialectics*, trans. E.B. Ashton, London: Routledge.

—— (1991) *The Culture Industry: Selected Essays on Mass Culture*, ed. J.M. Bernstein, London: Routledge.

Adorno, Theodor, Benjamin, Walter, Bloch, Ernst, Brecht, Bertolt and Lukács, Georg (1988) *Aesthetics and Politics: The Key Texts of the Classic Debate within German Marxism*, translation editor Ronald Taylor, London: Verso.

Arendt, Hannah (1963) *On Revolution*, New York: Viking.

Arnold, Matthew (1960–77) *The Complete Prose Works*, ed. R.H. Super, 11 vols, Michigan: University of Michigan Press.

—— (1987) *The Complete Poems*, Longman Annotated English Poets, second edition, ed. Miriam Allott, Harlow: Longman.

—— (1988) *Culture and Anarchy*, ed. J. Dover Wilson, Cambridge: Cambridge University Press.

Attridge, Derek, Bennington, Geoff and Young, Robert, eds (1987) *Post-Structuralism and the Question of History*, Cambridge: Cambridge University Press.

Baines, Jocelyn (1986) *Joseph Conrad: A Critical Biography*, Harmondsworth: Penguin.

Bakhtin, Mikhail (1981) *The Dialogic Imagination*, ed. Michael Holquist, trans. Caryl Emerson and Michael Holquist, Austin: University of Texas Press.

Barker, Francis, ed. (1977) *Literature, Society and the Sociology of Literature*, Colchester: University of Essex Press.

Barker, Howard (1989) *Arguments for a Theatre*, London: John Calder.

Barrell, John (1972) *The Idea of Landscape and the Sense of Place 1730–1840: An Approach to the Poetry of John Clare*, Cambridge: Cambridge University Press.

Barrett, Dorothea (1989) *Vocation and Desire: George Eliot's Heroines*, London: Routledge.

Barthes, Roland (1990) *A Lover's Discourse: Fragments*, trans. Richard Howard, Harmondsworth: Penguin.

172

Baudelaire, Charles (1987) *Les Fleurs du Mal*, trans. Richard Howard, London: Picador.

Beckett, Samuel (1970) *Proust and Three Dialogues with Georges Duthuit*, London: John Calder.

—— (1973) *Murphy*, London: Picador.

—— (1979) *The Beckett Trilogy: Molloy, Malone Dies, The Unnamable*, London: Picador.

—— (1980) *The Expelled and other Novellas*, Harmondsworth: Penguin.

—— (1988) *Watt*, London: Picador.

—— (1990) *The Complete Dramatic Works*, London: Faber and Faber.

Beer, Gillian (1985) *Darwin's Plots: Evolutionary Narrative in Darwin, George Eliot and Nineteenth-Century Fiction*, London: Ark/Routledge and Kegan Paul.

—— (1986) *George Eliot*, Key Women Writers, series ed. Sue Roe, Brighton: Harvester.

Benjamin, Andrew ed. (1991) *The Problems of Modernity: Adorno and Benjamin*, Warwick Studies in Philosophy and Literature, London: Routledge.

Benjamin, Walter (1973) *Illuminations*, ed. Hannah Arendt, trans. Harry Zohn, London: Fontana.

—— (1974) *Gesammelte Schriften*, ed. Rolf Tiedemann and Hermann Schweppenhauser, Frankfurt: Suhrkamp Verlag.

—— (1975) *Charles Baudelaire: A Lyric Poet in the Era of High Capitalism*, trans. Harry Zohn, London: New Left Books.

—— (1977) *The Origin of German Tragic Drama*, trans. John Osborne, London: Verso.

Bennington, Geoff (1988) *Lyotard: Writing the Event*, Manchester: Manchester University Press.

Berger, John (1972) *Ways of Seeing*, London: BBC and Penguin Books.

Bernal, Martin (1987) *Black Athena: The Afroasiatic Roots of Classical Civilisation*, vol. 1, *The Fabrication of Ancient Greece 1785–1985*, London: Vintage.

Bogue, Ronald (1989) *Deleuze and Guattari*, London: Routledge.

Brecht, Bertolt (1986) *Poems, 1913–1956*, ed. John Willett and Ralph Manheim, London: Methuen.

—— (1987) *Brecht on Theatre: The Development of an Aesthetic*, ed. and trans. John Willett, London: Methuen.

Brown, Norman O. (1959) *Life Against Death: The Psychoanalytical Meaning of History*, New York: Random Century.

Buckley, Jerome H. (1967) *The Triumph of Time: A Study of the Victorian Concepts of Time, History, Progress and Decadence*, Cambridge Mass.: Harvard University Press.

Burckhardt, Jacob (1990) *The Civilisation of the Renaissance in Italy* (first published 1860, Eng. trans. 1878), trans. S.G.C. Middlemore, Harmondsworth: Penguin.

Burke, Edmund (1990) *A Philosophical Enquiry into the Origin of Ideas of the Sublime and Beautiful*, ed. Adam Phillips, Oxford: Oxford University Press.

Burstein, Janet (1975) 'Victorian Mythography and the Progress of the Intellect', *Victorian Studies*, 18, pp.309–24.

Calvino, Italo (1989) *The Literature Machine*, trans. Patrick Creagh, London: Picador.

173

Carlyle, Thomas (1896) *Critical and Miscellaneous Essays*, London: Chapman and Hall.

—— (1987) *Sartor Resartus*, Oxford: Oxford University Press.

—— (1988) *Selected Writings*, ed. Alan Shelston, Harmondsworth: Penguin.

Carpenter, Mary (1984) 'The Apocalypse of the Old Testament: *Daniel Deronda* and the Interpretation of Interpretation', *Publications of the Modern Languages Association of America*, 99, pp. 56–71.

Carr, David (1986) *Time, Narrative and History*, Bloomington, Ind.: Indiana University Press.

Chandler, Alice (1971) *A Dream of Order: The Medieval Idea in Nineteenth-Century Literature*, London: Macmillan.

Chiaromonte, Nicola (1971) *The Paradox of History: Stendhal, Tolstoy, Pasternack and Others*, London: Weidenfeld and Nicolson.

Comte, Auguste (1865) *A General View of Positivism*, trans. J.H. Bridges, Stanford, Calif.: Stanford Academic Reprints.

Connor, Steven (1985) *Charles Dickens*, Rereading Literature, Oxford: Blackwell.

—— (1988) *Samuel Beckett: Repetition, Theory and Text*, Oxford: Blackwell.

Conrad, Joseph (1970) *Notes on Life and Letters* (first published 1921), London: J.M. Dent.

—— (1978) *Congo Diary and other Uncollected Pieces*, ed. Zdislaw Najder, New York: Doubleday and Co.

—— (1979) *Under Western Eyes* (first published 1911), Harmondsworth: Penguin.

—— (1980) (1) *The Secret Agent: A Simple Tale* (first published 1907), Harmondsworth: Penguin.

—— (1980) (2) *Lord Jim: A Tale* (first published 1900), Harmondsworth: Penguin.

—— (1981) 'Heart of Darkness' (first published 1902), Harmondsworth: Penguin.

—— (1983) *The Nigger of the 'Narcissus', Typhoon and Other Stories* (first published 1898, 1903), Harmondsworth: Penguin.

—— (1983–90) *The Collected Letters*, 4 vols, ed. Frederick R. Karl and Laurence Davies, Cambridge: Cambridge University Press.

—— (1984) *An Outcast of the Islands* (first published 1876), Penguin: Harmondsworth.

—— (1986) (1) *Nostromo: A Tale of the Seaboard* (first published 1904), Harmondsworth, Penguin.

—— (1986) (2) *The Shadow-Line; A Confession*, (first published 1917), Harmondsworth: Penguin.

—— (1988) *'The Mirror of the Sea' and 'A Personal Record'* (first published 1906, 1912) ed. Zdislaw Najder, Oxford: Oxford University Press.

Crosby, Christina (1991) *The Ends of History: Victorians and 'the Woman Question'*, London: Routledge.

Dale, Peter Allan (1977) *The Victorian Critic and the Idea of History: Carlyle, Arnold, Pater*, Cambridge, Mass.: Harvard University Press.

Dean, Susan (1977) *Hardy's Poetic Vision in 'The Dynasts': The Diorama of a Dream*, Princeton, N.J.: Princeton University Press.

Deiss, Joseph Jay (1966) *Herculaneum: A City Returns to the Sun*, New York: The History Book Club.

Deleuze, Gilles (1972) *Différence et Répétition*, Paris: Presses Universitaires de France.
—— (1990) *The Logic of Sense*, trans. Mark Lester with Charles Stirale, ed. Constantin Boundas, London: The Athlone Press.
Deleuze, Gilles and Guattari, Félix (1984) *Anti-Oedipus: Capitalism and Schizophrenia*, trans. Robert Hurley, Mark Seem and Helen R. Lane, London: The Athlone Press.
—— (1988) *A Thousand Plateaus: Capitalism and Schizophrenia*, trans. Brian Massumi, London: The Athlone Press.
De Man, Paul (1971) *Blindness and Insight: Essays in the Rhetoric of Contemporary Criticism*, New York: Oxford University Press.
Derrida, Jacques (1976) 'Limited Inc. abc . . ', *Glyph*, 2, pp. 27–60.
—— (1978) *Writing and Difference*, trans. Alan Bass, London: Routledge and Kegan Paul.
—— (1979) *Spurs, Nietzsche's Styles / Eperons, Les Styles de Nietzsche*, trans. Barbara Harlow, Chicago, Ill.: University of Chicago Press.
Dickens, Charles (1980) *The Old Curiosity Shop* (first published 1840–1), Harmondsworth: Penguin.
—— (1983) *Little Dorrit* (first published 1855–7), Harmondsworth: Penguin.
—— (1984) *Dombey and Son* (first published 1848), Harmondsworth: Penguin.
—— (1985) *David Copperfield* (first published 1849–50), Harmondsworth: Penguin.
—— (1986) *Great Expectations* (first published 1860–1), Harmondsworth: Penguin.
—— (1987) *Hard Times* (first published 1854), ed. Terry Eagleton, London: Methuen English Texts.
—— (1988) *The Pickwick Papers* (first published 1836–7), Harmondsworth: Penguin.
—— (1990) *A Tale of Two Cities*, (first published 1859), Harmondsworth: Penguin.
Dickinson, Emily (1984) *The Complete Poems*, ed. Thomas H. Johnson, London: Faber and Faber.
Dowling, Linda (1985) 'Roman Decadence and Victorian Historiography' *Victorian Studies*, 28/4, pp.590–607.
Dwight Culler, A. (1985) *The Victorian Mirror of History*, New Haven, Conn. and London: Yale University Press.
Eagleton, Terry (1976) *Criticism and Ideology*, London: New Left Books.
—— (1983) *Literary Theory: An Introduction*, Oxford: Blackwell.
—— (1985) *Marxism and Literary Criticism*, London: Methuen.
—— (1990) *The Ideology of the Aesthetic*, Oxford: Blackwell.
Eliot, George (1954–5) *The George Eliot Letters*, ed. Gordon S. Haight, 7 vols, New Haven, Conn: Yale University Press,
—— (1963) *Essays*, ed. Thomas Pinney, London: Routledge and Kegan Paul.
—— (1973) *Silas Marner: The Weaver of Raveloe* (first published 1861), Harmondsworth: Penguin.
—— (1981) *Middlemarch: A Study of Provincial Life* (first published 1871–2), Harmondsworth: Penguin.
—— (1982) (1) *Felix Holt: The Radical* (first published 1866), Harmondsworth: Penguin.

—— (1982) (2) *Scenes of Clerical Life* (first published 1858), Harmondsworth: Penguin.

—— (1983) *The Mill on the Floss* (first published 1860), Harmondsworth: Penguin.

—— (1984) (1) *Adam Bede* (first published 1859), Harmondsworth: Penguin.

—— (1984) (2) *Daniel Deronda* (first published 1876), Harmondsworth: Penguin.

—— (1984) (3) *Romola* (first published 1863), Harmondsworth: Penguin.

—— (1985) 'The Lifted Veil' (first published 1878), Reading: Virago Press.

—— (1989) 'Brother Jacob' (first published 1878), Reading: Virago Press.

—— (1990) *Selected Essays, Poems and Other Writings*, ed. A.S. Byatt and Nicholas Warren, Harmondsworth: Penguin.

Eliot, T.S. (1963) *Collected Poems: 1909–1962*, London: Faber and Faber.

—— (1975) *Selected Prose*, London: Faber and Faber.

Engels, Friedrich (1985) *The Origin of the Family, Private Property and the State*, trans. Alick West, Harmondsworth: Penguin.

—— (1987) *The Condition of the Working Class in England* (first published Germany, 1845), trans. Florence Wischnewetzky, Harmondsworth: Penguin.

Faucitt, Helena (1887) *On Some of Shakespeare's Female Characters*, Edinburgh: Blackwood's.

Flaubert, Gustave (1977) *Salammbô* (first published 1862), trans. A.J. Krailsheimer, Harmondsworth: Penguin.

—— (1984) *The Letters 1857–1880*, ed. and trans. Francis Steegmuller, London: Faber and Faber.

Fleishman, Avron (1971) *The English Historical Novel: Walter Scott to Virginia Woolf*, Baltimore, Md: Johns Hopkins University Press.

Fogel, Aaron (1985) *Coercion to Speak: Conrad's Poetics of Dialogue*, Cambridge, Mass.: Harvard University Press.

Forster, E.M. (1936) *Arbinger Harvest*, London: Edward Arnold.

Forsythe, R.A. (1968) 'The Buried Life: The Contrasting Views of Arnold and Clough in the context of Dr Arnold's Historiography', *English Literature and History*, 35, pp. 218–54.

Foucault, Michel (1967) 'Nietzsche, Marx, Freud', *Cahiers de Royaument Philosophie*, 6, pp. 25–52.

—— (1989) *The Order of Things: An Archaeology of the Human Sciences*, London: Tavistock/Routledge.

Freeman, Janet H. (1977) 'Authority in *The Mill on the Floss*', *Philological Quarterly*, 56, pp.374–88.

Freud, Sigmund (1931) 'Female Sexuality' in *Sexuality and the Psychology of Love*, trans. Joan Riviere, London: Hogarth Press.

—— (1979) *Case Histories II: 'Rat Man', Schreber, 'WolfMan', Female Homosexuality*, trans. ed. James Strachey, The Pelican Freud Library, vol. 9, Harmondsworth: Penguin.

—— (1985) *Civilisation, Society and Religion: Group Psychology, Civilisation and its Discontents and Other Works*, trans. ed. James Strachey, The Pelican Freud Library, vol. 12, Harmondsworth: Penguin.

—— (1987) *Case Histories I: 'Dora' and 'Little Hans'*, The Pelican Freud Library, vol. 8, trans. Alix and James Strachey, Harmondsworth: Penguin.

—— (1988) *The Interpretation of Dreams*, trans. James Strachey, The Pelican Freud Library, vol. 4, Harmondsworth: Penguin.

Fuller, Peter (1980) *Art and Psychoanalysis*, London: The Hogarth Press.

Genette, Gérard (1980) *Narrative Discourse: An Essay in Method*, trans. Jane Lewin, Oxford: Blackwell.

Gillon, Adam (1982) *Joseph Conrad*, Twayne's English Authors Series, Boston, Mass.: Northeastern University Press.

Goode, John (1988) *Thomas Hardy: The Offensive Truth*, Rereading Literature, Oxford: Blackwell.

Gordon, Jan B. (1976) 'Origins, History and the Reconstruction of Family: Tess' Journey', *English Literature and History*, 43, pp. 257–79.

Gray, Alasdair (1984) *Unlikely Stories, Mostly*, Harmondsworth: Penguin.

Greer, Germaine (1979) *The Obstacle Race: The Fortunes of Women Painters and their Work*, London: Secker and Warburg.

Haight, Gordon (1985) *George Eliot: A Biography*, Penguin Literary Biographies, Harmondsworth: Penguin.

Hardy, Barbara (1985) *Forms of Feeling in Victorian Fiction*, London: Peter Owen.

Hardy, Florence Emily (1986) *The Life of Thomas Hardy: 1840–1928*, (first published as two volumes 1928, 1930), London: Macmillan.

Hardy, Thomas (1974) *The Trumpet-Major* (first published 1880), New Wessex Edition, London: Macmillan.

—— (1975) *A Pair of Blue Eyes* (first published 1873), New Wessex Edition, London: Macmillan.

—— (1979) *Under the Greenwood Tree* (first published 1872), Harmondsworth: Penguin.

—— (1982) (1) *Jude the Obscure* (first published 1896), New Wessex Edition, London: Macmillan.

—— (1982) (2) *A Laodicean* (first published 1881), New Wessex Edition, London: Macmillan.

—— (1983) *The Return of the Native* (first published 1878), New Wessex Edition, London: Macmillan.

—— (1984) *The Complete Poems*, ed. James Gibson, New Wessex Edition, London: Macmillan.

—— (1985) *Tess of the d'Urbervilles: A Pure Woman* (first published 1891), Harmondsworth: Penguin.

—— (1986) *The Well-Beloved: A Sketch of a Temperament* (first published 1897), New Wessex Edition, London: Macmillan.

Harland, Richard (1987) *Superstructuralism: The Philosophy of Structuralism and Post-Structuralism*, London, Methuen.

Haskell, Francis and Penny, Nicholas (1981) *Taste and the Antique: The Lure of Classical Sculpture, 1500–1900*, New Haven, Conn. and London: Yale University Press.

Hawthorn, Jeremy (1979) *Joseph Conrad: Language and Fictional Self-Consciousness*, Lincoln, Neb.: University of Nebraska Press.

—— (1990) *Joseph Conrad: Narrative Technique and Ideological Commitment*, London: Edward Arnold

H.D. (Hilda Doolittle) (1985) *Tribute to Freud*, Manchester, Carcanet.

Hegel, G.W.F. (1956) *The Philosophy of History*, trans. J. Sibree, New York: Dover Publications.

—— (1977) *Phenomenology of Spirit*, trans. A.V. Millar, Oxford: Oxford University Press.

Herbert, Lucille (1970) 'Hardy's Views in *Tess*', *English Literature and History*, 37, pp. 77–95.

Hewitt, Douglas (1952) *Conrad: A Reassessment*, London: Bowes and Bowes.

Hill, Geoffrey (1984) *The Lords of Limit: Essays on Literature and Ideas*, London: André Deutsch.

—— (1985) *Collected Poems*, Harmondsworth: Penguin.

Hillis Miller, J. (1968) *The Forms of Victorian Fiction*, Notre Dame, Ind.: University of Notre Dame Press.

—— (1974) 'Narrative and History', *English Literature and History*, 41, pp.455–74.

—— (1982) *Fiction and Repetition: Seven English Novels*, Oxford: Blackwell.

—— (1985) *The Linguistic Moment; From Wordsworth to Stevens*, Princeton, N.J.: Princeton, University Press.

Holderness, Graham (1982) *D.H. Lawrence: History, Ideology and Fiction*, Dublin: Gill and Macmillan.

—— (1985) *Wuthering Heights*, Open Guides to Literature, Milton Keynes: Open University Press.

Homer (1987) *The Iliad: A New Prose Translation*, trans. Martin Hammond, Harmondsworth: Penguin.

Howe, Irving (1967) *Thomas Hardy*, London: Macmillan.

—— (1987) *Politics and the Novel*, New York: Horizon Press.

Hunter, Jefferson (1982) *Edwardian Fiction*, Cambridge, Mass.: Harvard University Press.

James, Alice (1987) *The Diary Of Alice James* (first published 1934), Harmondsworth: Penguin.

James, Henry (1983) *The Golden Bowl* (first published 1904), Harmondsworth: Penguin.

—— (1984) *The Portrait of a Lady* (first published 1881), Harmondsworth: Penguin.

—— (1987) *The Critical Muse: Selected Literary Criticism*, ed. Roger Gard, Harmondsworth: Penguin.

Jameson, Fredric (1971) *Marxism and Form: Twentieth-Century Dialectical Theories of Literature*, Princeton, N.J.: Princeton University Press.

—— (1981) *The Political Unconscious: Narrative as a Socially Symbolic Act*, Cambridge: Cambridge University Press.

Jones, Peter (1975) *Philosophy and the Novel*, Oxford: Clarendon Press.

Joyce, James (1986) *Ulysses: The Corrected Text* (originally published 1922), Harmondsworth: Penguin.

Kafka, Franz (1988) *The Collected Novels*, Harmondsworth: Penguin.

Kavanagh, James (1985) *Emily Brontë*, Rereading Literature, Oxford: Blackwell.

Keats, John (1982) *Poetical Works*, ed. H.W. Garrod, Oxford: Oxford University Press.

Kennedy, Alan (1979) *Meaning and Signs in Fiction*, London: Macmillan.

Kipling, Rudyard (1987) *Selected Stories*, ed. Andrew Rutherford, Harmondsworth: Penguin.

Kissane, James (1962) 'Victorian Mythology', *Victorian Studies*, VI, pp.5–29.

Klee, Paul (1989) *On Modern Art*, London: Faber and Faber.

Knight, Everett (1969) *A Theory of the Classical Novel*, London: Routledge and Kegan Paul.

Kroeber, Karl (1974) 'Experience as History: Shelley's Venice, Turner's Carthage', *English Literature and History*, 41, pp.321–40.

Kucich, John (1985) 'Narrative Theory as History: A Review of Problems in Victorian Fiction Studies', *Victorian Studies*, 28/4, pp.657–77.

Lacan, Jacques (1977) (1) *Écrits: A Selection*, trans. Alan Sheridan, London: Tavistock/Routledge.

—— (1977) (2) *The Four Fundamental Concepts of Psycho-Analysis*, trans. Alan Sheridan, Harmondsworth: Penguin.

Land, Stephen K. (1984) *Conrad and the Paradox of Plot*, London: Macmillan.

Lawrence, D.H. (1969) *Selected Literary Criticism*, ed. Antony Beal, London: Heinemann.

—— (1985) *D.H. Lawrence and Italy: Twilight in Italy, Sea and Sardinia, Etruscan Places* (first published 1916, 1921, 1932), Penguin Travel Library, Harmondsworth: Penguin.

—— (1988) *Kangaroo* (first published 1923), Harmondsworth: Penguin.

Leavis, F.R. (1980) *The Great Tradition*, Harmondsworth: Penguin.

Lévi-Strauss, Claude (1970) *The Raw and the Cooked: Introduction to a Science of Mythology,* I, trans. John and Doreen Weightman, London: Jonathan Cape.

—— (1989) *The Savage Mind*, London: Weidenfeld and Nicolson.

Lodge, David (1977) *The Modes of Modern Writing*, London: Edward Arnold.

Lowe, Donald M. (1982) *The History of Bourgeois Perception*, Brighton: Harvester.

Lukács, Georg (1962) *The Historical Novel*, trans. Hannah and Stanley Mitchell, London: Merlin Press.

—— (1969) *The Meaning of Contemporary Realism*, trans. Arthur Kahn, London: Merlin Press.

—— (1970) *Writer and Critic and Other Essays*, trans. Arthur Kahn, London: Merlin Press.

—— (1978) *The Theory of the Novel*, trans. Anna Bostock, London: Merlin Press.

Lyotard, Jean-François (1973) *Des Dispositifs Pulsionnels*, Paris: Union générale d'éditions.

Macaulay, Thomas Babington (1860) *Critical, Historical and Miscellaneous Essays,* I, New York: Sheldon and Co.

MacCabe, Colin (1979) *James Joyce and the Revolution of the Word*, London: Macmillan.

McCobb, E.A. (1985) '*Daniel Deronda* as Will and Representation: George Eliot and Schopenhauer', *The Modern Language Review*, 80, pp.533–49.

McGann, Jerome J. (1985) *The Beauty of Inflections: Literary Investigations in Historical Method and Theory*, Oxford: Clarendon Press.

Macherey, Pierre (1978) *A Theory of Literary Production*, trans. Geoffrey Wall, London: Routledge and Kegan Paul.

Marx, Karl (1965) *The German Ideology*, London: Sheldon and Co.

—— (1977) *Selected Writings*, ed. David McLellan, Oxford: Oxford University Press.

—— (1990) *Capital: Volume 1*, trans. Ben Fowkes, Harmondsworth: Penguin.

Mein, Margaret (1974) *A Foretaste of Proust: A Study of Proust and his Precursors*, Glasgow: Glasgow University Press.

Mill, John Stuart (1958) *Nature and the Utility of Religion*, Indianapolis: The Library of Liberal Arts.

—— (1980) *Mill on Bentham and Coleridge*, ed. F.R. Leavis, Cambridge: Cambridge University Press.

—— (1987) *On Liberty*, Harmondsworth: Penguin.

—— (1989) *Autobiography*, Harmondsworth: Penguin.

Milner, Ian (1966) 'Structure and Quality in *Silas Marner*', *Studies in English Literature 1500–1900*, 6, pp.717–29.

Moi, Toril (1985) *Sexual/Textual Politics: Feminist Literary Theory*, London: Methuen.

Morf, Gustav (1976) *The Polish Shades and Ghosts of Joseph Conrad*, New York: Astra Books.

Musselwhite, David E. (1987) *Partings Welded Together: Politics and Desire in the Nineteenth-Century English Novel*, Oxford: Oxford University Press.

Myers, F.W.H. (1881) 'George Eliot', *Century Magazine*, 23, Nov.

Newton, K.M., ed. (1991) *George Eliot*, Longman Critical Readers, Harlow: Longman.

Nietzsche, Friedrich (1910) *The Joyful Wisdom*, trans. Thomas Common, ed. Oscar Levy, London: T.N. Foulis.

—— (1966) *Beyond Good and Evil: Prelude to a Philosophy of the Future*, trans. Walter Kaufmann, New York: Random House.

—— (1967) *The Birth of Tragedy and The Case of Wagner*, trans. Walter Kaufmann, New York, Random House.

—— (1980) *Sämtliche Werke, Kritische Studienausgabe*, ed. G. Colli and M. Montinari, Berlin/New York: Edition Suhrkamp.

—— (1983) *Untimely Meditations*, trans. R.J. Hollingdale, Cambridge: Cambridge University Press

—— (1990) *Twilight of the Idols/The Anti-Christ*, trans. R.J. Hollingdale, Harmondsworth: Penguin.

Oakshott, Michael (1983) *On History and Other Essays*, Oxford: Blackwell.

Parry, Benita (1983) *Conrad and Imperialism: Ideological and Visionary Frontiers*, London: Macmillan.

Peckham, Morse (1972) 'Afterword: Reflections on Historical Modes in the Nineteenth-Century', Stratford upon Avon Studies, vol. 15, *Victorian Poetry*, London: Edward Arnold.

Pinkney, Tony (1990) *D.H. Lawrence*, Hemel Hempstead: Harvester Wheatsheaf.

Plath, Sylvia (1981) *Collected Poems*, ed. Ted Hughes, London: Faber and Faber.

Poe, Edgar Allan (1986) *The Fall of the House of Usher and Other Writings: Poems, Tales, Essays and Reviews*, ed. David Galloway, Harmondsworth: Penguin.

Poole, Adrian (1983) '"Hidden Affinities" in *Daniel Deronda*', *Essays in Criticism*, vol. 33, no. IV, pp.294–311.

—— (1991) (1) *Henry James*, Hemel Hempstead: Harvester Wheatsheaf.

—— (1991) (2) 'Henry James, War and Witchcraft', *Essays in Criticism*, 41/IV, Oct., pp.291–307.

Popper, Karl (1986) *The Poverty of Historicism*, London: Routledge.

Pound, Ezra (1988) *Selected Poems: 1908–1959*, London: Faber and Faber.

Proust, Marcel (1954) *A la recherche du temps perdu* (first published 1912–27), 8 vols, Paris: Editions Gallimard.

Pykett, Lyn (1987) 'Typology and the End(s) of History *Daniel Deronda*', *Literature and History*, 9, pp.62–74.

Reilly, Jim (1991) *Joseph Conrad*, Life and Works Series, Brighton: Wayland.

Rimmon-Kenan, Shlomith (1983) *Narrative Fiction, Contemporary Poetics*, London: Methuen.

Ruskin, John (1904) *The Stones of Venice*, Works, vol. 10, ed. E.T. Cook and Alexander Wedderburn, London: George Allen.

—— (1989) *Praeterita*, Oxford Letters and Memoirs, Oxford: Oxford University Press.

Ryan, Kiernan (1982) 'Revelation and Repression in Conrad's *Nostromo*', in *The Uses of Fiction: Essays in Honour of Arnold Kettle*, ed. Douglas Jefferson and Graham Martin, Milton Keynes: Open University Press.

Said, Edward W. (1966) *Joseph Conrad and the Fiction of Autobiography*, Cambridge, Mass.: Harvard University Press.

—— (1975) *Beginnings: Intention and Method*, New York: Basic Books.

Sanders, Wilbur (1968) *The Dramatist and the Received Idea*, Cambridge: Cambridge University Press.

—— (1987) *The Winter's Tale*, Harvester New Critical Introductions to Shakespeare, Brighton: Harvester.

Schaff, Adam (1976) *History and Truth*, Oxford: Pergamon.

Schopenhauer, Arthur (1958) *The World as Will and Representation*, trans. E.F.J. Payne, 2 vols, New York: Dover.

—— (1970) *Essays and Aphorisms*, trans. R.J. Hollingdale, Harmondsworth: Penguin.

Sève, Lucien (1978) *Man in Marxist Theory and the Psychology of Personality*, trans. John McGreal, Brighton: Harvester.

Shaffer, E.S. (1970) *Kubla Khan and the Fall of Jerusalem: The Mythological School in Biblical Criticism and Secular Literature 1770–1880*, Cambridge: Cambridge University Press.

Shakespeare, William (1985) *Coriolanus*, ed. Philip Brockbank, The Arden Shakespeare, London: Methuen.

—— (1982) *Othello*, ed. M.R. Ridley, The Arden Shakespeare, London: Methuen.

Shelley, Percy Bysshe (1970) *Poetical Works*, ed. Thomas Hutchinson, Oxford: Oxford University Press.

Sherry, Norman, ed. (1976) *Joseph Conrad: A Commemoration, Papers from the 1974 International Conference on Conrad*, London: Macmillan.

Shuttleworth, Sally (1984) *George Eliot and Nineteenth-Century Science: The Make-Believe of a Beginning*, Cambridge: Cambridge University Press.

Smith, Ann, ed. (1980) *George Eliot: Centenary Essays and an Unpublished Fragment*, London: Vision Press.

Sobel, Joshua (1989) '*Ghetto*: A Note From the Playwright', Programme note for *Ghetto*, First British production, National Theatre, 1989.

Steiner, George (1969) *Language and Silence: Essays 1958–1966*, Harmondsworth: Penguin.

Stendhal (1983) *The Charterhouse of Parma*, trans. Margaret R.B. Shaw, Harmondsworth: Penguin.

Stern, J.P. (1990) *Hitler: The Führer and the People*, London: Fontana Press.

Stewart, J.I.M. (1968) *Joseph Conrad*, London: Longman.

Sudrann, Jean (1970) *'Daniel Deronda and the Landscape of Exile'*, *English Language and History*, 37, pp.433–55.

Tanner, Tony (1986) *Jane Austen*, London: Macmillan.

Taylor, Richard H. (1982) *The Neglected Hardy: Thomas Hardy's Lesser Novels*, London: Macmillan.

Tennyson, Alfred (1971) *Tennyson's Poetry: Authoritative Texts, Juvenilia and Early Responses, Criticism*, ed. Robert W. Hill jr., New York: Norton.

Tobin, Patricia D. (1978) *Time and the Novel: The Genealogical Imperative*, Princeton, N.J.: Princeton University Press.

Tolstoy, Leo (1979) *War and Peace* (first published 1869), trans. Vicomte de Vogue, 3 vols, London: Heron.

Twain, Mark (1963) *The Complete Essays*, ed. Charles Neider, New York: Doubleday and Co.

Watts, Cedric (1990) *Nostromo*, Penguin Critical Studies, Harmondsworth: Penguin

Weiss, Robert (1969) *The Renaissance Discovery of Classical Antiquity*, Oxford: Blackwell.

White, Hayden (1973) *Metahistory: The Historical Imagination in Nineteenth-Century Europe*, Baltimore, Md.: Johns Hopkins University Press.

Wiesenfarth, Joseph (1970) *'Demythologising Silas Marner'* in *English Literature and History*, 37, pp.226–45.

Williams, Raymond (1976) *Keywords: A Vocabulary of Culture and Society*, Glasgow: Fontana.

Woolf, Virginia (1980) *Collected Essays*, vol. 1, London: Hogarth Press.

Wordsworth, William (1971) *The Prelude: A Parallel Text*, ed. J.C. Maxwell, Penguin English Poets, Harmondsworth: Penguin.

—— (1985) *Poetical Works*, ed. Thomas Hutchinson, revised Ernest de Selincourt, Oxford: Oxford University Press.

INDEX